THE EVERYTHING

GREEN BABY
BOOK

Dear Reader,

Before my kids were born, I *thought* I was doing a pretty good job of being an environmentalist. I was a park ranger for the National Park Service and I had the time, energy, and money to invest in making earth-friendly choices. But the moment I became pregnant with my first child, I was thrust into a world I had never known before—a world of disposable, plastic, energy-wasting, and planet-trashing everything. I was struggling to find the best solutions for my growing baby and the planet. And now I suddenly had no time, no energy, and a whole lot less money than I had before to devote to making eco-savvy choices for my family and the planet.

   Thus began my quest to find the easiest and healthiest ways to go green as a parent and to pass that information along to other parents. Going green does not have to be complicated, expensive, or labor intensive. In fact, the essence of going green is to keep things as simple and natural as possible. And it's one of the very best things that we as parents can do to protect our family's health and ensure that our children inherit a clean and abundant environment.

Jenn Savedge

Welcome to the EVERYTHING® Series!

These handy, accessible books give you all you need to tackle a difficult project, gain a new hobby, comprehend a fascinating topic, prepare for an exam, or even brush up on something you learned back in school but have since forgotten.

You can choose to read an *Everything*® book from cover to cover or just pick out the information you want from our four useful boxes: e-questions, e-facts, e-alerts, and e-ssentials.

We give you everything you need to know on the subject, but throw in a lot of fun stuff along the way, too.

We now have more than 400 *Everything*® books in print, spanning such wide-ranging categories as weddings, pregnancy, cooking, music instruction, foreign language, crafts, pets, New Age, and so much more. When you're done reading them all, you can finally say you know *Everything*®!

QUESTION

Answers to
common questions

FACT

Important snippets
of information

ALERT

Urgent
warnings

ESSENTIAL

Quick
handy tips

PUBLISHER Karen Cooper

DIRECTOR OF ACQUISITIONS AND INNOVATION Paula Munier

MANAGING EDITOR, EVERYTHING® SERIES Lisa Laing

COPY CHIEF Casey Ebert

ACQUISITIONS EDITOR Brett Palana-Shanahan

DEVELOPMENT EDITOR Brett Palana-Shanahan

EDITORIAL ASSISTANT Hillary Thompson

EVERYTHING® SERIES COVER DESIGNER Erin Alexander

LAYOUT DESIGNERS Colleen Cunningham, Elisabeth Lariviere, Ashley Vierra, Denise Wallace

Visit the entire Everything® series at *www.everything.com*

THE
EVERYTHING®
GREEN BABY
BOOK

From pregnancy to baby's first year—an easy and
affordable guide to help you care for your baby—
and the earth!

Jenn Savedge

Aadamsmedia

Avon, Massachusetts

*For Don, Emily, and Erin, without whom this
book would have never been born.*

An Everything® Series Book.
Everything® and everything.com® are registered trademarks of F+W Media, Inc.

Published by Adams Media, a division of F+W Media, Inc.
57 Littlefield Street, Avon, MA 02322 U.S.A.
www.adamsmedia.com

ISBN 10: 1-60550-367-3
ISBN 13: 978-1-60550-367-7

Printed in the United States of America.

10 9 8 7 6 5 4 3 2 1

Library of Congress Cataloging-in-Publication Data
is available from the publisher.

This publication is designed to provide accurate and authoritative information with regard to the subject matter covered. It is sold with the understanding that the publisher is not engaged in rendering legal, accounting, or other professional advice. If legal advice or other expert assistance is required, the services of a competent professional person should be sought.

—From a *Declaration of Principles* jointly adopted by a Committee of the
American Bar Association and a Committee of Publishers and Associations

649.122 SAV   OCLC   12/9/09

Many of the designations used by manufacturers and sellers to distinguish their products are claimed as trademarks. Where those designations appear in this book and Adams Media was aware of a trademark claim, the designations have been printed with initial capital letters.

The pages of this book are printed on 30% post-consumer recycled paper.

Fabric © ansem/123RF

*This book is available at quantity discounts for bulk purchases.
For information, please call 1-800-289-0963.*

Contents

Top 10 Ways to Green Your Baby **x**

Introduction **xi**

01 The Green Birth Plan / 3

Choosing a Green
Health Care Provider **4**

Choosing a Birthing Location **7**

Labor and Delivery Options **9**

Your Green Birth Plan **12**

Packing Your Green Bags **14**

Home Remedies for
Common Pregnancy Ailments **16**

02 Eating Your Greens / 20

What's in Your Food? **21**

Organic and Free-Range Foods **26**

Seafood and Mercury **27**

What's Your Beef? **29**

Steer Clear of Bacteria **30**

Reducing Your Food Miles **30**

Where to Buy Organic **31**

Most and Least
Contaminated Foods **31**

03 Detox Your Day / 33

What's in the Air? **34**

Breathe Easier **35**

Allergies and Asthma **36**

What's in Your Water? **37**

Clean up Your Water **38**

Toxins to Avoid **39**

Toxins in the Workplace **44**

04 Have a Green and Gorgeous Pregnancy / 45

Green Beauty Basics **46**

Skip the Chemical Cocktail **48**

Know Your Green Beauty Labels **49**

Hair Care **53**

Skin Care and Cosmetics **54**

Teeth **57**

Shaving **58**

Smelling Clean and Green **59**

Manicures and Pedicures **60**

Do It Yourself (DIY) Beauty **60**

05 Green Shopping / 61

Why Shop Green? **62**

Save Green by Going Green **64**

Minimize Waste **65**

B.Y.O.B. **67**
Buying Local **68**
Know Your Green Product Labels **68**
Don't Get Greenwashed **72**

06 **Green Maternity Clothes / 75**
Your Expanding Wardrobe **76**
Choosing Fabrics **76**
Use What You Have **79**
Pre-Loved Clothes **81**
Finding Organic Maternity Clothes **81**
Passing It On **83**
Green Dry Cleaners **83**

07 **Green Cleaning / 87**
Get Your Home Green and Clean **88**
Chemicals in Your Cleaning Products **89**
Natural Air Fresheners **91**
Dishwashing **92**
Laundry **93**
How to Make Your
Own Green Cleaners **95**
Eco-Friendly Cleaning Supplies **98**

08 **Save Your Energy! / 99**
Household Energy Consumption **100**
Home Energy Audits **100**
Conserve Energy at Home **101**
Energy-Saving Gadgets **107**
Renewable Energy **108**
Green Energy Suppliers **108**

09 **Put Your Trash
Can on a Diet / 109**
What's in Your Trash Can? **110**
Where Does All the Garbage Go? **110**
Reduce Your Trash **112**
Start Your Own Compost Pile **114**
Reuse **115**
Recycle **116**
The Waste-Can Weigh-In **121**

10 **Saving Water / 122**
Why Conserve Water? **123**
Conserve Water at Home **123**
Conserve Water at the Store **129**
Water-Saving Gadgets **129**
Collecting Rain Water **131**

11 **Make Your Grass
a Little Greener / 132**
Is Your Yard Green? **133**
Planting **133**
Mowing **135**
Watering **137**
Weeding **138**
Natural Fertilizers **139**
Start Your Own Garden **140**

12 **Green on the Go / 141**
Planes, Trains, and Automobiles **142**
Use Your Legs **142**
Public Transportation **143**

Driving Green **143**

Green Car Guide **145**

Car Maintenance **146**

Eco-Vacations **148**

Carbon Offsets **150**

13   Green Your Pets / 151

Greening Your Pet **152**

Feeding Fido **153**

Green Pet Gear **154**

Bathing **155**

Fleas **156**

Pet Poo **157**

Can't Have a Pet? **158**

14   Green Baby Essentials / 163

What Does Your Baby Really Need? **164**

Car Seats **165**

Strollers **167**

Changing Tables **168**

High Chairs and Boosters **168**

Slings and Babywearers **169**

Baby Tubs **171**

15   Baby Clothes / 172

The Green Layette **173**

The Dangers of Fabric Finishes **173**

Green Baby Clothing **175**

Safer Sleepwear **178**

Finding Green Baby
Clothes on a Budget **178**

Easy Homemade Baby Clothes **179**

Washing Baby's Clothes **180**

16   The Diaper Dilemma / 181

Diaper Options **182**

The Chemicals Used
to Make Disposables **186**

A Cost Comparison
of Cloth versus Disposable **187**

Cleaning Cloth Diapers **188**

Diaper Bags, Wipes, and Pails **190**

Elimination Communication **192**

17   The Nursery / 193

Sleep Options **194**

Remodeling or Adding On **194**

Paints and Finishes **196**

Floor Coverings **199**

Window Coverings **201**

Furniture **202**

Bedding **204**

18   The Green Baby Shower / 206

Greening a Baby Shower **207**

Green Baby Shower Themes **210**

How to Ask for Green Gifts **211**

Green Gift Registries **212**

Green Baby Shower Gift Ideas **212**

Thank-You Notes **214**

19 Healthy Mom/ Healthy Baby / 217

At the Hospital or Birthing Center **218**

Getting the Rest You Both Need **220**

Finding a Green Pediatrician **221**

The Vaccination Decision **223**

Finding Green Childcare **224**

20 Healthy Home Remedies / 227

The Green Medicine Cabinet **228**

Cradle Cap **228**

Colds **229**

Gas **230**

Ear Infections **231**

Diarrhea and Constipation **232**

Diaper Rash **232**

Teething **233**

Eczema **235**

Baby Massage **236**

21 Baby Foods / 237

Breast Milk or Formula? **238**

Nursing Gear **244**

Organic Formulas **246**

BPA-Free Baby Bottles and Sippy Cups **246**

Introducing Solid Foods **247**

Homemade Baby Food **247**

22 Caring for Baby's Skin / 249

Green Your Baby's Bath **250**

Washing Baby's Delicate Skin **251**

Baby Wash **252**

Homemade Baby Lotion **252**

Homemade Bubble Bath **253**

Bath Toys and Books **254**

Sun Protection **255**

Natural Bug Repellents **257**

23 It's Play Time / 260

Green Arts and Crafts for Baby **261**

Outdoor Play **263**

Baby Toys **264**

Homemade Baby Play **267**

Great Green Reads for Baby **269**

24 Baby's First Birthday! / 271

Throwing a Great Green Party **272**

Invitations **273**

Food **275**

Decorations **277**

Table Settings **278**

Entertainment **279**

Party Favors **280**

Thank-You Notes **281**

Appendix A: Green Glossary **282**

Appendix B: Green Resources **284**

Index **289**

Acknowledgments

I am so very thankful to all of my friends, family, and coworkers who helped this book become a reality. First and foremost, I owe a special thanks to Melanie Renzulli, for connecting me with the right people to bring this book to life. And thank you to Bob Diforio, my agent, and Brett Palana-Shanahan, my editor at Adams Media, for their encouragement and patience throughout the book writing process.

Thanks to Megan Williams, Liz Lewis, Missy Forder, Sandy Schaberl, Brooke Downing, and the all the gals of the Luray Mom's Club for providing me with countless hours of support as well as adequate supplies of caffeine, wine, and chocolate! Thank you to all of the moms of the Green Moms Carnival (*www.organicmania.com/green-moms-carnival*), who shared their expertise, questions, concerns, and experiences on green parenting. And finally, thank you, thank you, thank you to my family: my mom, my brother, my mother- and father-in-law, my sisters-in-law, my husband, and of course, my beautiful daughters, whose love and support I cherish more than words can say.

Top 10 Ways to Green Your Baby

1. Breastfeed.

2. Use cloth diapers.

3. Walk with your baby whenever possible.

4. Borrow or purchase gently used baby gear.

5. Reuse and then recycle.

6. B.Y.O.B. (Bring Your Own Bag/Bottle).

7. Green your baby's bath.

8. Install CFLs.

9. Buy organic.

10. Teach your baby to love her planet.

Introduction: Why Go Green?

THERE ARE FEW PHASES in life more overwhelming and exciting than becoming a new parent. Life changes from the moment you learn your new baby is on the way, as you are suddenly faced with a barrage of decisions to make about the health and welfare of your baby. And even if you never thought about it before, you will probably begin to see the environment you live in—the environment your baby will grow up in—from a whole different set of eyes. For the first time, issues such as global warming, air quality, water pollution, food security, and biodiversity stand to affect your child's future as well as your own.

No parent wants to raise his or her child in a world full of toxins. Yet we are often too overwhelmed by the magnitude of environmental concerns, and what we perceive as the necessary steps that must be undertaken by communities, industries, and the government, to make a difference. Environmental issues such as global warming, hazardous waste, loss of rain forests, endangered species, acid rain, the ozone layer, and heaving landfills seem out of our control. There is just too much trash, too much pollution, too few resources, and too little time to really make a difference, right? WRONG!

Each of the decisions that you must make as a new parent, from how to feed your baby to what diapers to use will have an impact on both your baby and the planet. Even the method you use to deliver your baby affects the environment. But the good news is that it is easier than you think to make savvy decisions to go green.

As a busy parent, you may not have time to spend hours researching what you could do to protect the environment. Should you buy organic or buy local? Which items are the most important to recycle? How can you get the most green for your green? Let's face it, in the modern household, time is as precious a commodity as any other. But the fact of the matter is, whether this is your first baby or your tenth, the decisions you make each day affect the environment. And even small changes can make a big difference.

If you are concerned about the environment your baby will grow up in and concerned about the impact your expanding family will have the planet, then *The Everything® Green Baby Book* is a must read for you. This book offers easy-to-understand information and easy-to-implement ideas to help you go green, from pregnancy to your baby's first birthday! This book gives parents nonjudgmental, real-life, and comprehensive information about raising a green baby.

The Everything® Green Baby Book is a book that you will earmark and return to time and time again as you and your baby enter new stages of development. During pregnancy, it will show you how to go green at home and on the go to protect yourself and your developing baby from environmental toxins. After your baby is born, you can turn to *The Everything® Green Baby Book* as your ultimate resource for choosing the green options that work best for your family when it comes to diapering, feeding, bathing, and clothing your newborn baby. And it will also show you simple ways to reduce your whole family's impact on the environment.

Even more importantly, *The Everything® Green Baby Book* will show you how to introduce your baby to nature, and plant the seed for a lifetime of environmental stewardship. Because teaching your children to understand and cherish their connection to the environment is one of the best ways that you as a parent can protect the planet for today and for your child's future.

part one

Your Healthy Green Pregnancy

CHAPTER 1

The Green Birth Plan

Congratulations! With a new baby on the way, you are sure to be excited and maybe even a little nervous about all that lies ahead. You will want to make sure your baby gets the healthiest, greenest start to life. And that begins right now. The choices you make during your pregnancy about the health and care of your baby will go a long way toward greening her future. Get ready to enjoy this wonderful green pregnancy as you prepare to welcome your new little sprout to the planet!

Choosing a Green Health Care Provider

The first step in caring for yourself and your baby is to assemble your "green team" of folks that will help guide and care for you through this pregnancy and help you welcome your new little one into the world. Your team will likely include your partner, close family members and friends, and a staff of health care personnel who will all work together to help you meet your needs and the needs of your growing baby.

One of the most important decisions you will make during your pregnancy is finding the health care provider who will guide you through the next nine months. Even if you decide not to have your health care provider present during the actual birth of your baby, you will want to be seen throughout your pregnancy to ensure that you and your baby are as healthy as possible. Your health care provider will also help answer any questions you have about your pregnancy, the birthing process, and your growing baby, so you want to make sure that you choose someone you can trust. Depending upon your location and health insurance options, you may be able to choose between an obstetrician and a midwife for your prenatal care. Here is a closer look at the differences between these two professions.

Obstetricians

An obstetrician (OB/GYN if he or she practices both obstetrics and gynecology) is a doctor who specializes in treating the medical aspects of pregnancy and childbirth. Most women rely on OB/GYNs to care for them during their pregnancy and deliver their babies. OB/GYNs generally see patients only in their office and will attend the birth of the baby only in a hospital setting, not at home or in any other nonmedical setting.

If this is the type of birth you envision, than an OB/GYN may be just right for you. In addition, if you have any significant health problems that might make your pregnancy "high risk," such as diabetes, cancer, or high blood pressure, you may feel more confident about seeing an OB/GYN for your prenatal care.

Midwives

A midwife is a certified nurse who is legally registered or licensed to deliver babies. Midwives are generally much more flexible about where they can practice. Most will deliver a baby anywhere: at your home, in a hospital, or in a birthing center. Midwives also tend to be more flexible about the setting and birthing choices of pregnant moms.

ESSENTIAL

If you don't already have an established relationship with an OB/GYN or midwife, ask friends, family, and coworkers to recommend a provider to care for you throughout your pregnancy. Don't be afraid to interview several practitioners to ensure that you select the health care provider with whom you feel the most comfortable.

During your labor and delivery, an OB/GYN will more than likely be delivering other babies at the same time, all while also seeing regularly scheduled office visits. He will likely check in on you once or twice during your labor and be paged to your room when you are ready to push for delivery.

A midwife, on the other hand, will stay with you throughout the labor and delivery process. She can recommend pain management techniques, update you on the status of your progress, and prepare you for what's to come. If you deliver your baby in a hospital, she can also advocate for you and your green birth plan and act as a go between with hospital staff.

Doulas

A doula is a professional birthing assistant whose primary responsibilities are to provide physical, emotional, and informational support to expecting moms and their partners throughout the labor and delivery process. She would not take the place of a medical provider such as an OB/GYN or a midwife. Rather she would work alongside your primary provider to help you care for yourself and your baby throughout your pregnancy and during your delivery.

If you decide to hire a doula, she will likely meet with you throughout your pregnancy to discuss your birth plan and answer any questions you may have about your baby's delivery. She can suggest alternative pain management techniques, help you make an informed decision about where to deliver your baby, and provide emotional support throughout your pregnancy and your labor. Similar to a midwife, a doula can act as a liaison between you and the hospital staff to ensure that your birth plan preferences are honored. Your doula may even be responsible for making sure that certain eco-friendly items like organic cotton sheets and nontoxic lotions are brought to the delivery room. After delivery, your doula can help answer questions about your postpartum recovery, newborn care, breastfeeding, and coping with a new baby.

FACT

Clinical research shows that having a doula present during your delivery can reduce the need for invasive and/or unwanted medical intervention. In clinical studies, the presence of doulas resulted in a 50 percent decrease in cesareans, a 36 percent decrease in the use of pain medication, and a 70 percent decrease in the use of Pitocin.

Questions to Ask During Your Pregnancy

Whether you choose an OB/GYN or a midwife to care for you during your pregnancy, you will want to make sure that you are on the same page regarding your prenatal care and the delivery of your baby. Your health care provider will be your guide to caring for the medical and emotional needs of you and your baby throughout your pregnancy and even after your baby's birth. Talk to him about your concern for the environment and your desire to have a green pregnancy and delivery. Use these questions as a guide to determine whether or not he will support you in this endeavor.

1. Do you support my decision to make my pregnancy and delivery as environmentally conscious as possible?
2. Can you suggest ways that I can make my delivery and pregnancy greener?
3. What types of pain management do you recommend for delivery?
4. How many of your patients deliver via C-Section as compared to vaginally?
5. What is your criteria for performing (or recommending) a C-Section?
6. What can I bring with me (or have at home) to ensure that my delivery room is as green as possible?

If your health care provider is an OB/GYN, he may have limited control over the eco-friendly practices at the hospital where you deliver. But he may be able to help support your choices and offer suggestions to ensure that your needs, and the needs of your baby, are met in a way that is as gentle and environmentally friendly as possible.

Choosing a Birthing Location

In many parts of the United States, women can choose between a hospital birth, a birth center birth, or a homebirth. Where you decide to have your baby will play a major role in determining the atmosphere in which your new baby will be born.

If you decide to have your baby delivered by an OB/GYN, you will more than likely deliver at the hospital where your doctor has admitting privileges. That's an important consideration to keep in mind when you choose your health care provider. If you prefer to have your baby in a birthing center or at home, you will need to find a midwife who will consider these options.

Hospitals

In the United States, most women deliver their babies in hospitals. Many women feel more comfortable in a hospital because hospitals have the staff and facilities to give pregnant moms and newborn babies immediate medical attention should the need arise. If you have a medical history that puts you at risk for complications during your delivery, then a hospital delivery may be the safest choice for you and your baby.

ESSENTIAL

If you decide to have your baby in a hospital or birthing center, you will not be able to control the amount or type of energy used during your stay. But you can "offset" the energy used during your baby's delivery by purchasing carbon credits (try *www.carbonfund.org*) or planting your own carbon-absorbing trees to commemorate the occasion.

If you do decide to deliver in a hospital, make sure you take a tour of the facilities before you go in to labor so that you will feel comfortable with the rooms, staff, and equipment that is available to you. Many hospitals are making strides at incorporating green designs, such as solar panels, natural lighting, and outdoor walking paths, into their facilities. So don't be afraid to ask what, if any, steps the hospital is making to go green. Be sure to also ask questions about what you are allowed to bring in to your room and what may be forbidden.

Birthing Centers

A birthing center is a facility that allows you to take advantage of the medical facilities of a hospital in a more natural "home-like" setting. Birthing centers are designed for expectant moms with low-risk pregnancies who are unlikely to need medical intervention during their delivery but want the assurance of nearby medical care.

Most birthing center facilities are designed to look more like someone's home than a hospital, with wallpaper on the walls, cushy pillows on the beds, and an open kitchen for you to use during your stay. Birthing centers are also much more open to respecting the wishes of your green birth plan. They will generally allow you to make your own decisions on issues like how many people to have present during the delivery, pain management, and so on.

ALERT

Many major health insurers will cover the birth of a baby at a free-standing birthing center just as they would in a hospital. However, if you are thinking about having your baby in a birthing center, contact your health insurance carrier ahead of time to ensure that all tests, procedures, and therapies will be covered.

Another significant difference between a birthing center and a hospital is that in a birthing center, the tests, bathing, and care given to your newborn baby will take place right in your room after delivery. In a hospital, newborns are usually moved to another room for a short period after delivery for testing before they are returned to their mothers.

Home Birth

A home birth, just as its name implies, is when a pregnant mom delivers her baby at home. Many women decide to have their babies at home so that they can maintain control over the labor and delivery process and ensure that it remains as natural as possible. Home births are only recommended for expectant women who have had no complications during their pregnancy and who are not likely to need medical intervention during delivery.

If you choose to have your baby at home, you will have complete control over the foods you eat, the pain management techniques you use, and the exercises you do during delivery. You can choose where to deliver, on a bed or in a tub, without asking for permission. And you can ensure that the cleansers, lotions, diapers and creams used on you and your baby are healthy, nontoxic, and eco-friendly.

The disadvantage of a home birth is that it should an emergency arise, it will take longer for you and your baby to be transported to a medical facility and receive medical attention. If you do decide to have a home birth, you should have an emergency backup plan in place. And be sure that all members of your birthing team know what to do in case of an emergency so that you and your baby can get medical help quickly should the need arise.

Labor and Delivery Options

If you haven't already done so, you will want to talk to your health care provider about the different types of delivery options available to you and the amount of control you will have over the decision. Of course, it is impossible to determine how your labor and deliver will proceed until it is already in progress. So keep in mind that any number of things can happen during your labor and delivery that will simply be out of your control. And in the end, the ultimate goal of your labor and delivery is the arrival of a healthy baby from a healthy mom. But talking with your health care provider ahead of time will give you both a clearer picture of each other's concerns and expectations.

Nonmedicated Vaginal Delivery

When it comes to going green, a nonmedicated vaginal delivery is considered the most eco-friendly option. It is green because it reduces the waste and energy consumed during medical intervention and also protects the mother and unborn baby (as well as the environment) from the side effects of medication.

ESSENTIAL

For more information about taking a childbirth class, talk to your health care provider or the staff at the hospital or birthing center where you will deliver. Or check out the International Childbirth Education Association (*www.icea.org*) to lookup a listing of local classes. Ask around among friends, family members, and coworkers to find out which classes they recommend.

If you decide that you want to try for a nonmedicated vaginal delivery, make sure you talk to your health care provider about the entire birthing process so that there won't be any (or as many!) surprises. Even if you will be delivering your baby at home, it is important that you know what to expect during labor and delivery. A childbirth class that specializes in nonmedicated pain management techniques like deep breathing, hypnosis, visualization, muscle relaxation, and massage can help you learn different ways for relieving and dealing with pain that do not rely on medication. The two most popular types of "natural" childbirth techniques are Lamaze and the Bradley Method.

Lamaze

Lamaze is the oldest and most commonly referred to method for managing pain during labor and delivery. The program uses patterned breathing, visualization, guided imagery, massage, and coaching assistance to help women block pain messages before they get to the brain. Check out Lamaze International (*www.lamaze.org*) to learn more about this technique and find a class location near you.

The Bradley Method

The Bradley Method emphasizes the teamwork approach to labor and delivery, with particular emphasis on the role of the coach. Instead of trying to block pain messages, the Bradley Method encourages the mother to trust her body and overcome the pain through abdominal breathing and relaxation techniques. Learn more about the Bradley Method (*www.bradleybirth .com*).

Medicated Vaginal Delivery

While most women consider nonmedicated vaginal delivery to be the only true form of "natural" childbirth, it is also important to note that using certain types of medication can help ease the pain of labor and delivery, which may help some women enter new motherhood in a calmer and more refreshed manner than without medication. If you decide to have an OB/GYN or midwife present during your delivery, talk to her ahead of time about the pain medications she recommends and is able to administer.

FACT

According to the American Pregnancy Association, over 50 percent of women giving birth at hospitals use epidural anesthesia to ease the pain of labor and delivery. If you are considering using an epidural, talk to your health care provider about the different types of epidurals that she recommends, how an epidural is administered, and the benefits and potential risks of the medication.

The pain medications most commonly used during labor and deliver are analgesics and anesthetics. Narcotic analgesics should be considered a last resort to use during delivery, as they transfer across the placenta and into your unborn baby. They may cause sleepiness and slowed breathing for both you and your baby. The anesthetics most commonly used during labor (such as in an epidural), on the other hand, will not directly affect your baby. Although according to the American Pregnancy Association, some studies indicate that when an epidural is used during delivery, some babies may initially have trouble latching on or may experience other difficulties with breastfeeding after birth.

C-Section

A C-section, or cesarean section, is often not the first choice for an expectant mom to deliver her baby. It is a major surgery in which a surgeon must cut an incision in the mother's abdomen and uterus in order to remove the baby. The pain, expense, and recovery time from a C-section are all much greater than that from a vaginal delivery.

However, a C-section may be necessary to deliver a baby that is in fetal distress, an exceptionally large baby, a baby that is premature, or a baby in a breech position, or in a labor and delivery that is placing the mother's health at risk. In this situation, it is much more important to consider the health and safety of both you and your baby than to worry about being green. Remember, the end goal of your delivery is a healthy baby and mother. If you need to have a C-section, don't stress out about it. The only thing that truly matters is that you and your baby are healthy.

VBAC

Women who have had a C-section during a previous pregnancy may be able to choose between a vaginal or cesarean delivery for subsequent babies. Of course, this depends on the circumstances of the initial C-section and the medical history of the mother. But if this is something you would like to consider, talk to your health care provider about having a VBAC: vaginal birth after cesarean.

Your Green Birth Plan

Now that you've talked to your health care provider and made some decisions about where you will deliver your baby and the type of delivery you hope for, you can start to put together your green birth plan. A green birth plan is a written checklist of your preferences during labor, deliver, and, if applicable, your hospital stay. Basically, a green birth plan puts your wishes down on paper so that you can discuss them with your health care provider ahead of time. A green birth plan can also help guide you through the labor and delivery process and assist your green team in providing the care you want. Use these tips as a starting point for developing your own comprehensive green birth plan.

1. My baby will be delivered:

   A. At home.
   B. In a freestanding birthing center.
   C. In a hospital birthing center.
   D. In a hospital delivery room.

2. My green team will consist of:

   A. My partner or other lay coach.
   B. A doula.
   C. A midwife.
   D. An OB/GYN.

3. I would like to use the following pain management techniques:

   A. Deep-breathing techniques.
   B. Visualization.
   C. Guided imagery.
   D. Abdominal stretches and exercises.
   E. Medication: narcotics or epidural.
   F. Medication only as a last resort.

4. I would like to bring the following items with me to use during my labor and delivery:

   A. Natural-fiber sheets and diapers.
   B. A natural-fiber birthing gown.
   C. Natural-fiber bedding and baby clothing.
   D. Nontoxic lotions and cleansers.
   E. A CD player or iPod.
   F. A birthing ball.

5. I would like my baby's first meal to be:

   A.   Breast milk.
   B.   Hospital-supplied baby formula.
   C.   Organic formula that I will bring from home.
   D.   Formula offered in BPA-free baby bottles.

6. After my baby is born:

   A.   I would like to hold and feed her as soon as possible.
   B.   I would like her to remain with me for as long as possible.
   C.   I would like to meet with a lactation consultant as soon as possible.

Talk with your partner and your green team about your preferences ahead of time so that on the big day, you can focus your concentration on taking care of yourself and your new little bundle of joy.

Packing Your Green Bags

As your pregnancy progresses, you will want to start thinking about the items you will take to the hospital or birthing center with you when you go in to labor. By the time you are about seven months pregnant, it is a good idea to gather these items in one location so that you can quickly access them when the time comes. Look over your green birth plan to see which items, like nontoxic lotions and organic cotton bedding, you have decided to bring along. Use this checklist to help you make sure that you have everything you need.

PAPERWORK

❑ Green birth plan
❑ Health insurance card

FOR YOU

- ❏ Organic snacks and ice pops
- ❏ Organic cotton pillowcase
- ❏ Cozy socks and slippers
- ❏ Organic robe
- ❏ Organic toiletries
- ❏ Nontoxic massage oils and lotions

FOR YOUR PARTNER

- ❏ Cell phone and charger
- ❏ Prepaid calling card (cell phones are often prohibited in hospitals)
- ❏ Digital camera and/or video camera with rechargeable batteries and chargers
- ❏ Cash for parking meters, vending machines, and payphones
- ❏ Phone list
- ❏ Healthy snacks and treats

FOR BABY

- ❏ Organic cotton T-shirts or onesies
- ❏ Organic cotton baby bedding and blankets (check with the hospital first to make sure these are allowed)
- ❏ Nontoxic soaps, lotions, and creams
- ❏ Eco-friendly diapers
- ❏ Organic socks, booties, and cap
- ❏ Organic going-home outfit
- ❏ Infant car seat
- ❏ BPA-free baby bottles and organic formula (if you choose to use formula instead of breastfeeding)

POSTPARTUM

- ❏ Comfy organic nightgown
- ❏ Nursing bras (if breastfeeding)
- ❏ Comfy, organic going-home outfit

EXTRAS

❑ iPod or CD player
❑ DVD player
❑ Laptop (some hospitals now have wireless Internet for instant labor updates)
❑ Extra pillows
❑ Birthing ball

This list is just a guide. Feel free to add to it as you see fit. The important thing is to make sure that you gather all of the items you may need ahead of time so that when your labor begins you can easily grab them or have a friend pick them up for you.

Putting It All Together

Talk over your green birth plan with your partner, health care provider, and doula and make sure that everyone understands your preferences for a green and healthy delivery of your baby. If you will have your baby in a hospital or birthing center, make sure you know what you will be allowed to bring for your big day. By your eighth month, you should have these items packed up together and ready to go for the big day!

Home Remedies for Common Pregnancy Ailments

Minor conditions can become major maladies when they are combined with the discomforts and other ailments of pregnancy, especially because you may not be able to take the over-the-counter remedies that you usually reach for treat your discomfort. Be sure to talk with your health care provider about the remedies you can use to care for some of these common ailments that occur during pregnancy.

Morning Sickness

Roughly half of all pregnant women suffer from periods of nausea and vomiting known collectively as morning sickness (although it can strike at any time of day). These are usually caused by a combination of low blood sugar, dehydration, and an overflow of hormones.

The best way to ward off morning sickness is to get plenty of rest and to eat a number of small meals throughout the day to make sure that your stomach is never completely empty. Place a few crackers on your bedside table to nibble on throughout the night and when you wake up in the morning. It is also a good idea to eat slowly and avoid drinking and eating at the same time. Steer clear of greasy, spicy, or high-fat foods that might aggravate your nausea. Also avoid strong odors, overheating, and smoke. If nausea continues to be a problem, try one of these home remedies:

- Sniff a fresh lemon peel.
- Dissolve 1 teaspoon wheat germ in 1 cup of warm milk and sip.
- Drink a mixture of 1 tablespoon apple cider vinegar, 1 tablespoon honey, and 1 cup cold water at bedtime.
- Suck on a piece of ginger candy or sip ginger ale.
- Drink peppermint, chamomile, or spearmint tea.
- Wear motion sickness bands.

These tricks may help you through the temporary bouts of nausea that accompany your pregnancy. If morning sickness continues to be a problem, change the time of day you are taking you prenatal vitamin, talk to your health care provider about increasing your intake of vitamin B6, and take heart, for most women morning sickness dissipates somewhere around the fourteenth week of pregnancy.

ALERT

Although morning sickness is common during pregnancy, some pregnant women are affected by a more extreme form of the condition called *hyperemesis gravidarum*. This ailment is characterized by severe nausea, vomiting, weight loss, and dehydration. Talk to your health care provider if you are experiencing any of these symptoms.

Heartburn

It may be hard to imagine, but as your baby grows and develops inside your uterus, other organs in your body will get pushed around to make room.

As your stomach gets pushed up from its normal position, you may begin to experience acid reflux, indigestion, and heartburn.

If this becomes a problem, trying eating smaller meals throughout the day and remaining upright for an hour or two after eating. Avoid spicy and/ or greasy meals and increase the amount of milk you drink throughout the day. Drink a cup of peppermint tea or eat a few spoonfuls of yogurt to settle your stomach. Also, talk to your health care provider about taking a natural, over-the-counter antacid to soothe you stomach as needed.

Constipation and Hemorrhoids

Hormonal changes can cause food to move through your digestive system more slowly than before, leading to constipation. The strain and pressure of constipation can, in turn, cause the development of hemorrhoids. Stress and poor diet can also cause or aggravate these conditions. The best remedies for constipation are regular exercise, a high-fiber diet, and an increased intake of water. For hemorrhoids, try applying witch hazel and lemon juice to the area to reduce swelling or dissolve baking soda in a warm bath and soak for fifteen to twenty minutes. Talk to your health care provider if you are bothered by these conditions for more than a few days or if your symptoms increase in severity.

Headaches

Even if you've never been bothered by headaches before, surging hormones can cause headaches to occur on a regular basis during pregnancy. They may even lead to migraines, which can cause severe discomfort, nausea, and vomiting. Most of the time, resting and increasing your intake of water will help you soothe a headache naturally. You could also try drinking lavender or chamomile tea to help you relax and ease the discomfort of a headache. If headaches continue to be a problem, talk to your health care provider about the over-the-counter remedies you can use to alleviate them.

Stretch Marks and Dry Skin

Stretch marks are another nasty side effect of pregnancy. Seventy-five to ninety percent of pregnant women are affected by this common condition that typically occurs on the abdomen but may also appear on the breasts, butt, thighs and upper arms. In addition, many women are bothered by dry skin or the appearance of red patches that develop during their pregnancies.

FACT

Stretch marks are caused by changes in the elastic supportive tissue that lies just beneath the skin. They start out pink, reddish brown, purple, or dark brown, depending on your skin color. They usually fade after pregnancy, but for most women they never totally disappear.

Genetics play a large role in determining whether or not you will develop stretch marks or have other skin problems during your pregnancy. If you do, try nontoxic, coconut oil lotions to help moisturize skin and promote healthy stretching. Tea tree oil may also help to reduce the appearance of blemishes and spots that can occur during pregnancy.

CHAPTER 2

Eating Your Greens

Your mother always told you to eat your greens, right? Well now more than ever it is important that you do so. Pregnant moms are the only source of nutrition for their growing babies. So the foods you eat will not only help your baby develop and thrive, but they may also be filling her up with toxins. Make sure you *green* your greens by selecting eco-friendly foods that are healthy for you, your baby, and the planet.

What's in Your Food?

Your doctor or midwife will give you lots of information about eating a balanced diet and the types of foods you should and shouldn't eat while pregnant. Now that you are eating for two, you need to pay even closer attention to the amount of calcium, iron, protein, vitamins, and minerals that you eat each day. You also need to think carefully about the health and safety of all the foods in your diet.

The foods you eat during your pregnancy give you the energy you need to get through each day and provide your baby with the nutrients she needs to grow. Your food selections also make a difference to the health of the environment in which you will raise your baby. It is important to avoid toxins in your diet to improve your health, lower your risk of illness, and reduce your growing baby's exposure to dangerous toxins.

The next time you sit down to a meal, take a good look at the food on your plate. There was a time when you could take for granted that these foods contained nothing but the most natural ingredients. But that's no longer the case. Now, foods that you once considered healthy like fruits, vegetables, and meats are laden with chemicals, like pesticides, hormones, antibiotics, and genetically modified ingredients.

In addition, almost 90 percent of foods sold at the grocery store are processed in some way. During this processing, chemical additives and preservatives are added to improve the food's flavor, appearance, or shelf life.

Fortunately, it is easy to make better decisions about the foods you put on your plate and in your body. By avoiding foods that you know are heavily contaminated and selecting locally produced, organic varieties instead, you can significantly reduce the amount of toxins in your diet, and the amount of toxins that your baby will be exposed to during your pregnancy.

Additives and Preservatives

Chances are any ingredient on a food's ingredient label that you don't recognize (or cannot pronounce) is a chemical food additive or preservative. Most processed foods contain additives and preservatives in order to improve their flavor, make them look more natural, and help them last longer on the shelf. Processed foods lose many of their natural flavors and colors during the heating and preparation required to can or package them, so food manufacturers also rely on these chemicals to restore foods to a more natural appearance, texture, and flavor. For instance, "chicken flavor" is added to McDonald's Chicken McNuggets to make them taste like chicken again after processing.

ALERT

According to the U.S. Food and Drug Administration, the agency responsible for overseeing the food manufacturing industry, more than 3,000 food additives are currently approved for use in the United States. These chemicals have all been approved for humans to eat, but many are still linked to a number of frightening health effects like allergies, asthma, cancer, and even birth defects.

Some food additives, like sulfites and monosodium glutamate (MSG), are so commonly associated with reactions like nausea, shortness of breath, headaches, or dizziness that they are required by law to be listed prominently on a product's packaging.

During pregnancy, your health care provider will probably talk to you about avoiding certain food additives called nitrates. Nitrates are added to cured meats like hot dogs, bacon, and sausages to improve flavor and prevent spoiling. But once they get in your body, nitrates form nitrosamines—carcinogenic (cancer-causing) compounds that are harmful for both pregnant moms and their growing babies.

Unfortunately, you may not always realize that there are additives in the food you eat. The U.S. Food and Drug Administration (FDA) requires food manufacturers to list all ingredients on product labels. But some additives are simply listed as *spices* or *artificial flavoring*, making it difficult for consumers to know exactly what's on their plate.

Here is a list of some of the most common chemicals you will find in processed foods:

- **Aspartame:** Used as a sweetener.
- **Benzoates:** Used primarily in acidic foods to prevent bacterial growth.

- **Butylated Hydroxy Anisole (BHA) and Butylated Hydroxytoluene (BHT):** Used as flavor enhancers.
- **Carrageenan:** Used to create a smooth texture and thicken foods.
- **Cochineal:** Added to improve the coloring and appearance of foods.
- **Disodium Guanylate:** Added to enhance flavor.
- **FD&C Red No. 40:** Used to improve color.
- **Nitrates and Nitrites:** Added to prevent discoloration in meat.
- **Potassium Sorbate:** Used for killing mold.
- **Propionic Acid:** Used to prevent the growth of mold.
- **Propylene Glycol:** Used to thicken and improve texture of food.
- **Titanium Dioxide:** Added to give foods a whiter coloring.

Inspect food labels carefully and look for those that contain the minimum number of food additives and preservatives. Opt for fresh fruits, vegetables, meat, and dairy products to limit your exposure.

Genetically Modified Ingredients

A few decades ago, scientists started looking for ways to improve our food supply by altering the genetic makeup of certain crops and livestock. For instance, by tinkering with the genetic code of a corn plant, scientists were able to create a strain of corn that is more resistant to pests, disease, and weather conditions. This genetic modification, therefore, improves the success of the crop and makes it easier and cheaper for farmers to produce food. However, a number of concerns have been raised regarding the health and safety of these genetically modified crops both for humans and the environment as a whole.

QUESTION

How can I find eco-friendly food on the go?
Patronize restaurants that use local and organic foods in their selections. Ask your server if they incorporate healthier green foods into their recipes. On the web, review the Eat Well Guide (*www.eatwell guide.com*) for a list of restaurants that use local, sustainable ingredients. Try to minimize waste by using the minimum amount of paper napkins and plastic silverware and cups.

The majority of genetic modifications of crops are engineered to improve a plant's resistance to pesticides. That way, farmers can douse crops with pesticides meant to kill weeds and pests without harming the intended crop.

Scientists are also researching ways to genetically engineer farm animals. Chickens, for instance, have been genetically modified to lay lower cholesterol eggs and certain salmon species have been engineered to grow five times faster than wild species.

The problem is that there are a lot of unanswered questions about the safety of these genetically modified foods, for both environmental and human health. Because the science is so new, researchers don't yet have solid information about the future consequences of changing the genetic makeup of plants and animals. In Europe, foods made with genetically modified ingredients must be clearly labeled as such on their packaging, so that consumers know if the foods they are eating have been altered. Unfortunately, there is no such law yet requiring the labeling of genetically modified foods that are sold in the United States.

ALERT

About 70 percent of the processed foods on store shelves contain genetically modified ingredients. Genetically modified versions of the following foods have been approved for commercial use: alfalfa, cherry tomatoes, chicory, corn, cotton, flax, papayas, potatoes, rapeseed (canola), rice, soybeans, squash, sugar beets, and tomatoes. To be safe, choose organic varieties of these foods or look for products labeled *GMO Free*.

Pesticides

Pesticides are the chemicals that farmers use to kill the pests, like weeds, rodents, and insects that might otherwise harm a crop and hinder its growth. About 300 different pesticides are used to grow the foods you see on supermarket shelves every day. These pesticides harm the environment by polluting the soil, air, and water, and altering the environment of fish, birds, and other wildlife. The farm workers who come in contact with these pesticides are also at risk. According to the Environmental Protection Agency (EPA), pesticides are responsible for 20,000–40,000 work-related poisonings each year in the United States.

There are also concerns about the health risks associated with pesticides once they hit your plate. One study published in the peer-reviewed journal, *Environmental Health Perspectives*, found pesticides present in the urine and saliva of children who ate conventionally grown produce. The most prominent pesticides found were malathion and chlorpyrifos, two chemicals that are banned for use in homes, but are still widely used on crops. These types of pesticides work by poisoning the nervous system in pests. In humans, they can cause damage to the nervous system, organ damage, behavior disorders, immune system dysfunction, behavioral abnormalities, and hormone disruption.

In other words, they really are not chemicals that you want in your body, especially when you are pregnant. Fortunately, you can minimize or even eliminate your exposure to most pesticides by making the switch to organic fruits, vegetables, meats, and dairy products. In the study mentioned above, when children were switched to a diet that consisted of only organic produce, the pesticides disappeared almost immediately.

Synthetic Hormones

Hormones are compounds that are found in all animals, including humans. In the body, they naturally control important functions such as growth, development and reproduction.

However, for a number of years, synthetic hormones have been injected into certain types of farm animals in order to increase production or increase an animal's weight gain. The USDA and FDA contend that these hormones are safe, but many health advocates argue that hormone residues in meat and milk might be harmful to human and environmental health.

The major concern surrounding the use of hormones in farm animals is that the hormone residues may disrupt the hormone balance of the humans who eat them. Birds, fish, and other wildlife are also vulnerable to the hormone residues left behind in the environment through animal feces.

The European Union does not allow the use of hormones in cattle farming, and, since 1988, they have banned the import of hormone-treated beef. The United States, however, currently allows six hormones—estradiol, progesterone, testosterone, zeranol, trenbolone acetate, and melengestrol acetate—to be used in food production.

Look for meats and dairy products that are certified organic or specifically labeled *hormone-free* to minimize your baby's exposure to synthetic hormones.

FACT

In 1950, the average dairy cow produced roughly 5,300 pounds of milk each year. Today, a typical dairy cow produces more than 18,000 pounds of milk each year. Why the increase? America's dairy cows are now given a genetically engineered hormone called rBGH to increase milk production.

Organic and Free-Range Foods

Organic foods are a great choice for pregnant women and the planet because they are produced without the use of any synthetic chemical pesticides, hormones, additives, or genetically modified ingredients. They are safer for the environment, safer for farm workers, and better for your family's health because they keep these unwanted toxins off your plate.

Organic foods may also contain more nutrients than conventional produce. A recent ten-year study by researchers at the University of California at Davis found that some organic foods, like tomatoes and corn have twice as many antioxidants as conventionally grown produce.

ESSENTIAL

All grocers are legally required to place organic foods (especially fruits and vegetables) where they won't be exposed to the pesticide-laden water runoff from conventional produce. If your local store has forgotten that rule, remind them. If they still don't move the organic food, shop somewhere else.

But be wary of foods labeled only *free range* rather than *organic*. The free-range label commonly found on poultry, eggs, and beef, may make you think of animals grazing in open fields and drinking from fresh, cool streams. But this is hardly the reality. For starters, the term is only legally defined for labeling poultry, not beef or eggs. So a *free-range* label on eggs is meaningless. And unfortunately, it doesn't indicate much when it comes to poultry. The U.S. Department of Agriculture (USDA) requires that poultry labeled free range must have access to the outdoors for "an undetermined period each day." Opening a coop door for five minutes each day is considered adequate to get a free-range stamp of approval, regardless of whether the chickens saw the door and went outside.

Seafood and Mercury

Seafood is a lean protein that has always been considered a healthy alternative to fatty meats and poultry. It is also rich in the omega-3 fatty acids that are important for a growing baby's brain development. However, many species of fish have become so contaminated with chemicals and heavy metals that they are no longer safe to eat, especially for pregnant women. The EPA estimates that 630,000 babies are born in this country each year with high levels of mercury—a condition that can lead to neurological, developmental, and cognitive problems for your baby down the road. But fear of mercury doesn't mean you need to eliminate all seafood from your diet. Just be very cautious about the types and quantity of seafood that you eat.

Safer Seafood

The FDA and EPA currently recommend that pregnant women avoid eating shark, swordfish, king mackerel, and tilefish as these fish are known to contain high levels of polychlorinated biphenyls (PCBs) and mercury, two contaminants that are particularly harmful to a developing fetus. Many OB/GYNs and midwives also suggest that expectant moms limit their consumption of tuna, oysters, salmon, marlin, halibut, and sea bass.

Wild or Farmed?

Choose wild-caught fish over farmed varieties whenever possible. Farm-raised fish are often raised in tanks or net enclosures that are stressful for the fish and may facilitate the spread of disease and contamination.

Farm-raised fish also tend to contain significantly higher concentrations of PCBs, dioxin, and other contaminants.

ALERT

Shrimp is a popular type of seafood that is relatively low in toxins and healthy to eat. However, the fishing practices used to harvest shrimp are often harmful to the environment. Shrimp trawling causes a large number of by-catch whereby other species are inadvertently killed, as well as destruction of coastal wetlands and mangrove forests.

You should also avoid eating refrigerated, smoked seafood labeled lox, nova style, kippered, or jerky that has not been cooked, as these may be contaminated with *Listeria*. And avoid fish caught locally from contaminated lakes and rivers. Contact your local health department to find out which fish are safe to eat in your area.

Wild-caught fish, on the other hand, are harvested directly from their natural habitat. Depending upon the species of fish, they may have a lower risk of disease and contamination than farm-raised varieties.

According to the Marine Stewardship Council, an independent agency that certifies the sustainability of various fishing industries, the following fish species are the most likely to have been harvested sustainably:

WILD-CAUGHT FISH
- Anchovies
- Atlantic herring
- Atlantic mackerel
- Crab (blue, Dungeness, snow, and stone)
- Flounder
- Herring
- Mahi Mahi
- Salmon
- Scallops (bay)
- Sardines
- Shrimp (northern, Oregon, and spot)

FARM-RAISED FISH

- Abalone
- Catfish
- Caviar
- Clams
- Mussels
- Oysters
- Scallops (both sea and bay)
- Striped Bass
- Sturgeon
- Trout

The FDA recommends that pregnant women can safely eat about twelve ounces of cooked fish each week. Use this list as you guide to finding fish that have been harvested with concern for the environment and talk to your health care provider about the risks and benefits of eating seafood while pregnant.

What's Your Beef?

The production of beef makes more of an impact on the environment than any other type of food. According to a report produced by the World Wildlife Fund, more pasture is used for cattle than all other domesticated animals and crops combined. Cattle also eat an increasing proportion of grain produced from agriculture, are one of the most significant contributors to water pollution, and are a major source of greenhouse gas emissions.

The average American eats roughly four servings of beef each week. Skip the beef in just one meal each week and you can dramatically reduce your overall impact on the environment. A vegetarian or vegan diet can be a great option for pregnant women, as long as you pay close attention to the amount of vitamins, calcium, and protein your diet provides. Talk to your health care provider about the food selections and vitamin supplements that would work best for you.

Steer Clear of Bacteria

There are certain types of microscopic bacteria that can be harmful to pregnant women their babies. *Listeria* is a bacteria that is occasionally found in soft cheeses like brie, camembert, feta, and *queso fresco*; in deli meats and cheeses; in processed meats (like hot dogs, meat spreads, and *pate*); in smoked seafood; and in raw or unpasteurized milk. Although most people can safely be exposed to *Listeria* without experiencing a problem, pregnant women are ten times more likely to get sick from the same exposure. To be safe, avoid any of the foods that could be contaminated with the bacteria.

Reducing Your Food Miles

Thanks to the global marketplace, consumers now have access to a wide variety of fruits, vegetables, meats, and grains regardless of location or season. But shipping foods across the country or even around the world creates an enormous amount of pollution and waste. Unfortunately, due to the industrialization of the farming industry, food is more likely to come from a distance than it is to come from one's nearby farms and markets.

The term, *food miles* refer to the distance that food must travel from where it is produced to where it is consumed. By reducing the food miles of the foods on your plate, you can significantly reduce the environmental impact caused by their production.

FACT

Most produce travels roughly 1,500 miles between the farm where it was produced and your dinner plate. About 40 percent of fruit in the United States is imported from other countries and, even though broccoli is commonly grown within 20 miles of the average American's house, most broccoli travels an average 1,800 miles from where it is grown to the grocery store.

Opt for local, in-season foods, whenever possible. If you cannot find a local source for organic foods, purchase the conventional varieties to avoid the pollution and waste associated with transporting organics to your location. Check out Sustainable Table (*www.sustainabletable.org*) for a state-by-state list of seasonal produce availability.

Where to Buy Organic

Shopping for organic foods is easier now than ever, as both large and small grocers are expanding their organic selections in response to the explosion of demand. To find wholesome, fresh, organic food that is also locally grown, check out your local farmers' market, where you can find organic growers selling produce without the supermarket premiums. For listings of local farmers' markets, check out *www.ams.usda.gov/farmersmarkets* or *www.localharvest.org*.

ESSENTIAL

Don't get hit by organic sticker shock. Stretch your budget for organic foods by seeking out the deals. Purchase generic, store-brand varieties of organic selections. Sign up for the free shopper's-club savings card at your favorite store, buy in bulk whenever possible, and search the web for printable coupons for your favorite items.

Community-supported agriculture (CSA) is another great way to get organic foods from a local source. CSAs usually require a seasonal subscription ranging from $300 to $500. But for this investment, which works out to about $10 to $15 per week, you will get a weekly supply of fresh, organic foods that often cost less than the same nonorganic foods on your grocer's shelf. Check out Local Harvest (*www.localharvest.org*) to find a CSA in your area.

Most and Least Contaminated Foods

You will get the best health and environmental benefits when you purchase organic foods that would require the use of a lot of chemicals if they were grown conventionally. Use this list as a guide to the foods that are the most and least important to buy organic.

MOST CONTAMINATED FOODS

- Apples
- Bell Peppers
- Celery
- Cherries
- Grapes (imported)
- Nectarines
- Peaches
- Pears
- Potatoes
- Red raspberries
- Spinach
- Strawberries

LEAST CONTAMINATED FOODS

- Asparagus
- Avocados
- Bananas
- Broccoli
- Cauliflower
- Kiwi
- Mangoes
- Onions
- Papaya
- Pineapples
- Sweet corn
- Sweet peas

If your budget is tight, don't worry about organic when it comes to the foods that are grown with the least amount of synthetic chemicals, as these are the least harmful to your health and that of the environment.

CHAPTER 3

Detox Your Day

Now that you are thinking, drinking, eating, and breathing for two, your immediate environment is more important than ever. You probably already know that you need to avoid cigarette smoke and lead, but what about the other chemical toxins lurking in your home, at your office, and in your car? The world may suddenly seem fraught with peril for both you and your baby. But don't worry, there a number of things that you can do to reduce your exposure to these toxins and make your world a healthier place for your family.

What's in the Air?

Ah, there's nothing like a breath of fresh air, right? Well, it all depends on what's in that air! Air pollution is a common problem in our modern society. And both you and your baby are affected by the quality of the air around you.

In a recent study at the Columbia University Center for Children's Environmental Health in New York, researchers evaluated sixty newborns whose mothers wore portable air monitors during their last trimester. They found that a baby's genetic makeup can be damaged by the polluted air his mother breathes during pregnancy. Additional studies have also linked air pollution to decreases in lung function and increases in heart attacks.

Still, it won't do you or your baby any good if you are stressed out about every breath you take. Breathe easier by knowing what to look for and what to do to protect yourself and your baby from air pollution.

Outdoor Air Quality

Outdoor air pollution occurs when the air in the atmosphere becomes contaminated with gases and particulates that don't belong there. It is caused by both natural and human activity. Natural causes of air pollution, such as volcano eruptions, soil erosion, and forest fires, emit toxic gases and particulates into the atmosphere.

But by and large, it is human activities, like fossil fuel combustion from cars and power plants, that account for most of the pollution in outdoor air. This is why outdoor air pollution is often greatest in and around cities where human concentrations are largest.

Indoor Air Quality

If all of that information about outdoor air pollution has you headed for the indoors, it may alarm you to realize that indoor air pollutants are often more dangerous than those outside. Chemicals in your cleaning supplies, paint, furniture, and even in your household dust can become trapped inside your home, making the indoor air pollutant levels as much as 25 to 62 percent greater than outdoor levels.

Between work and home activities, most Americans spend an average of 80 to 90 percent of their time inside, making exposure to harmful indoor pollutants a serious concern for human health.

Indoor plants can help filter toxins out of your indoor air and improve the air quality for your whole family. But with a new baby on the way, it is important to look for plants that are safe for little children. Look for baby-safe indoor plants like spider plants, snake plants, wandering jews, begonias, geraniums, corn plants, and pothos.

Breathe Easier

You may think that there is not much you can do to prevent or control air pollution. But there are actually a number of things you can do to minimize your contribution to air pollution and ensure that the air you and your baby are breathing is the freshest air possible.

Here's how to minimize your exposure to air pollution, both indoors and outside:

OUTDOORS

❑ Pay attention to air-quality advisories, especially if you live in or near a big city. If the levels are high, don't spend a lot of time outdoors.

❑ When traveling by car, try to limit the amount of time you spend sitting in heavy traffic. Seek out less traveled routes or walk instead.

❑ Hold your breath or turn your head when you see exhaust spurting out of the car in front of you or when you are filling your car with gas.

INDOORS

❑ Do not smoke and avoid exposure to others who do.

❑ Ventilate your home well by opening windows and doors regularly, especially when dusting, vacuuming, and painting.

❑ When entering your home, leave your shoes at the door and ask your guests to do the same to avoid tracking harmful chemicals indoors.

❑ Do not dry clean your clothes. If you cannot avoid dry cleaning, make sure you air-out your clothes before bringing them indoors, or select an environmentally safe dry-cleaning service that does not use perchloroethylene.

❑ Use natural cleaning agents like baking soda and vinegar around your home instead of synthetic chemical compounds.

❑ Wet-mop your floors frequently to reduce your exposure to dust.

❑ Do not use synthetic chemical pesticides or fertilizers in your home, on your lawn, or in your garden.

By taking control of your indoor and outdoor environments, you can significantly reduce the number of pollutants that you and your baby are exposed to with every breath you take.

Allergies and Asthma

Chemicals, fumes, airborne toxins, and particulate pollution are common in the environment, and they may be making you sick. Exposure to pollution can cause allergy-like symptoms such as headaches, cough, fatigue, dizziness, rashes, and nausea. It can also trigger or aggravate asthma attacks.

ESSENTIAL

The American College of Obstetrics and Gynecology recommends that pregnant women get thirty minutes of moderate physical activity every day. Exercise can help improve muscle tone, strengthen bones, increase flexibility, and boost your body's immune system. If you have never exercised before, talk to your health care provider about the types of exercise that would work well for you.

If you think that you are suffering from allergies or asthma attacks as a result of environmental pollution, try the techniques above to reduce your exposure to pollution at home and at work. If you have been diagnosed with asthma prior to your pregnancy, take special care to avoid triggers like allergens, dust mites, and cigarette smoke, which may aggravate your condition.

And be sure to talk to your health care provider about the effects that environmental pollution can have on your pregnancy.

What's in Your Water?

You know it is important to drink a lot of water while you are pregnant. But concerns about lead, mercury, and other potential contaminants lurking in your water may make you think twice before taking your next sip. How can you make sure that you and your baby are drinking the purest water available?

Water Pollution

Water pollution occurs when the Earth's waterways become contaminated with organisms that don't belong there. More often than not, water pollution is caused by human activities, such as industrial and agricultural manufacturing, food processing, petroleum use, and the improper storage of chemicals. Water pollution has a harmful effect on drinking water supplies and on the environment as a whole.

Bottled versus Tap

More than 90 percent of the water in the United States meets the tap water quality standards set forth by the EPA. Your local water authority is required by law to send you an annual report detailing the quality of your drinking water and alerting you to any contaminants that have been detected. You may even be able to access you water quality report online at *www.epa.gov/ safewater/ccr/whereyoulive.html*.

Unfortunately, according to the Environmental Working Group, a nonprofit agency that specializes in identifying toxins, more than half of the contaminants found in local water systems are unregulated and therefore do not appear on the water tests or reports produced by water facilities. The group reported that the EPA tests and regulates less than 20 percent of the chemicals found in drinking water, forty-one of which have been linked to reproductive health risks.

At one time, most Americans had no choice but to get their water from the tap. In recent years, however, sales of bottled water in the United States have exploded, largely as a result of a public perception of purity driven by advertisements and packaging labels featuring pristine glaciers and crystal-clear mountain springs.

Yet, according to the Natural Resource Defense Council's (NRDC) four-year study on the bottled water industry, water that comes from a bottle is no cleaner or safer than water that comes from the tap. In fact, NRDC's study found that at least 25 percent of bottled water is actually just tap water that has been packaged in a bottle.

And bottled water takes a much greater toll on the environment than tap. Bottled water uses more energy and resources in its production and shipping than tap water, and it creates the production of disposable plastic bottles that fill up landfills at an alarming rate. Think again before purchasing bottled water. Save money and resources by carrying your own reusable bottle filled with filtered tap water instead.

FACT

In 2007, American consumed more than 8.8 billion gallons of bottled water, making it the second largest commercial beverage in the country (next to carbonated beverages). According to the Earth Policy Institute, nearly a quarter of all bottled water must be transported long distances by boat, train, and truck to reach American consumers.

Clean up Your Water

Don't take the purity of your drinking water for granted. According to the NRDC, many cities around the United States rely on ancient water delivery systems and treatment technology that may not be very effective at removing toxins. In addition, many water treatment facilities have aging pipes that can break and leach contaminants into the water they carry. Here's how to make sure that you and your baby are drinking the cleanest water you can.

Water Tests

If you are concerned about the health and safety of the tap water in your area, there are measures you can take to test it for toxicity. Many water contaminants are colorless and odorless, so testing is the only way to know for sure if your water is clean and safe.

In addition to concerns about the contaminants that don't show up on your local water facilities annual water quality report, you may want to be sure that the pipes, joints, and faucets in your home are not leaching toxins (like lead) into your water.

Water Filters

Another way to make sure the water you drink is clean and free of contaminants is to invest in a high-quality water filter. Most decent filters will remove lead, chlorine, mercury, and other chemicals. A water filter may even improve the taste of your drinking water, giving you an incentive to drink more of it each day!

If you don't already have one, this is a great time to look in to getting a home water filtration unit. The first step in choosing a water filter is to decide which types of toxins you are trying to filter out. The next section of this chapter will give you a better idea of the toxins you should avoid during pregnancy.

Toxins to Avoid

Toxins are everywhere in your environment, the air you breathe, the water you drink, and the foods you eat. Many are dangerous chemicals that may cause significant health risks with daily or repeated exposure. In today's modern society, it is not practical to try to avoid all exposure to toxins. But you can minimize your exposure to the most harmful toxins by paying special attention to the following compounds.

Volatile Organic Compounds

Volatile organic compounds (VOCs) are a major class of both indoor air pollution and outdoor smog. Indoors, they can be found in paints, carpets, furniture, glues, stains, finishes, copy paper, printers, cleaning products, air fresheners, and craft supplies.

VOCs can cause immediate reactions like eye, nose, and throat irritation, headaches, and nausea. They have also been linked to more serious health effects such as neurological disorders, liver and kidney damage, and even certain kinds of cancer. Babies and children, because of their developing immune systems, are especially susceptible to VOCs.

ESSENTIAL

According to the EPA, VOC concentrations are generally ten times higher indoors than outdoors. You can significantly reduce your exposure to VOCs by using nontoxic cleaners, paints, and rugs in your home and office and airing out your indoor space whenever possible.

Dioxins

Dioxins are a group of environmental pollutants that are known to affect a number of the human body's organs and systems. They are released into the environment by a number of human activities; most notably, the manufacture and disposal of chorine. They are also highly persistent in the environment, meaning they stick around and accumulate rather quickly in both the air and water.

ALERT

If you use cling wrap to store your foods, you may be exposing yourself to polyvinyl chloride (PVC), a toxic chemical known to release dioxins. Look for nontoxic cling wrap like Glad Cling Wrap, Saran Cling Plus, and Saran Premium Wrap, which use low-density polyethelyene instead of PVC. Butcher paper, wax paper, and reusable containers are even better alternatives.

Lead

Lead exposure can be extremely harmful to an unborn baby. It can cause premature birth, low birth weight, and permanent damage to a baby's developing nervous system. If your home was built before 1978, the walls may still be covered in lead-based paint. Chips from lead paint can be tracked along floors and kicked up during dusting. If you think your house may contain lead paint, contact a certified lead abatement contractor before removing or sanding the old paint. You can also test for lead using a test kit available at your local hardware store or from the National Safety Council (*www.nsc.org*).

Chlorine

Chlorine is present in the environment as both a liquid and a gas. The majority of chlorine that you are exposed to is found in your water supply as it is used in water treatment facilities to clean water and remove the presence of harmful bacteria. The EPA regulates the amount of chlorine that may be present in treated wastewater discharges. However, there is still likely chlorine present in the water that comes out of your tap. Not only will you be exposed to chlorine when you drink and cook, but also when you shower or take a bath. You can purchase a simple at-home water filter to remove chlorine from your home's water supply.

If you are concerned about chlorine in your water, you might also want to pour your water into a pitcher of water and allow it to sit uncovered in the refrigerator overnight. Most of the chlorine will evaporate (unfortunately into the air) reducing the content of the chemical in the water and improving its taste.

FACT

Thirty-five percent of the chlorine used worldwide is utilized to make PVC, or polyvinyl chloride. PVC is used in plastic packaging, cling wrap, bottles, credit cards, records, imitation leather, window frames, cables, pipes, flooring, wallpaper, and window blinds. Looking for PVC-free products can help reduce the amount of chlorine and other toxic byproducts found in the environment.

Chlorine is also released into the environment through manufacturing processes. For instance, chlorine is used to bleach paper and to produce some types of plastic packaging. When chlorine is used in manufacturing, the process can also result in the formation of harmful chemicals such as dioxins and furans, which are known to cause cancer in humans. You can minimize the amount of chlorine that is released into the environment by purchasing unbleached or chlorine-free paper products and avoiding any packaging or products made with PVC (#3) plastic.

Asbestos

Asbestos is the name for a family of mineral fibers that occur naturally in certain types of rock. It is strong, durable, noncombustible, and an efficient insulator, so for many years it was used in and around homes in products such as vinyl flooring, vinyl tiles, insulation, shingles, siding, textured paints, ceiling tiles, and certain types of insulation.

Today, the health risks associated with asbestos, namely lung cancer, are well known. But homes built or renovated between 1930 and 1970 may still contain asbestos products.

If you think your home or workplace may contain asbestos, talk to your health care provider immediately about the potential health risks to your pregnancy. You may also need to consult an asbestos removal professional about getting the asbestos out of your home. Minimize your exposure to asbestos by staying away from household or workplace renovations, especially when asbestos-containing materials are known to be present.

Tobacco Smoke

By far, one of the most dangerous toxins that you and your baby can come in contact with is tobacco smoke. The list of health problems associated with smoking during pregnancy is long. The most devastating side effect is the strong link between smoking and SIDS (sudden infant death syndrome). Smoking during pregnancy, and when a child is first born, doubles the baby's risk of dying from SIDS. And you don't even have to be the one doing the smoking. Exposure to secondhand smoke during pregnancy is linked to lower birth weight and increased risk of cancer in both mothers and babies.

ALERT

If you smoke, now is the time to quit. Check out one of these resources for help and support: Smoke Free (*www.smokefree.gov*), Quit Now (1-800-QUIT-NOW), and the American Legacy Foundation (*www.americanlegacy.org*). Do whatever it takes to get the help you need, for your own health as well as your baby's.

Don't smoke when you are pregnant or after your baby is born, and avoid those who do. At work, try not to hang out in a breakroom that is commonly frequented by smokers. And don't let anyone smoke in your home, near your work space, or in your car.

Mercury

Mercury is a cumulative heavy metal that is extremely toxic to both humans and the environment. It can be absorbed the through the skin, ingested through eating, or breathed in through the lungs.

QUESTION

How can I safely dispose of mercury?
Mercury is found in a number of household items like electronics, watch batteries, old-style glass thermometers, and fluorescent light bulbs. Because of its toxicity and persistence in the environment, you should never toss any products containing mercury into the waste stream. Instead, contact your local waste management service to find out how to safely dispose of mercury-containing items in your area.

Mercury destroys the central nervous system and many other organs. Sufficient exposure can result in brain damage, insanity, and death. Mercury is also a persistent toxin in the environment.

Nitrates

In Chapter 2, you learned about avoiding nitrates that are found in processed meats. But that's not the only place that nitrates are found. Approximately 4.5 million people in the United States have drinking water that exceeds the EPA's maximum allowable contaminant levels for nitrates. So it is a good idea to check your local water quality report and make sure the level of nitrates is at an acceptable level.

Nitrate contamination in water occurs due to fertilizers, animal waste, and septic tank waste. So it is more prone to occur in agricultural areas. If your water does test positive for nitrates, you can install an ion-exchange water softener, reverse-osmosis, or distillation filtration system to reduce the levels of nitrates in your water.

Toxins in the Workplace

The levels and types of toxins that you are exposed to at work will vary depending upon the type of work that you do. In the typical office setting, exposure is likely to be similar to what you would find in your home (chemical compounds from cleaning agents, dust, furniture, etc.). In general, you should make an effort to avoid exposure to harmful fumes from glues, paints, household cleaners, new carpets, dry-cleaned clothing, gasoline, pesticides, incinerators, smog, cigarette smoke, and flame retardants. If you work in an industrial environment or in any type of job that requires frequent exposure to chemicals, talk with your employer and your health care provider about the potential hazards you may be encountering during your pregnancy and the best ways to minimize them.

CHAPTER 4

Have a Green and Gorgeous Pregnancy

Your body will go through tremendous physical changes over the next nine months, so this is the perfect time to indulge in a beauty routine that makes you feel gorgeous inside and out. But you have to be careful; many of the products on store shelves that claim to make you beautiful may actually be harmful to you, your baby, and the planet. Use the tips in this chapter to pamper yourself with eco-savvy style.

Green Beauty Basics

Over the next nine months, every inch of your body will change in one way or another. As your body expands to accommodate your growing baby, you may notice differences in your skin, your hair, and even your fingernails. And at a time when you may be feeling most self-conscious about your body, it can be easy to fall prey to the constant bombardment from the global cosmetics industry as it aims to sell you products that claim to make you look younger, thinner, and more gorgeous.

Unfortunately, many conventional beauty products contain ingredients that are known to be harmful to human and environmental health. You might think that if they are on the store shelves, they must be safe, but there is actually minimal oversight over the safety of products that come from the personal care industry.

More than 1,110 personal-product ingredients have been banned for use in cosmetics in the European Union because of concerns that they may cause cancer, birth defects, or reproductive disorders. By contrast only ten are banned in the United States.

ALERT

According to the Environmental Working Group: 89 percent of the 10,500 ingredients used in personal care products have not been evaluated for safety by the FDA (the agency that regulates the personal care product industry), the Cosmetic Ingredient Review (an in-house panel appointed by the cosmetics industry), or by anyone else.

Also remember that every personal care product you use in your beauty regimen, whether it is soap or mascara, will eventually wash off of your body and into the environment, where its presence may affect plants, birds, fish, and other wildlife.

Does this mean that you have to go without washing your hair or applying cosmetics in order to be green? Certainly not! Fortunately it is easy to green your beauty regimen, as long as you know what to look for. Here's how to enjoy a green and gorgeous pregnancy.

Use a Little Less

Now that you have a baby on board, it may be time to reevaluate just how many beauty products you use each day. Sure, cosmetic companies want you to think that you need every lotion and potion on the store shelves in order to look beautiful, but you will find that when you use clean, all-natural beauty products, you only need the basics to look and feel your best. All the rest is a waste of money for you and a waste of energy and resources for the planet.

Also, be conscious of the amount of each product that you use each day. Do you consistently squeeze a huge dollop of styling products into your hand only to wash most of it away? Make an effort to use a little less of each of your beauty products to make them go further. It will save you money and minimize the amount of chemicals that eventually wash down the drain.

Be Kind to Animals

You don't have to be a vegetarian to realize that animal testing is unnecessary, unethical, and just plain cruel. Look for products labeled with the *Leaping Bunny*. This symbol, created by the Coalition for Consumer Information on Cosmetics (*www.leapingbunny.org*) is the only international standard label for personal care products indicating that they are cruelty-free and they have not been tested on animals.

FACT

In the past, manufacturers had to choose between minimal safety testing of their products and safety testing that used animals. But now, scientists can now use cultures of human skin cells and tissues to test the reaction and absorption rate of chemicals, or combination of chemicals, on the skin.

Go Oil-Free

You probably already know that the consumption of fossil fuels is not so great for the planet. But you may not realize that petroleum is also used for a number of products in your bathroom vanity. Petroleum derivates may be found in personal care products such as lip balm, lotions, and lubricants, as well as the plastics used in sanitary products. Pass on products that use petroleum or its derivatives (paraffin oil, propylene glycol, and ethylene) and look for alternatives such as beeswax, cocoa butter, and vegetable oils instead.

Skip Disposables

According the environmental news website Grist.org (*www.grist.org*), 2 billion disposable razors end up in U.S. landfills each year. Add this to the 50 million pounds of used toothbrushes that are tossed annually into the dump and you end up with quite a heap of personal care garbage. Invest in a reusable and refillable razor to save money and take a knick out the waste stream. For your teeth, try a Preserve toothbrush from Recycline (*www .recycline.com*) that's made from recycled yogurt cups and can be sent back to the company when you are through with it.

Avoid Aerosols

The chemicals used in aerosols are no longer a hazard to the ozone layer, but these chemicals have been replaced with petroleum propellants whose production creates the greenhouse gases that lead to global warming. Choose nonaerosol or pump-style products for your personal care routine.

Skip the Chemical Cocktail

There are a number of dubious chemical ingredients such as phthalates, parabens, formaldehyde, and mercury that are used to create many of the personal care products you find on store shelves. By themselves, each of these chemicals may pose a threat to both human and environmental health.

But FDA officials and health experts throughout the world are even more concerned about the "cocktail effect" that may occur when these chemicals and toxins are mixed in the body and then subsequently in the environment. Daily exposure to these chemicals, in combination with the myriad other chemicals found in your environment, may cause irreparable harm to both you and your baby.

Know Your Green Beauty Labels

So how can you make sure that the beauty products you use are healthy for you, your growing baby, and the environment? Read the labels. Sophie Uliano, author of *Gorgeously Green*, estimates that women spend an average of 400 hours per year on their beauty routine. Surely it is worth spending five extra minutes at the store to make sure the products you choose are healthy for you and the environment.

You don't have to be a scientist to know which ingredients to look for, and which to avoid on your personal care products. It is actually pretty simple —if you can pronounce the ingredient and you wouldn't be afraid to eat it, than it is more than likely safe to use on your skin. By contrast, if it sounds like a toxic chemical, than it probably is. Put that product down and move on to another.

ALERT

Many companies have introduced nanoparticle-sized ingredients to their formulations. Nanoparticles allow ingredients to permeate the skin more easily, boosting the product's effect. They are commonly used in sunscreens and lotions to improve absorption. But because of their small size, they may become uncontrollable and unpredictable in the body. Make sure your skin care products are labeled nano-free.

Ingredients to Look For

Want to make sure your personal care products are safe? Look for ingredients, such as these, that you can read and that you wouldn't be afraid to eat (not that your shampoo will be very tasty):

- Aloe Vera
- Beeswax
- Cocoa butter
- Essential oils
- Glycerin
- Herbs (green tea, chamomile, and lavender)
- Honey

- Lanolin
- Lemon
- Plant-based oils (almond, apricot, coconut, grape seed, jojoba bean, macadamia nut, olive, sesame, and tea tree)
- Vitamins
- Witch hazel

These ingredients are not only safe and healthy for you to use, they are also likely to be as, or more effective, than their synthetic chemical counterparts.

Ingredients to Avoid

Most commercial beauty products contain a number of harsh and toxic ingredients that are anything but beautiful. Take five seconds to read the label and put down any product that contains the following ingredients:

- BHA
- Formaldehyde
- Fragrance
- Lead
- Mercury
- Parabens
- Petroleum distillates
- Phthalates
- Polyethylene glycol
- Sodium Laurel Sulfate
- Toluene

These chemicals are considered the most detrimental to human and environmental health. Here's why.

BHA. BHA, or beta hydroxyl acid, is a preservative used in some skin care products. It is intended to reduce fine lines and wrinkles and other effects of aging. It may be listed as *BHA*, *salicylic acid*, *salicylate*, *sodium salicylate*, *willow extract*, *beta hydroxybutanoic acid*, *tropic acid*, or *trethocanic acid*. According to the Environmental Working Group (*www.ewg.org*), BHA is linked to certain types of cancer as well as organ system toxicity.

Formaldehyde. Also known as *formalin*, *DMDM hydantonin*, *diazolidinyl urea*, and *quaternium-15*, formaldehyde is found in eye shadows, mascaras, and other cosmetics. According to the National Toxicology Program, formaldehyde is a likely human carcinogen. Formaldehyde can be absorbed through the skin and nails.

Fragrance. A major loophole in the laws that govern health and safety standards for personal care products allows manufacturers to include virtually any ingredient in their product under the name *fragrance* without actually listing the chemical. About 2,600 chemicals are commonly used to create a single fragrance, and 95 percent of chemicals used as fragrances in cosmetics are synthetic compounds derived from petroleum. Because perfumes are of low molecular weight, they can easily penetrate the skin. In addition, products that contain ambiguous *fragrance* ingredients could contain formaldehyde, phthalates, or parabens. Some artificial fragrances, such as artificial musk, accumulate on the skin and have even been found in breast milk.

ALERT

Products labeled "unscented" are not necessarily free from chemical fragrances. More often than not, these products just use more synthetic chemicals to mask their original odor. Look for products labeled fragrance-free and carefully check the ingredient list to make sure no fragrances are included in the formula.

Lead. Lead is a brain- and nervous-system toxin as well as a known carcinogen and hormone disruptor that can accumulate in the bones. It is found in lead acetate in hair dyes and makeup.

Mercury. Your health care provider may have talked to you about the importance of limiting the amount of seafood you eat while pregnant in order to minimize your exposure to mercury. But he may not have mentioned that it is also possible to be exposed to mercury in your personal care products. Also known as *thimersol*, mercury is found in certain types of eye drops and some makeup products, such as mascara and eye shadow.

ALERT

Just because a product is labeled natural or all-natural does not mean that it is. In fact, many beauty products that claim to contain botanic ingredients actually only contain a small amount of natural ingredients combined with a formulation of chemicals. Skin care products only need to contain 1 percent natural ingredients in order to be called natural.

Parabens. Parabens are chemical compounds that are used as preservatives and can be found in shampoos, commercial moisturizers, shaving gels, cleansing gels, and personal lubricants. Parabens may cause skin irritation, itching, or allergic skin reactions. They have also been found to disrupt normal hormone function, as they mimic the natural hormone estrogen. Steer clear of products that list parabens such as methylparaben, ethylparaben, propylparaben, or butylparaben in their ingredients.

Petroleum distillates. Petroleum and petroleum derivates are commonly found in cold creams, lipsticks, lip protection, baby creams, and eye shadows. Petrolatum distillates can cause allergic reactions in sensitive individuals. And their production leads to the depletion of petroleum, a nonrenewable resource, and contributes to global warming.

Phthalates. Phthalates are synthetic, human-made substances that are used in the cosmetics industry to stabilize fragrances and make their aromas last longer. These chemicals have also been linked to some really frightening health risks, such as hormone disruption and reproductive changes known to cause birth defects, sperm damage, infertility, and the feminization of baby boys. Dibutyl and diethylhexyl phthalates have been banned in the European Union but not in the United States.

Polyethylene glycol. Polyethylene glycol, also known as *propylene glycol*, *isopropyl alcohol*, and *butylenes glycol*, is used in cleansers and as a thickening agent in a number of skin care products. It is a caustic ingredient used to dissolve grease. In fact, it is the same ingredient used in oven cleaner.

Sodium laurel sulfate. Also known as *sodium dodecyl sylfate* or *SDS*, sodium laurel sulfate is a foaming agent that may be carcinogenic and is often contaminated with the known carcinogenic 1,4 dioxane. It is commonly found in sudsy beauty products like shampoo, bubble bath, soap, and toothpaste.

Toluene. Found in nail polish and nail polish removers, toluene is a neurotoxin that affects the kidneys and can also cause birth defects. Steer clear of nail products that contain toluene or any of its derivatives, such as phenylmethane, toluol, and methylbenzene.

Hair Care

Hormone surges do some interesting things to a pregnant woman's hair. For some women, pregnancy makes their hair thicker and more lustrous than ever before, while others experience the opposite effect. Whatever effect pregnancy has on your hair, you will want to make sure that it is healthy by using eco-friendly hair care products that protect both your hair and your baby from toxins.

Your scalp, like the rest of your skin, is extremely absorbent, and it will easily soak in your hair products, especially those applied in the hot, moist conditions of the bath. Steer clear of shampoos and conditioners that contain petroleum products or coal tar. Coal tar is a known carcinogenic that is used in hair dyes and some dandruff and psoriasis shampoos. Also avoid hairsprays and hair gels that contain petroleum derivatives, formaldehyde, phthalates, and synthetic fragrance. Try the hair care products from Jason Natural (*www.jason-natural.com*) or Jane Carter Solution (*www.janecarter solution.com*).

Hair styling products. Some styling mousses contain triethanolamine, a toxin used to make chemical weapons. Also, commercial brands of hair spray and other styling agents use alcohol, polyvinylpyrrolidone plastic (a carcinogen), and formaldehyde, as well as artificial fragrances.

ESSENTIAL

Talk with the stylist at your salon to find out which beauty products they use and if they will use organic hair and skin care products upon request. Aveda Salons (*www.aveda.com*) use only Aveda products, which are made from organic, plant-based, and nonpetroleum ingredients. The company also offsets all of their manufacturing practices with wind energy programs, and it continually campaigns to raise money for environmental and social causes.

Hair dryers. You don't have to give up drying your hair just to go easy on the planet. Look for an ionic hair dryer or an Energy-Star rated model that uses less energy than comparable products.

Hair dye. The European Union has recently banned twenty-two ingredients that are commonly used in hair dyes citing concerns about the chemicals' possible links to bladder and bone marrow cancer. Not much is known about the safety of hair dyes in pregnancy. Talk to your health care provider about any hair coloring treatments you are considering.

If you do decide to color, try henna or an eco-friendly hair dye like Tints of Nature (*www.tintsofnature.com*) or Eco Colors (*www.ecocolors .net*).

Skin Care and Cosmetics

Beauty may only be skin deep, but the products you place on your skin to make yourself more beautiful go all the way into your body and your baby. Your skin is your largest organ and roughly 60 percent of the products you apply to your skin are absorbed directly in to your bloodstream. The average person uses about ten different skin care products in the form of lotions, soaps, toners, and moisturizers on her body every day. Sound familiar? If so, then you are likely absorbing the nearly 130 chemicals found in those products on a daily basis.

Cleansers. Just how clean is your bar of soap? Not only will the soap you use be absorbed into your body, but it will also run off of your body, down the drain, and directly into your local waterways. So, look for natural, plant-based soaps to get you clean without leaving a chemical residue. Choose bar soap over liquid soap to save money and packaging. Try skin cleansers from Dr. Bronner (*www.drbronner.com*), Evanhealy (*www.evanhealy.com*), or Nude Skincare (*www.nudeskincare.com*).

Also, avoid the waste that comes with disposable cleansing products like sponges, tissues, or cotton balls. Instead, use a quality organic facecloth that can be washed and reused over and over again.

QUESTION

Are self-tanners safe to use during pregnancy?
No. Self-tanners contain ingredients such as parabens, phthalates, and petroleum-based derivatives that are unhealthy for anyone, especially pregnant women. Most self-tanners also rely on dihydroxyacetone (DHA) to change the color of the skin by reacting with the skin's amino acids. This chemical increases the production of damaging free radicals in the skin, thus potentially increasing the risk of premature aging and skin cancer.

Lotions and oils. Many moisturizers use petroleum and petroleum derivates in their formulas. Look for healthier, greener products made from fruit and nut oils instead of petroleum. Ecco Bella (*www.eccobella.com*) and Dr. Hauschka (*www.drhauschka.com*) both make luscious moisturizing lotions that are as good for your skin as they are for the planet.

For stretch marks, try Erbaviva Stretch Mark Oil (*www.erbaviva.com*), Tummy Rub Bitter by Mama Mio (*www.mamamio.com*), or Mambino Organics Oh Baby! Belly Butter (*www.mambinoorganics.com*).

Sunscreen. According to the Environmental Working Group, 86 percent of sunscreen products offer inadequate protection from the sun or contain ingredients with significant safety concerns. Some may increase the production of free radicals that lead to premature aging and skin cancer. Look for a mineral-based sunblock that will protect your skin from the sun without exposing it to dangerous chemicals. Try Alba Botanica, (*www.albabotanica.com*), Avalon Organics (*www.avalon organics.com*), Burt's Bees (*www.burtsbees.com*), California Baby (*www .californiababy.com*), or Jason Natural (*www.jason-natural.com*).

Bubble bath and bath salts. It goes without saying that a water-hogging bath is not nearly as eco-friendly as a shower; a regular size tub uses twenty gallons of water compared to the three gallons used to take the average shower. But when you are pregnant, the weightlessness of a bath is often a welcome relief for sore muscles and aching joints.

For a natural, cleansing bath, try adding Epsom salts to warm water. Epsom salts are made from a combination of two minerals: magnesium and sulfate, which can help lower your blood pressure, alleviate headaches, and flush toxins from the body.

ALERT

Pregnant women should avoid using hot tubs or getting in a bath tub with water that is over 98°F. And unless you plan on giving birth at home and have prepared a special bath to do so, do not take a bath after your water breaks, or you risk introducing toxins to your baby during birth.

Cosmetics. Every woman has her favorite must-have product; for some it is mascara, for others it's lip gloss, and still others won't leave the house without a swipe of blush. Many women think that green beauty means going without cosmetics, but there's no reason why you cannot enjoy your favorite must-haves and still be eco-friendly. Just choose your products carefully.

Most commercial cosmetics contain some combination of toxic chemicals, parabens, phthalates, synthetic dyes, and harmful additives and preservatives. Look for nontoxic plant-based cosmetics in recyclable and/or reusable containers, like those from Honeybee Gardens (*www.honeybeegardens.com*), Afterglow Cosmetics (*www.afterglow cosmetics.com*), Josie Maran Cosmetics (*www.josiemarancosmetics .com*), and Iredale Mineral Cosmetics (*www.janeiredale.com*).

Teeth

Want a clean, bright, eco-friendly smile? The first step to going green while you are taking care of your teeth is to turn off the water while brushing. You can save 1,200 gallons of water each year with this one simple step. Here are more ways to go green while taking care of your pearly whites.

Toothpaste. Most toothpaste contains chemicals like parabens, sodium laurel sulfate, titanium dioxide for whitening, and high levels of fluoride.

For an effective, all-natural tooth cleaner, try using baking soda. Or if you prefer something with a bit more flavor, try the toothpastes from Jason Natural (*www.jason-natural.com*), Burt's Bees (*www.burtsbees .com*), or Tom's of Maine (*www.tomsofmaine.com*).

Toothbrushes. Most dentists recommend that you change your toothbrush at least four times per year. That adds up to 50 million pounds of used toothbrushes that end up in landfills each year in the United States alone. Unfortunately, there are not many reusable options when it comes to brushing your teeth. To minimize your impact, try the Preserve toothbrush from Recycline (*www.recycline.com*). They·are made from recycled plastic and come with a postage-paid envelope so that they can be returned to Recycline and recycled to create new toothbrushes.

ALERT

While fluoride is great for fighting tooth decay, high levels can be poisonous, and many health advocates worry about the level of fluoride that most people are exposed to every day in their toothpaste and drinking water. Since mid-1997, the FDA has mandated that all toothpastes containing fluoride must carry a poison warning.

Mouthwash. If you enjoy the fresh, clean feeling you get from mouthwash but don't want to pour a cocktail of chemicals in your mouth to get it, try making your own mouthwash with a mixture of lemon juice and water. Another good option is Tea Tree Oil Mouth Wash from Desert Essence (*www.desertessence.com*).

Floss. Most tooth floss is made with petroleum-based waxes. Eco-Dent Gentle Floss (*www.eco-dent.com*) is a vegan, waxed floss made with a blend of natural essential oils and enzymes to reduce plaque and help you maintain healthy teeth and gums.

Shaving

There are lots of easy ways to green your shaving. For starters, don't forget to turn off the tap while you shave, even if you are shaving in the shower. Just shaving your armpits could waste as much as four gallons of water if the water is running.

Razors. Americans throw away about 2 billion razors every year. Reusable electric razors can help to reduce this waste, and reduce the amount of hot water and chemical-laden shaving products that you use. Of course, they also require electricity to operate. If you do choose electric, be sure to purchase an Energy-Star rated model that uses less energy than comparable models. Reusable razors, or those made from recycled content (like the Preserve razor from Recycline (*www.recycline.com*), made from recycled plastic) can also help to reduce the waste associated with shaving.

Shaving creams and gels. Like other cosmetics and skin care products, many shaving creams contain petroleum-based derivatives, BHA, and parabens—chemicals linked to a number of serious health risks. They are also usually packaged in canisters that use a petroleum-based propellant. Before you lather up, check to make sure your shaving cream or gel uses organic plant-based ingredients in a reusable and/or recyclable container. Try Pacific Shaving Oil (*www.pacificshaving.com*), a blend of natural ingredients like sunflower oil, avocado oil, cucumber extract, and essential oils.

Smelling Clean and Green

Your sense of smell goes on high alert during pregnancy. You may be more sensitive to perfumes and find that some scents make you nauseated, light-headed, agitated, or more prone to headaches. To prevent these unnecessary side effects, try to keep your environment as clean and fragrance-free as possible.

Perfume. Most commercial perfumes contain a mixture of approximately 4,000 synthetic chemicals, many of which have never been tested for safety. And as mentioned earlier, cosmetic manufacturers do not even have to list all of the ingredients found in their proprietary fragrance formulas. If you want to smell pretty, try using a lightly scented nontoxic lotion. Some scents, such as citrus, peppermint, ginger, and cardamom, can help reduce nausea in addition to smelling good. Other scents that may be pleasant include lavender, rose, and chamomile.

ALERT

Essential oils are natural, concentrated, aromatic liquids excreted from plants. However, some essential oils are not recommended during pregnancy and can be toxic when used on the skin, so be sure to talk with your health care provider about the types of scents you can use during your pregnancy.

Antiperspirant and deodorant. Most antiperspirants use aluminum as their active ingredient. Aluminum has been found to cause skin irritation and general inflammation. It also blocks the pores, which prevents the body from eliminating toxins through perspiration and reduces the body's natural ability to regulate temperature. The mining of aluminum is also harmful for environmental health in that it scars the landscape, pollutes water, and consumes enormous amounts of energy. Instead of using antiperspirant, try using a natural deodorant brand that doesn't contain aluminum such as Jason Natural (*www.jason-naturals.com*), Desert Essence (*www.desertessence.com*), or Kiss My Face (*www.kissmyface.com*), or using a crystal stick deodorant made from natural mineral salts.

Manicures and Pedicures

Your health care provider may caution you against having any manicures and pedicures during your pregnancy. Most commercial nail care products contain harmful chemicals that could be particularly harmful to a developing baby. Toulene, a major component of both nail polish and nail polish remover, can lead to birth defects and cancer. Dibutyl phthalate (DBP) and formaldehyde are additional offenders often found in nail products. That doesn't mean you have to skip the manicure altogether, but your best option is to pass on the polish and instead buff nails to a shine.

Nail polish and remover. If you cannot live without a little color on your nails, opt for a formula that is toluene, DBP, and formaldehyde free such as soy-based Priti Nail Polish (*www.pritiorganicspa.com*). When it is time to take the polish off, try the organic, acetone, ethyl acetate, and cruelty-free Vegan Nail Polish Remover from No Miss (*www.veganessentials.com*).

Fake nails. Acrylic nails damage the health of your fingernails by depriving them of oxygen and light and causing nails to become weak and brittle. They also provide a harbor for moisture, which can lead to a fungal infection. Removing acrylic nails requires the powerful and toxic solvent *acetonitrile*, which can irritate the respiratory system and damage your thyroid gland. Acrylic nails are not healthy for any women and you should certainly avoid them during pregnancy.

Do It Yourself (DIY) Beauty

One way to ensure that your personal care products contain only the most natural, eco-friendly ingredients is to make them yourself. It is not as hard as you might think. Yes, it will take more time than purchasing a product from the store, but it is also an inexpensive and satisfying way to get great green beauty products. Check out *Naturally Healthy Skin: Tips & Techniques for a Lifetime of Radiant Skin* by Stephanie Tourles, or visit My Beauty Recipes (*www.mybeautyrecipes.com*) for recipes for everything from shampoo to mouthwash.

CHAPTER 5

Green Shopping

One of the best places to show your support for the environment is in the marketplace. Going green while you shop minimizes waste, reduces pollution, conserves resources, promotes fair treatment for workers, and sends a powerful message to businesses about the importance of environment. By educating yourself about the products you buy and the products you might want to avoid, you have a direct influence over the protection of the planet. This chapter will show you how to tread lightly on the environment while you shop.

Why Shop Green?

Green shopping means thinking about all of the ways that a product impacts the environment throughout its *lifecycle*—or from the time it is created to the time it hits the waste stream. This takes into account everything from the materials used to manufacture a product to the energy used to transport it to the store, to the way you will dispose of it when you are finished with it.

ESSENTIAL

Co-op America operates two websites to help shoppers go green. The National Green Pages (*www.greenpages.org*) provides a directory of green businesses throughout the country, while Responsible Shopper (*www.greenamericatoday.org/programs/responsibleshopper*) provides detailed information about the social and environmental impacts of major corporations.

In the past, it was difficult to find products that were made from eco-friendly materials or via manufacturing processes that were easy on the environment. But over the last decade, the marketplace for environmentally friendly goods has exploded so that there is now an eco-savvy alternative for just about any purchase you need to make.

Reduce Waste and Conserve Resources

Of course, the greenest items are those that you already have. Every new item you purchase at the store creates pollution, uses resources, and will eventually create waste when its life is over.

The essence of going green is to buy less stuff, and to be more discriminating about the stuff you do buy. Eco-savvy products made from recycled materials reduce the amount of virgin resources that are consumed each day and keep the old materials from wasting away in a landfill.

Reduce Pollution

Every item you buy at the store created some pollution in its manufacturing and transportation to the store shelf. And products like cleaning agents, lawn and garden chemicals, appliances, and cosmetics create pollution with every use. Green products, like appliances that are Energy-Star rated or natural cleaning agents, will minimize the amount of pollution created with each use.

ESSENTIAL

If you've got twenty minutes, check out the Story of Stuff (*www.story ofstuff.com*). Hosted by Annie Leonard, this fun video helps you digest some rather frightening information, like just how each product we buy impacts the Earth in its manufacture, use, and disposal.

Promote Fair Treatment of Workers

Due to intense competition in the marketplace, manufacturers are always under pressure to make cheap stuff even cheaper. But unfortunately, many fill this need through the use of sweatshop labor to produce their materials. Sweatshops exploit workers with long hours, unfair pay, and unsafe working conditions. They are most common in poorer countries where labor practices and health and safety violations often go unreported. But these factories have also popped up in the United States, as poor immigrant workers are lured with the promise of high pay and good benefits, only to essentially become indentured servants.

ALERT

Just because a product is labeled *Made in the USA* does not mean it is sweatshop-free. According to the Department of Labor, over 50 percent of U.S. garment factories are actually sweatshops. To be sure that a product was not made in a sweatshop, look for local or second-hand items, or those that carry the *Fair Trade* label.

Low wages are still better than no wages, right? Wrong. Forced overtime, low wages, worker intimidation, child labor, and physical abuses for mistakes or slow work are common practices in sweatshops. These factories are also notorious for forcing workers to labor in unsafe or even downright dangerous working conditions.

It is important to remember the real costs of the stuff you see in the store. Sure that $5 T-shirt is cheap, but is it really worth the social and environmental costs that come along with it? That cheap price tag means that the people who made it weren't paid a fair wage, so they are likely being held in a cycle of poverty, it means that trees were cut down excessively and water and land was polluted without cost to the company, and it means that the materials that were used to make it are probably not going to be good for the environment or your family. By shopping green and purchasing items from trusted companies, you can rest easy that your dollars do not go to support sweatshops.

Save Green by Going Green

New babies come with lots of new expenses, both short term (food, clothing, health care) and long term (college, cars, prom dresses). It can be scary to think about finances when a little one is on the way. Many new parents think that going green is too expensive. But if you are on a budget, going green is a great way to save money.

There are tons of eco-friendly choices you can make that will save you money on your energy bill, your water bill, your trash removal bill, and even your shopping bills. It pays big, for both your wallet and the planet, to be a green shopper.

Think Green

The best way to save your green at the store is by thinking green. Shop with the environment in mind and ask yourself if you *really* need each purchase. Can you get by without it? Is it possible to rent, borrow, or swap with a friend instead? If you are looking for maternity wear or baby gear, check in with friends about items they may have available. Curb impulse buying to save money and protect the environment. Remember, even an item you buy on sale is a 100 percent waste of money and resources if you don't really need it.

Buy in Bulk

Save money and the planet by purchasing items in bulk whenever possible. Buying in bulk is cheaper than purchasing several smaller items, and it will minimize the amount of packaging that you need to toss. Need two cans of soup? Buy the larger can. Are you feeding a pet? Buy the largest bag of food you can afford. But be careful: If you cannot actually eat that whole five-pound bag of pretzels, then you are better off buying a smaller bag.

Look for the Stars

Look for the EPA's Energy Star label the next time you are shopping for items like appliances, electronics, or even doors and windows. Products that carry the Energy Star label will use less water and energy over their lifetime than similar models that don't. The EPA estimates that the typical American household can save over $600 each year using Energy Star appliances instead of less eco-efficient models.

Minimize Waste

Help protect the planet by looking for products that will generate the least amount of waste in their manufacture, use, and disposal. Ease the impact on landfills by looking for products made from recycled content or those that use the least amount of packaging.

Buy Recycled

Look for items that contain recycled content, rather than virgin materials. Recycled content is used in a number of eco-friendly products from pencils to notebooks, jackets to sneakers, and even dog beds. Purchasing these products reduces the consumption of new materials, reduces landfill waste, and supports the market for recycling. And recycled content is now easier than ever to find. Take a peek at product labels and you will find insulation made from recycled denim, sweatshirts made from recycled cotton, and even toothbrushes made from recycled yogurt containers.

Minimize Packaging

Most of the products you will find on store shelves come packaged in plastics, boxes, and bags. If you have a choice between two products at the store, opt for the item with the least packaging or with packaging that you can reuse around your house.

Avoid Nonrecyclable Packaging

Any product can label itself as recyclable, but that doesn't necessary mean that it is recyclable in *your* area. For instance, most yogurt brands are packaged in cups made from #5 plastic. This type of plastic is technically recyclable, but facilities that accept #5 plastic are few and far between.

FACT

To find out what types of products are recyclable in your area, surf over to Earth 911 (*www.earth911.org*). This website lets you plug in your zip code to find the closest places for you to recycle everything from paper to plastic to motor oil.

If your local recycling center does not accept certain types of plastic or paper, try to avoid bringing any home. Instead, choose products in containers that are easily recyclable in your area.

Skip Disposables

Disposable products take a toll on the environment in the resources they use and the pollution and waste they create. And while they may seem inexpensive at first glance, their costs add up each time they must be replaced. According to Earth 911, a family of four can save $1,000 each year by purchasing reusable products instead of disposables. Here's how they break it down:

- **Batteries:** In the months and years to come, you will go through a mountain of batteries in toys, flashlights, baby monitors, and radios. Earth 911 estimates that by switching to rechargeable batteries instead of disposables in even one CD player, you can save $200 each year.
- **Camera:** You are sure to take loads of pictures in the months ahead. If you take a roll of pictures each month, you will save $144 each year by investing in a reusable camera rather than a disposable (go digital and you will save even more on film and processing).
- **Diapers:** You can save $600 a year by using cloth diapers (even with a diaper service) instead of disposables.

- **Kitchen supplies:** Save over $260 each year on paper towels and napkins by using reusable napkins, sponges, and cloth towels instead of the throw-away variety.

The money you save by going green, will help you afford more important expenses, like college, vacations, and babysitters!

B.Y.O.B.

Americans are blazing through plastic, disposable products at an alarming rate—as much as 60,000 plastic bags every five seconds and 4 million disposable plastic bottles every hour! These products create litter, consume resources, waste energy, and produce the greenhouse gases that cause global warming. Remember to B.Y.O.B. (bring your own bag and bottle), and you can completely eliminate your contribution to this growing environmental problem.

ALERT

A key concern about the use of plastic bags is the litter they create as they find their ways into trees, roadways, and waterways. According to Planet Ark (*www.planetark.com*), an international environmental group, about 100,000 whales, seals, turtles, and other marine animals are killed by plastic bags each year worldwide.

Bring Your Own Bag

For decades, disposable bag manufacturers argued over which was better for the environment, paper or plastic. Paper bags require trees and lots of them, whereas plastic bags are made with petroleum. And that's not to mention the vast amounts of energy, chemicals, and other resources required to produce each bag and ship it to the store.

The next time you are at the store and a clerk asks you if you want "paper or plastic," respond with a resounding "NEITHER!" Bring your own reusable bag to the store to reduce waste.

Bring Your Own Bottle

According to Treehugger (*www.treehugger.com*) approximately 1.5 million barrels of oil are used to make plastic water bottles every year. That's enough to run 100,000 cars for a whole year; and transporting these bottles burns even more oil. In addition, it takes millions of gallons of water to produce plastic water bottles; and an additional two gallons of water must be wasted in the purification process for every gallon that goes into the bottles. What's worse, nearly 90 percent of water bottles are not recycled and wind up in landfills where they take thousands of years to decompose. Toss a reusable drinking bottle in your purse, diaper bag, briefcase, backpack, car, or bike bag to eliminate your use of disposable water bottles.

Buying Local

Locally produced foods help to minimize the pollution and depletion of resources that go along with transportation and packaging. Organic produce that is transported from another country creates enough pollution to negate its environmental benefit. Local farmers' markets are great places to find fresh produce and other locally produced goods, often at bargain prices. If you have to choose between local and organic, go local. If you can get local products that are also organic, you've hit the jackpot.

Know Your Green Product Labels

It can be difficult to tell if a product is green just by looking at it. Fortunately, there are a number of labels you can look for on a product's packaging that indicate just how eco-friendly it is. Look for these green labels on the products you buy at the store to be sure you are getting the real green deal.

Cradle to Cradle. Cradle to Cradle certification analyzes the environmental impact of a product throughout its entire life cycle. Products that bear this label use environmentally safe materials, are designed for reuse, use energy- and water-efficient technology, and incorporate socially responsible strategies into their design. The certification is found on a wide range of products such as diapers (gDiapers), cleaning agents (Begley's

Best) and surfboard wax (Wet Women Surf Wax). Check out the Cradle to Cradle website (*www.c2ccertified.com*), to learn more about the standards behind this label.

QUESTION

Where can I find green products online?
Green goods are popping up at retailers all over the web. But just as you would in a store, look for green certifications to ensure that a website's products are as green as they claim. You can trust the green products you find at retailers like Gaiam (*www.gaiam.com*), the Green Home (*www.greenhome.com*), and the Green Store (*www.greenstore.com*).

Dolphin Safe. Several decades ago, consumer watchdogs blew the whistle on the dangerous fishing practices of the tuna industry, an industry that was damaging the environment and decimating millions of dolphins in its by-catch. In 1990, the Dolphin Protection Consumer Information Act was created to prohibit the use of fishing methods that are harmful to dolphins and other marine mammals.

In popular tuna fishing grounds, the *dolphin-safe* claim is verified by the National Marine Fisheries Service. However, tuna caught outside of these waters can be labeled *dolphin-safe*, even if it is not. The nonprofit group Earth Island Institute (*www.earthisland.org*) acts as an independent watchdog by sending its representatives on surprise field visits to canneries and docks in order to inspect the premises and report violations to the Feds. They also have onboard observers who are granted access to inspections at the discretion of the company.

Today, almost all tuna sold in the United States bears the *dolphin-safe* label. But it is still a good idea to check for it, especially if you are shopping in a new store or buying a brand you've never purchased before.

Energy Star. The EPA created the Energy Star label (*www.energy star.gov*) as a means of certifying products that use less energy and less water than comparable models. There are more than fifty different categories of products that are eligible for the Energy Star label, including battery chargers, dehumidifiers, ceiling fans, dishwashers, televisions, cordless phones, computers, printers, and even windows and doors. Look for the Star before making your next purchase.

Fair-Trade Certified. If you are concerned about the environmental and social implications of the products you purchase, then seek out the *Fair-Trade* label on foods such as coffee, tea, chocolate, rice, sugar, and bananas. The Fair-Trade Certification is an independently verified label that ensures that farmers in developing nations receive a fair price for their product.

The Fair-Trade program also prohibits forced child labor, supports sustainable agriculture, limits the use of harmful pesticides, and supports community-building programs such as health care, credit plans, and training workshops. Check out Transfair USA (*www.transfairusa.org*), to learn more about the fair trade certified label.

FACT

The United States produces 90 million tons of paper annually and consumes about 100 million tons, making it the single largest market for paper products in the world. Despite improved technologies, only 35 percent of the current consumption is met by using recycled paper. You can improve these numbers by recycling paper and purchasing products made from recycled content.

FSC (Forest Stewardship Council) Certified. The Forest Stewardship Council (*www.fsc.org*) is an international accrediting organization that has developed standards for certifying wood and wood products produced from sustainable forests. Wood certified under FSC standards is rated according to ten principles that take into account the environmental, social, and economic impacts of the timber industry. Look for the FSC label on wood, paper, and wood products such as furniture, cabinets, and windows.

Greenguard. The Greenguard Environmental Institute (*www.greenguard.org*), is an industry-independent, nonprofit organization that oversees certification of low-emitting products for the indoor environment. A product that carries the Greenguard seal will off-gas the minimum amount of VOCs and other harmful toxins. Look for the Greenguard seal on building materials, furniture, household cleaning products, electronic equipment, and personal care products.

Green Seal. Green Seal (*www.greenseal.org*), is an independent organization that sets standards for certifying environmentally sound products. Green Seal standards take into account the environmental impacts of a product from manufacturing to use to disposal. Look for this label on paper, wood products, household cleaners, and personal care products.

Leaping Bunny. The Leaping Bunny logo (*www.leapingbunny.com*) can be found on products that adhere to cruelty-free standards developed by the Coalition for Consumer Information on Cosmetics, a coalition of animal protection groups. Companies that use this logo on their products sign a pledge not to conduct or commission animal testing of their products or product ingredients. Look for the Leaping Bunny on cosmetics, personal care products, and other household products.

Organic. In 2002, the USDA's National Organic Program (*www.ams.usda .gov/nop/indexNet.htm*) established the organic certification label to indicate that a product has been produced in an eco-friendly manner. In order for food items such as fruits, vegetables, meat, poultry, and dairy products to bear the organic seal, they must be produced without the use of synthetic pesticides and fertilizers, antibiotics, genetic engineering, irradiation, and sewage sludge. Animals raised for organic meats must have access to the outdoors and must be fed 100 percent organic feed that does not contain animal byproducts or growth hormones. However, the USDA draws a distinction between chickens and other animals. So cows that are raised to produce organic beef or milk must have continuous access to the outdoors without confinement, whereas chickens are not guaranteed access and can be confined.

There are three different organic labels you may see on the shelves:

- **100% Organic:** Products bearing this label can only contain organically produced ingredients.

- **Organic:** Products can use the *Organic* label if 95 percent of their ingredients are organically produced and the remaining 5 percent are nonorganic ingredients that have been approved by the National Organic Program.
- **Made with Organic Ingredients:** This label indicates that at least 70 percent of a product's ingredients are organic, with at least three listed on the back of the package. The remaining 30 percent of ingredients must be approved by the National Organic Program.

Look for the organic label of vegetables, meats, dairy products, and processed foods. But don't be fooled if you see the term *organic* used on seafood as this industry is not yet regulated by organic standards.

Processed Chlorine-Free. Products that claim to be "processed chlorine-free" must be processed without the use of environmentally damaging chlorine, which produces dioxin as a by-product. Look for the PCF label on all paper products. Check out the Chlorine Free Products Association (*www.chlorinefreeproducts.org*) to learn more about this label.

Rainforest Alliance Certified. The Rainforest Alliance (*www.rainforest-alliance.org*) is a nonprofit agency dedicated to preserving rainforests, and the people and wildlife that depend on them, throughout the world. Under their SmartWood program, the Rainforest Alliance grants FSC certification to forest products that are verified as originating from responsibly managed forest in accordance with FSC principles and criteria.

Don't Get Greenwashed

The demand for environmentally friendly products is booming, and manufacturers have responded by advertising their green. But, buyer beware. Not all products are as eco-friendly as they look. Many products are actually just *greenwashed*, meaning they are made to *appear* eco-friendly without actually being eco-friendly. Greenwashed products may contain labels such as biodegradable, cruelty-free, eco-safe, environmentally friendly, environmentally preferable, environmentally safe, or nontoxic. These terms are generally meaningless as they are not legally defined or enforced. Want to make sure you are getting the real deal? Here's a quick list of the labels that should catch your eye. If these labels are not accompanied by a true green certification, then they are probably not as green as they claim to be.

Biodegradable. A number of cleaning solutions, paper products, and personal care products claim to be biodegradable. According to the Federal Trade Commission (FTC), the biodegradable label *should* mean that a product will break down and decompose within a short time of disposal. However, neither the FTC nor any other organization currently verifies product claims.

Just because a product will break down quickly does not necessarily mean that it is good for the environment. For example, the now notorious chemical DDT is biodegradable, but it breaks down into components that are actually more harmful to the environment than the chemical in its original form.

FACT

DDT, or dichloro-diphenyl-trichloroethane, is a synthetic insecticide that was used in agriculture around the time of World War II. In 1962, American biologist Rachel Carson proved that that DDT was detrimental to both humans and wildlife, particularly birds. Her book, *Silent Spring*, became an environmental classic and was one of the primary reasons that DDT was banned from use in the United States in 1972.

Cruelty-free. This label is a response to the animal testing boycotts of the 1990s. It can be found on cleaning solutions and personal hygiene products and is intended to imply that the product was not tested on animals. However, this term is not legally defined and there is no agency that verifies the claim. Look for the *Leaping Bunny* label instead to backup this claim.

Free range. The *free range* label is found on poultry, eggs, and beef products. But the term is only legally defined for labeling poultry, not beef or eggs. The USDA requires that poultry labeled *free range* must have access to the outdoors for an undetermined period each day. Five minutes of open-air access is considered adequate to get a stamp of approval from the USDA. Incidentally, open air access just means the coop door is opened, not that the birds are actually outside.

Nontoxic. Under the Federal Hazardous Substances Act, the Consumer Product Safety Commission (CPSC) defines *toxic substances* as those that are directly responsible for an injury or illness to humans when they are inhaled, swallowed, or absorbed through the skin. Products must also be labeled as *toxic* if it can be shown that long-term exposure can cause chronic effects such as cancer or birth defects. However, the CPSC does not legally define the term *nontoxic*, so any manufacturer can use this label without actually backing up their claim.

Recyclable. Products labeled *recyclable* can be collected, separated or recovered from the solid waste stream and used again in some form or another. But just because a product is labeled recyclable does not mean that you will actually find anywhere to recycle it. Contact your local recycling center to find out what products are accepted in your area.

Recycled. The Federal Trade Commission (FTC) has developed guidelines on how the *recycled* label should be used; however, they do not verify its authenticity. They also do not distinguish between pre-consumer (materials like shavings from a paper mill that have never been used) and post-consumer waste (yesterday's newspaper.) If you want to know just how recycled a particular product is, you will have to contact the manufacturer.

CHAPTER 6

Green Maternity Clothes

Clothing may not be the first thing that comes to mind when you are thinking about going green. You probably don't think twice about the environment when you are eyeing a cute baby outfit or the latest maternity fashions. But the truth is that the clothing you wear comes at a heavy cost to the environment. It pays to be picky about your maternity clothing—for the sake of your baby, your planet, and your wallet.

Your Expanding Wardrobe

Trying to decide what to wear? Now that you have a baby on the way your selections are about to get a whole lot more, um, interesting. What fit yesterday may not necessarily fit today. You may need to set some of your favorite pieces aside and replace them with clothes that accommodate both you and your growing baby.

But one thing that you probably don't need is a brand new wardrobe of clothing that will only fit you for the next few months. The production of clothing is rough on the environment. One-quarter of all the pesticides used throughout the entire world are used in the production of cotton. In addition, most conventionally produced clothing is made using dyes and finishes that are loaded with chemicals. And to keep clothes cheap, many items are produced using child labor forces in deplorable sweatshop conditions.

QUESTION

Why is organic and sustainable clothing so expensive?
Sustainable clothing is generally more expensive than conventional mass-produced clothing. This is because it is produced in a labor-intensive manner, without the use of harmful chemicals, and its production does not exploit workers with unfair labor practices. With increased demand, the price of sustainable clothing has come down. But it will never be as cheap as clothing mass-produced in sweatshops.

The good news is that sustainable maternity clothing and eco-fashion have hit the mainstream. Gone are the days of scratchy burlap pullovers and horrid potato sack–looking dresses. Earth-friendly maternity clothes now come in every style, fabric, color, and price range you can imagine. It is entirely feasible to find beautiful, comfortable clothes that are free of chemicals and produced by workers who have earned a fair wage.

Choosing Fabrics

Many folks think that natural and organic fibers are the same thing. But in the clothing industry, natural fiber clothing simply refers to clothing made from fibers found in nature, such as wool, cotton, silk, or hemp. It has nothing to do with the purity of the clothing or the production and manufacturing processes.

Natural Fibers

Natural fibers are either plant-based (cotton, hemp, and flax), or animal-based (wool, alpaca, silk, and cashmere). In comparison, human-made or synthetic textiles, such as rayon, acetate, and polyester, are fibers that have been chemically and structurally produced to form a fiber.

Synthetic Fibers

The most common synthetic fibers used to make clothing include acrylic, polyester, rayon, and nylon. Each of these fibers wreaks havoc on the environment in its production.

ESSENTIAL

Do not buy your maternity clothing too far in advance. It is difficult to estimate just how (and where) your body will expand and change during pregnancy. What looks good today may be too small by your eighth month. If you do need to purchase maternity clothing, buy a few items at a time that you can grow into.

Acrylic fabrics are made from a class of chemical compounds called *polycrylonitriles*, which may be carcinogenic. Nylon and polyester are made from petroleum-based chemicals, whose production creates nitrous oxide, a gas that pollutes the environment and contributes to global warming. Rayon is made from wood pulp that has been treated with chemicals, including caustic soda and sulphuric acid.

Fabric Finishes

Most garments that are produced from natural fibers are not organic. Conventionally manufactured fabrics, whether they are natural or synthetic, rely heavily upon chemicals to clean and bleach the fibers and to prepare them to be spun into yarns. Most conventionally produced clothing is made using dyes and finishes that are loaded with chemicals. During finishing, most fabrics are chemically treated to be stain-resistant, wrinkle-resistant, odor-resistant, or any of a number of the other toxic chemical treatments used in our modern society.

FACT

According to the Environmental Justice Foundation, it takes more than 500 gallons of water to produce one cotton T-shirt. In addition, the worldwide production of cotton is responsible for the release of $2 billion worth of pesticides every year, and accounts for more insecticide release than any other single crop.

All of these chemicals leach into the environment, leaving an impact on groundwater, wildlife, air, and soil. They are also harmful to consumers as they may be absorbed or inhaled into the body.

There are also social costs, in addition to the environmental and health costs, associated with the production of clothing. To keep clothes cheap, many garments are produced using child labor forces in deplorable sweatshop conditions. Natural fibers may originate from nature, but they take a heavy toll on the planet before they are made into clothing.

Organic Fibers

Clothing that is certified as organic has not been subject to any of these chemical processes mentioned above. Fabrics that bear the organic label must be free from synthetic chemicals for at least three years. In other words, the cotton or hemp crops, or the sheep used to produce the wool must be farmed without the use of synthetic chemicals. Organic clothing must also be produced without the use of genetically modified crops. Cotton, linen, wool, and hemp can all be grown organically and used to produce green clothing.

Still, it is sometimes unclear just which fibers are actually organic because there are no global or even national standards for organic clothing like there are for foods. But because cottonseeds and cotton oils can be considered food products, they may fall under the USDA standards for organic certification.

In other words, a cotton T-shirt may bear a label claiming that it is made from 100 percent certified organic cotton, but that just means that the cotton used to make the shirt was free of chemicals. After production, that organic cotton T-shirt may have been exposed to chemical finishes and heavy metal dyes.

ESSENTIAL

If you buy items without paying attention to where they come from, you may unknowingly be supporting the cycle that causes sweat-shops. In an effort to make cheap stuff even cheaper, sweatshops exploit workers with long hours, unfair pay, and unsafe working conditions. Look for clothing that is locally made or has been independently verified as sweat-free.

Eco-Fibers

The eco-category in between natural and synthetic fibers is known as naturally derived human-made fibers. Wood pulp, bamboo, soy, and corn can all be used to create clothing. The process used to turn these fibers into garments is an energy-intensive industry, but they are considered more eco-friendly than synthetics like polyester or rayon because they can be composted when they are no longer useful. Still, soy- and corn-based clothing tends to come from genetically modified crops. And bamboo and wood pulp are often harvested unsustainably, so use caution before investing all of your money in these supposedly eco-friendly duds.

Use What You Have

Your best bet to greening your maternity wardrobe is to make full use of the clothing that is already in your closet. Wear the clothes you already own as long as possible throughout your pregnancy. You will be surprised at just how far your favorite pants and shirts can stretch when you need them to! Here's how to use the clothes you have throughout your pregnancy.

First Trimester

During your first trimester of pregnancy, especially if this is your first pregnancy, you will probably be able to wear most of the items already hanging in your closet. Most women don't start showing until sometime in the early second trimester. But even before your belly forms that tell-tale bump, your pants and undergarments may begin to feel tight against your swelling belly. Move the button on your favorite pants, or forgo it all together to give your baby room to grow.

Second Trimester

Once you hit your fourth month of pregnancy, you will probably need to get a little more creative in order to expand your current wardrobe to meet your needs. A rubber band can work wonders at extending the life, and girth of your pants well into your pregnancy.

FACT

A Belly Belt (*www.belly-belt.com*) offers the same function as a rubber band but with a little more fashion sense. Each kit comes with four different size belts and three fabric panels (in white, denim, and black) that can be inserted into the waistband of pants or skirts to extend their use throughout your pregnancy.

You can also purchase a bra extender, which essentially hooks into your bra's hooks, to give you another couple of inches. This is a great way to save money and reduce the number of new bras you will go through as your breasts grow steadily bigger and fuller throughout your pregnancy.

You can also learn how to sew a button or stitch a hem (or make friends with someone who can) to increase the lifespan of your family's clothing. Too boring? Consider giving new life to old clothes by re-tailoring worn out duds. For a fraction of the cost of new, you can turn worn out pants into shorts or a pre-pregnancy dress into a shirt or skirt to use throughout your pregnancy.

Third Trimester

By now, your stomach and the rest of your body may feel like they are expanding at an alarming rate. Some of your clothes, like close-fitting tops or button-up pants, may no longer be an option. But other clothes, like large T-shirts, button-down shirts, low-rise jeans, and stretchy pants may take you all the way through your pregnancy. If you do need more clothes to wear during these last few months, look for items that you will be able to wear comfortably after your baby is born as well.

Pre-Loved Clothes

One of the best ways to save money and go green when looking for maternity clothes is to ask for hand-me-downs from friends and family. Pre-loved maternity duds save money and reduce the use of new materials while keeping the old items out of the landfill. They also help extend the life of clothes that have likely only been worn for a few months by their previous owner.

ESSENTIAL

Want to have a little fun while you get something for free? Check out a Swap-O-Rama-Rama (*www.swaporamarama.org*), event in your area where you bring a bag of your gently worn duds to exchange for another. The events also host sewing and fashion workshops so that you can learn to get the most from your wardrobe.

If you've never worn pre-loved clothes before, this pregnancy is the perfect time to try them out. Think of it this way, with all of the money you will save by not buying clothes, you will have more money to pamper yourself with an eco-savvy massage or professional housecleaning.

Finding Organic Maternity Clothes

If your old wardrobe no longer fits and pre-loved is not an option, you may need to purchase new maternity clothes to wear throughout your pregnancy. Look for organic fabrics that minimize the environmental impact of the garment's production. And skip cheap and poorly made clothes that will fall apart after the first washing. Instead, save the planet and protect your overall investment by purchasing clothes that are built to last. Look for sturdy stitching, strong fabrics, and a minimum number of *appliqués*.

Check out your local clothing store to see if they offer maternity clothing made from organic fibers. If not, don't be afraid to ask if they'll consider carrying them in the future. Online, check out Jessica Scott (*www.jessicascottltd.com*), Baby Nut (*www.babynut.com*), Hip and Little (*www.hipandlittle.com*), MollyAnna (*www.mollyanna.com*), and Pristine Planet (*www.pristineplanet.com*).

ESSENTIAL

One item that you may need to purchase is maternity underwear. Your old undies just may not provide the coverage they once did before your pregnancy. Check out your favorite eco-retailer to find organic cotton maternity underwear to wear throughout your pregnancy.

You will also need at least one pair of comfortable, supportive shoes during your pregnancy. Not only are you going to be putting a lot of stress on your feet, but they also may swell later in pregnancy. Look for shoes that offer both foot and arch support. Also stick with shoes that slip on easily and do not use shoelaces, Velcro, or buckles, as later in your pregnancy it may be difficult to get them on. If you need to purchase a new pair that meet these criteria, look for shoes made from organic, recycled-content, and vegan materials like those from Simple Shoes (*www.simpleshoes.com*).

For shoes, try Timberland (*www.timberland.com*), a company that makes environmental commitments that go beyond a *greenwashed* label. A number of the company's global retail stores are carbon neutral, they use renewable energy at several of their facilities, and they provide a $3,000 incentive for employees who purchase hybrid cars. In addition, many of their most popular products now include a *Green Index* label that informs consumers about the chemicals and materials used and climate-impact created to produce each item. Another company that is working toward providing friendlier footprints is Simple Shoes (*www.simpleshoes.com*). They have great looking casual shoes for the whole family made from organic fibers, water-based glues, and recycled materials.

FACT

After your pregnancy, as you continue to search for green clothing, look for organic and sustainably produced garments made from eco-savvy retailers such as Patagonia (*www.patagonia.com*), Lotus Organics (*www.lotusorganics.com*), Blue Canoe (*www.bluecanoe.com*), and Stewart + Brown (*www.stewartbrown.com*).

Passing It On

After you've gotten all of the use you can out of your maternity clothes, be sure to pass them on to another expecting mom or to a local charity or thrift store in your area. Check out the following websites to find out more information about where and how to donate your old maternity clothing:

- Goodwill Industries International (*www.goodwill.org*): Collects both usable and unusable clothing (such as garments with holes, torn hems, broken zippers, and so on).
- The Salvation Army (*www.salvationarmyusa.org*): Accepts all types and sizes of clothing.
- Soles 4 Souls (*www.soles4souls.org*): Collects gently used shoes for children and adults in need.

If a garment is simply too worn out, cut it up to make baby doll clothes, blankets, or cleaning rags.

Green Dry Cleaners

Dry clean–only clothing and new babies go together like oil and water. Steer clear of any clothes that require dry cleaning, but if that is not possible, consider hand washing delicates or seek out a dry cleaner that uses green technology to reduce its toxic load. Conventional dry cleaners use an industrial solvent called perchloroethylene (PERC) that is seriously toxic to humans and a common ingredient in smog. Seek out a dry cleaner that uses environmentally friendly technology. Thanks to government regulations and increased demand, green dry cleaners are spreading. Eco-friendly dry cleaners skip the chemicals and use either liquid carbon (high pressure and liquid CO_2), Green Earth (silicone-based solvents), or wet cleaning (soap and water) to get clothes clean.

FACT

Check out Earth 911 (*www.earth911.org/master.asp?s=ls&serviceid=139*) for a directory of wet cleaners; find CO_2 (*http://findco2.com*) for information about dry cleaners that use liquid CO_2; or look up Green Earth Dry Cleaners (*www.greenearthcleaning.com/rostersearch.asp*) for a directory of Green Earth dry cleaners.

Check out the information in the next chapter to learn more about how to keep your maternity wardrobe clean and green.

part two

Greening
Your Home

CHAPTER 7

Green Cleaning

Feeling the need to nest? With a new baby on the way, you will want to make sure every inch of your home is squeaky clean and ready for your little bundle of joy. But you don't need a laundry list of chemicals to get your house clean. In fact, many cleaning products contain ingredients that are harmful to your health and that of your growing baby. Use natural cleaners instead to get your house clean and green without a residue of toxic chemicals.

Get Your Home Green and Clean

Just what is in your favorite cleaning products? You may not want to know. Most cleaning product manufacturers would have you believe that you need an arsenal of chemicals in order to get your house clean. But the truth is that not only are those chemicals unnecessary, they could also be putting your health, the planet's health, and the health of your baby at risk.

Why Clean Green?

Many health experts now believe that chemical exposure, even at very low levels, can have adverse impacts on the reproductive system. For growing babies, this exposure can lead to developmental effects, such as birth defects, low birth weight, and behavioral development.

And don't forget that all of these chemicals eventually make their way into the environment as they wash down the drain or are sprayed into the air. Their impact on natural ecosystems can be devastating.

Don't wipe your house down with dangerous chemicals. Instead, choose green cleaners that will not only get our house clean, but make sure its safe for little ones.

No More Waste

Don't forget to reach for a reusable cloth to do your cleaning. Switching from paper products to reusables in your cleaning will save you money and cut back on tons of waste.

Cut up T-shirts that are beyond repair to use as cleaning rags or pick up a few old pre-loved dish towels at the thrift store. If you prefer to clean with a sponge, look for natural sponges that are biodegradable and can even be composted when they are no longer useful as sponges. Just be sure your sponges came from a sponge farm and were not harvested from a natural ecosystem.

At the store, check out Target's (*www.target.com*) line of organic cotton cloths and towels. Method (*www.methodhome.com*) makes microfiber cloths that are specialized for a variety of surfaces such as stainless steel, wood, or windows. Or, for a new twist on cleaning, try the new line of sponges and cleaning cloths available from Twist (*www.twistclean.com*). All of their products are biodegradable and packaged in recyclable paper packaging that can be reused for fun craft projects (check out their website for craft ideas). And don't forget that you can reuse those clean cotton diapers as dust cloths once your baby is potty trained.

ESSENTIAL

If you use a cleaning service, you can get a green clean by asking staff to either use your green products or bring their own. There is not yet a one-stop location for finding a green cleaner in your area. Check with friends for a recommendation or talk with your current cleaning agency to see if they will comply.

Chemicals in Your Cleaning Products

Fifty years ago, consumers used natural items like vinegar, baking soda, and pure soap to clean their homes. But after World War II, many of the chemicals that had been developed for the military were marketed to the general public in the form of plastic wrap, pesticides, and chemical cleaning agents.

ALERT

Don't toss your old chemical cleaning agents in the trash. These chemicals certainly don't belong in the home, but they also too toxic for the drain or the landfill. Check with your local community disposal organization to find out when and where you can dispose of these products properly.

Today, the average home contains about ten gallons of harmful chemicals in the form of cleaning agents. Children under the age of six are more likely to be poisoned by liquid dish soap than anything else in the home. In fact, roughly 20 percent of all childhood poisonings occur as a result of exposure to chemical cleaning agents. Get the chemicals out of your home and clean with natural ingredients that are safer for you, your baby, and the planet.

Chemicals to Avoid

There are so many chemicals used in cleaning products that it is virtually impossible to list them all in one spot. But as a new or expecting parent, you should be on the lookout for three particular types of chemicals in your cleaning products: glycol ether, APEs, and phthalates.

Glycol Ethers

Glycol ethers such as 2-butoxyethanol, are solvents commonly found in glass cleaners. Research shows that pregnant women who were exposed to glycol ethers in their work environments were significantly more likely to have children with birth defects such as neural tube defects and cleft lip. In laboratory studies, glycol ethers have also been associated with low birth weight in exposed mice.

APEs

Alkylphenol ethoxylates (APEs) are a type of surfactant found in laundry detergents, citrus cleaners, disinfecting cleaners, and stain removers. According to the Washington Toxics Coalition, a nonprofit agency that evaluates chemicals for toxicity, more than 450 million pounds of APEs are produced each year, and half of these wind up down the drain. The most common APE, nonylphenol ethoxylate (NPE), is an endocrine disruptor that is clearly linked to impact on aquatic ecosystems. These chemicals can cause harm to fish, frogs, turtles, and other aquatic life. Studies have shown that even low-level exposure can damage the reproductive health and survival of a number of fish species. The United States Geological Survey found NPEs in 70 percent of North American streams.

ALERT

A truly green cleaning product will be nontoxic, biodegradable, and made from renewable resources. Unfortunately, manufacturers are not required to list all the ingredients in their products, and there is not yet an industry standard to define terms such as *natural*, *green*, or *eco-friendly* for cleaning products. Look for products that offer complete ingredient list on their labels.

Phthalates

Remember those nasty phthalates that are found in many of your personal care products? You will get a double dose of them if you use chemical cleaning products. Many conventional cleaning products use phthalates to stabilize fragrance. They can be found in glass cleaners, deodorizers, laundry detergents, and fabric softeners. Phthalates have been linked to adverse health effects and reproductive disorders such as reduced sperm count, allergies, and asthma.

Natural Air Fresheners

We all want our home to smell fresh, which is why air fresheners and deodorizers have become so popular these days. But breathing in the fresh scent provided by these products also causes you to inhale harmful chemicals such as phosphates, chlorine bleach, or ammonia. These chemicals can cause headaches, nausea, allergic reactions, asthma attacks, and lung irritation. In addition, many air fresheners work by using a nerve-deadening agent that interferes with your ability to smell or by lining your nasal passages with an odor blocking oil film. Commercial air fresheners can be especially noxious for expecting women, who are sensitive to strong odors in the air.

And the chemicals used to create those scents don't just disappear as they are sprayed into the air. They linger on as they land on surfaces and floors and sink into carpets. What's worse, these chemicals are among those that cross the placenta easily. A study released by the University of Bristol found that expecting moms who used air fresheners on a daily basis, especially during pregnancy and when their babies were newborn, were far more likely to have babies with minor infections such as ear infections or diarrhea, than families who used these products less than once a week. This same study also found that the moms themselves experienced ailments such as headaches and depression more frequently than their peers.

You don't need a bottle of chemicals to make your home smell great. Here are some simple, homemade air fresheners to try:

- **Baked treats:** If you like your house to smell like fresh baked apple pie or chocolate chips cookies, why not treat yourself to some goodies and actually bake some?

- **Baking soda:** Baking soda absorbs odors, so place a few open boxes throughout the home.
- **Essential oils:** Essential oils like cedar and lemon can be used in a number of ways to clean and freshen the air in your home. Dilute essential oils in water and spray into the air.
- **Household spices:** Add any one of your favorite smelling herbs such as cinnamon, cloves, ginger, basil, or rosemary to boiling water and allow it to simmer on the stove and release its fragrances into the air.
- **Natural candles:** Standard paraffin candles are made from petroleum and off-gas VOCs into the air. Instead, burn soy or beeswax candles for a pleasant fragrance without the chemicals.
- **Plants:** Indoor plants are another great way to keep indoor air fresh and clean. They won't necessarily remove odors, but they work great as air filters.
- **White vinegar:** Vinegar can be diluted in water and wiped on surfaces or sprayed in the air to clean and freshen naturally.

In warmer weather, be sure to open up windows and doors to freshen the air and remove toxic air particles from your home.

Dishwashing

When it comes to washing dishes, you might guess that it is more environmentally friendly to wash by hand than by machine. But that's actually not the case.

A study by German researchers at the University of Bonn showed that most modern dishwashers actually use as little as half the energy, a sixth of the water, and less soap than even the most conservative hand-washing techniques.

Green Dishwashers

Get the most out of the energy and water used to run your dishwasher by washing full loads. If your machine has an energy-efficient setting, use it. If your dishwasher doesn't come with that option, you can simply shut the machine off after the final rinse and let it drip dry, with the door open. If you are in the market for a new dishwasher, be sure to choose an Energy Star model that uses less energy and water than comparable models.

Hand Washing

If you need to wash dishes by hand, use as little water as possible. Don't leave the tap water running. If you have a double basin sink, fill each basin halfway or less—one with soapy water to wash and one with clean water to rinse. If you only have one basin in your sink, just give your dishes a quick burst of water each time you need a rinse.

When choosing soaps and detergents, whether for the sink or the dishwasher, look for all-natural brands, like Seventh Generation (*www.seventh generation.com*) or Ecover, (*www.ecover.com*). Natural soaps are cheaper and more widely available than ever before, and they are far less damaging to the eco-system.

Laundry

After your baby is born you may begin to wonder how anyone so little can produce so much laundry. And while these clothes will likely be some of the dirtiest you've ever seen, you will also want them to come out the cleanest they've ever been. Ironically, the very products you may be using to clean your clothes may be filling them up nasty chemicals that could harm you, your baby, and the environment.

ALERT

One of the biggest culprits in ocean pollution is phosphates, a common ingredient in laundry detergents and some cleaning products. High phosphate levels can kill aquatic life in rivers, streams, and oceans by causing algae blooms that suffocate marine life. Make sure your laundry detergent is phosphate-free.

Your laundry pile will expand even before your baby is born as you begin washing her clothes, bedding, and blankets. Here's how to make sure all of your laundry gets green and clean.

Green Your Machine

As with dishwashing, be sure to wash full loads of laundry whenever possible to maximize your machine's energy and water efficiency. If you do need to wash a smaller load, adjust your machine's settings as necessary. Also, use the lowest temperature possible to minimize the energy needed to heat water.

Detergents

If your clothes are not really dirty, you can simply wash them in cold or warm water to remove roughly 45 percent of the dirt. But if 45 percent just won't cut it, you will need to use detergent to get your clothes clean. Steer clear of chemical-laden laundry detergents and opt for an eco-savvy product from Seventh Generation (*www.seventhgeneration.com*), Ecover (*www.ecover.com*), or Planet (*www.planetinc.com*). Get the most out of your detergent by treating your clothes with these natural laundry boosters.

Fabric softener. Add one-quarter cup of white vinegar during your washing machine's rinse cycle to remove odors and leave clothes soft and fresh.

Stain remover. Soaking clothes in laundry soap for about a half hour before washing is often all you need to remove a stain. But for tough stains (like spit-up or diaper stains), try using a paste made of baking soda and water. Apply to the stain and let stand for one hour before washing.

Use lemon juice and water to remove stains from white clothing. Rub into the stain and let stand for one hour before washing. Hydrogen peroxide can also be used as a bleach alternative to brighten and whiten clothes.

Detergent booster. You can cut down on the amount of laundry detergent you need to use by adding a little baking soda to boost your detergent's cleaning power. If you use a liquid detergent, add one-half cup baking soda at the beginning of the wash. For powdered detergent, add one-half cup baking soda during the rinse cycle.

Starch. Mix one heaping teaspoon of cornstarch with one cup of hot water until the cornstarch is completely dissolved. Pour into a spray bottle and use immediately while ironing clothes.

How to Make Your Own Green Cleaners

Save money and the environment by making your own cleaning agents from natural, nontoxic ingredients. Making your own cleaning agents will save you a fortune in cleaning supplies, simplify your cleaning routine, and go a long way toward protecting the planet. Here's a list of some of the basic ingredients you will need:

- **Baking soda:** Acts as a water softener, odor remover, and scrubbing agent.
- **Castile soap:** Use as an all-purpose cleaner to cut grease and disinfect throughout the whole house.
- **Lemon juice:** Can be used as an all natural bleach, deodorant, stain-remover and grease-cutter.
- **White vinegar:** Kills bacteria and eliminates odors. It also works to remove mildew, wax buildup, lime buildup, and grease.

To put these natural ingredients to work, try out some of these simple yet effective recipes. As always, be careful when trying a new product or ingredient in your home. Test the cleaner in a small area first, especially on rugs and carpets, which could stain permanently.

General cleaners. For most household cleaning, use a simple mix of vinegar and water to remove dirt and germs. You can use this mixture to clean windows, floors, and countertops. Add a sprinkle of baking soda for scouring power to clean toilets, sinks, and bathtubs.

All-purpose disinfectant. Mix two teaspoons borax, four tablespoons vinegar, and three cups hot water in a spray bottle for an all-natural, all-purpose disinfectant. Need to cut through kitchen counter grime? Add one-quarter teaspoon liquid soap to the mixture.

Furniture polish. Mix a one-to-one ratio of olive oil and vinegar to clean and polish wood furniture.

Oven cleaner. Avoid oven cleaning altogether by placing a cookie sheet on the bottom rack of the oven to catch spills. When spills do occur, use baking soda to get your oven clean. Simply make a paste using one cup of baking soda and water. Apply to grimy spots and let stand. Lift off large deposits with a spatula and scrub surface with a scouring pad.

Windows. Mix three tablespoons of vinegar with one quart of water in a clean spray bottle. If the windows are really dirty, mix of one-half teaspoon of liquid soap, with three tablespoons of vinegar, and two cups of water. And to get those windows streak-free, use recycled newspaper rather than paper towels to wipe them clean.

Metal cleaners. Use sliced lemons to clean the tarnish from brass, copper, bronze, and aluminum. For extra dirty jobs, sprinkle the item with baking soda and then rub with lemon. To clean sterling silver, line a plastic or glass bowl with aluminum foil. Sprinkle the foil with a little salt and baking soda and then fill the bowl with warm water. Soak silver items in this mixture and the tarnish will migrate from your silver to the aluminum foil. Rinse and dry the silver, then buff it with a soft, clean cloth.

Floors. To get floors clean without harmful chemicals, add one cup of vinegar per pail of hot water. For linoleum floors, combine one-quarter cup washing soda, one tablespoon of liquid soap, one-quarter cup vinegar, and two gallons hot water. This will work on everything from muddy footprints to greasy spills. But do not use this formula on waxed floors.

Tubs and sinks. Baking soda and liquid soap can work wonders in your bathroom. Simply sprinkle baking soda on porcelain tubs and sinks. Add a little of the liquid soap to a wet cloth and use it to rub in the baking soda. Rinse well to avoid leaving a hazy film.

Toilets. Make your toilet sparkle by adding one-half cup vinegar to the toilet bowl. Allow it to sit for thirty minutes and then scrub with a toilet brush. Alternatively, sprinkle a little baking soda inside the bowl and scrub. To clean the outer surfaces, sprinkle a wet cloth with baking soda and wipe down toilet.

Drain cleaner. Clean sink and tub drains by pouring one-half cup of baking soda down the drain, followed by one cup vinegar. Let the mixture sit for fifteen minutes and then rinse with hot water. For tough clogs, use the same mixture but allow it to sit overnight before rinsing.

Carpeting and rugs. Few areas of the home get dirty faster than the floor. Fabric flooring tends to soak up the odors of the home, whether they are related to a pet or child. To absorb odors and clean your carpet naturally, sprinkle baking soda over the surface of the carpet and let it stand for fifteen to thirty minutes before vacuuming. For more intense cleaning, check out these recipes from Sierra Club Canada (*www.sierraclub .ca*) for handling heavy-duty dirt and stains.

- **Chocolate:** Make a paste from borax and water. Rub into the stain.
- **Coffee:** Rub club soda into the coffee spot and wipe up with a towel or sponge.
- **Grease:** Cover with cornstarch or cornmeal, let sit a while, rub in, and vacuum.
- **Heavy-duty carpet cleaner:** Make a paste from one-quarter cup each of salt, vinegar, and borax. Rub into the spot and let dry before vacuuming.
- **Mud:** Rub salt into the mud. Let dry for one hour and vacuum.
- **Red wine:** Cover the stain with salt while wet. Let dry completely, and then vacuum.

Your little one will likely to spend the better part of her first year crawling around on the floor, so it is important to make sure your carpets are as clean and nontoxic as possible.

Mold cleaner. Prevent mold and mildew, by repairing leaks and using an exhaust fan in bathrooms or a dehumidifier in areas where there is a lot of humidity in the air. To clean mold and mildew, mix one-half cup of borax in one gallon of hot water. Spray on and wipe off. Scrub mildew spots with a mixture of borax and water and a scouring pad. Machine wash fabric shower curtains adding one cup of vinegar to the rinse cycle.

Porcelain cleaner. Clean porcelain with a paste made from baking soda and water. Rub the paste into the item, let set, wipe clean, and rinse. Use a fine grain wet/dry sandpaper (400 grit) to remove stains from porcelain sinks.

Eco-Friendly Cleaning Supplies

The DIY alternatives listed above are not for every parent. If you don't have the time or desire to make your own, look for nontoxic, earth-friendly cleaning agents the next time you shop.

ESSENTIAL

If you have carpeting or large rugs that cannot be shaken outside, you will need to vacuum them frequently to remove all of the dust, toxins, allergens, and dirt that build up in their fibers. Look for a vacuum with a bagless HEPA (high efficiency particulate air) filter that can trap even the tiniest particles and keep them from recirculating in your home.

Companies that make trustworthy green cleaning products include Ecover (*www.ecover.com*), Seaside Naturals (*www.seasidenaturals.com*), Method (*www.methodhome.com*), and Seventh Generation (*www.seventh generation.com*). Actor Ed Begley, Jr., puts his name and his environmental reputation on the line with an all-purpose cleaner called Begley's Best All Purpose Cleaner (*www.begleysbest.com*) that is child-safe, vegan, nontoxic, non-caustic, non-allergenic, and 99 percent biodegradable within seven days. For more information about green cleaning products, check out Green Seal (*www.greenseal.org*) a nonprofit agency that certifies environmentally responsible products.

CHAPTER 8

Save Your Energy!

Need an energy boost? It can be hard to keep up your energy reserves when you are pregnant or taking care of a young child. But you also need a lot of energy in the form of fossil fuels (coal, oil, or natural gas) for the electricity required to keep your baby warm, cool, clean, clothed, and fed. Here are some easy ideas for reducing energy consumption in your home to help you save money and the planet.

Household Energy Consumption

Americans use nearly a million dollars worth of energy every minute—night and day—every day of the year. The largest portion of your energy bill goes toward keeping your home a comfortable temperature. Heating accounts for 66 percent of your annual energy bill, followed by 22 percent for cooling. Other big energy users in the home are appliances and the hot water heater. Every kilowatt you conserve and every battery you save can significantly trim your monthly energy bill while helping you protect the planet.

Home Energy Audits

The first step in making your home more efficient is to take a closer look at just how much energy you and using and where. A home energy audit can help you assess your home's energy use and understand what measures you can take to conserve it. You can do it yourself, or have one done by a professional. Either way, an energy audit is a great tool that can help you save loads of money and energy at home.

DIY Home Energy Audits

It is not difficult to perform your own home energy audit. And the knowledge you will gain from knowing how your home uses energy will be priceless down the road. To get started, gather up your last twelve months of utility bills, and take note of when you use the most and least energy throughout the year. Check out Energy Star's Home Energy Yardstick (*www.energystar.gov*) to compare your home's energy efficiency to similar homes across the country. If you don't have a copy of your bills for the last year, call your utility company and ask for a twelve-month summary.

QUESTION

How can I tell if my home has an energy leak?
On a windy day, take a lightweight piece of yarn or ribbon and test your windows and doorjambs for leaks. Hold the ribbon near the windowsills or doorjamb. If it is fluttering, you have a leak.

Now take a look around your home to see where your energy is going. Look for leaks around electrical outlets, switch plates, window frames, baseboards, weather stripping, pipes, doors, fireplace dampers, attic hatches, and wall- or window-mounted air conditioners. Check out your home's level of insulation to be sure it meets at least the minimum standard building requirements. Inspect your heating and cooling equipment to make sure that vents and filters are cleaned properly. Next, assess how much energy you are using in the form of lighting, computers, and electrical appliances.

The Home Energy Saver (*www.hes.lbl.gov*), sponsored by the U.S. Department of Energy, can help you as you complete an at-home energy audit. This site helps users calculate energy costs, research conservation, and calculate future savings.

Hiring a Professional

For a detailed look at your home's energy use, you may want to contact a professional home energy auditor. A professional auditor will inspect your home and use a variety of techniques and equipment to evaluate its energy efficiency. The audit will look at your existing utility bills and assess the efficiency of your home's heating and cooling systems, lighting, insulation, appliances, and windows. Thorough audits often use equipment such as blower doors, which measure the extent of leaks in the building envelope, and infrared cameras, which reveal hard-to-detect areas of air infiltration and missing insulation.

Contact your utility company to see if they offer free or discounted energy audits to customers. If not, you can hire a home energy professional to evaluate your home's energy efficiency. Check out Energy Star's Home Partner Locator (*www.energystar.gov*) or RESNET (Residential Energy Services Network; *www.resnet.us*) to find a certified home energy auditor in your area. In California, contact CHEERS (California Home Energy Rating Services; *www.cheers.org*).

Conserve Energy at Home

Making your home more energy efficient can help to reduce high energy bills, improve comfort, and reduce your impact on the environment. And there are lots of ways to do it. Don't be overwhelmed by the number of different ways to save energy around your home. Try taking the steps one at a time and before long your home will be humming along at maximum efficiency.

Heating and Cooling

As much as half of the energy used in your home goes to keeping it warm in the winter and cool in the summer. So making smart decisions about your home's heating, ventilating, and air conditioning (HVAC) system can have a big effect on your utility bills and your family's comfort. Take these steps to improve the efficiency of your heating and cooling system.

Control your temp. Two-thirds of your home's energy consumption is used to keep you warm and another big chunk is used to keep you cool. Even a minor adjustment in your thermostat can slash your energy use. During the summer months, bump up the thermostat to 78°F and open the windows when there is a fresh breeze. In the winter, set it to around 68°F and turn it down even more (try 55°F) when you go to sleep or are away for the day.

Adjust your drapes. In the summer, keep the drapes closed over sunny windows to reduce heat from the sun. If you live in a warm climate, take advantage of drapes with an insulating lining that will keep the sun's rays from heating your home. In the winter, take advantage of the sun's energy by leaving shades and blinds open on sunny days, and then closing them at night to reduce heat loss.

Close it off. Cut your energy costs further by making sure the hot (or cold) air stays where you need it. If you have rooms in your house that you rarely go into, keep them sealed off by closing doors and air vents.

Insulate yourself. Simple steps like insulating and weather stripping can reduce your energy use by 20 to 30 percent. Caulk and weather-strip around doors and windows to stop air leaks. Door sweeps are an easy cheap solution for drafty doors. Storm windows and doors can reduce heat loss by 30 percent.

Be sure to install appropriate insulation in your walls and ceiling for the climate in your area to improve your home's energy efficiency. You don't even have to tear down walls to add insulation. Contractors can pump foam insulation into a one-inch hole in your wall, insulating the whole house in just a few hours.

ALERT

Clean the filters on heating and air conditioning units to keep them operating efficiently. Dirty filters make your air conditioners and hot-air furnaces work harder and use more energy. Cleaning a dirty air conditioner filter can reduce energy use by 5 percent.

Water Heaters

Most Americans are fortunate enough to have an ample supply of clean, hot water available directly from the tap. Unfortunately, this easy access sometimes leads to a tremendous amount of waste. Hot water accounts for almost 15 percent of your home's annual energy bill.

Turn it down. The easiest way to save money on water heating is to turn the temperature on your water heater down to 120°F. The lower temperature will protect your new baby from scalding at the tap while saving you energy and money.

Bundle up. If you have an older water heater, keep it bundled up with a blanket or insulating jacket to trap heat inside the tank. Be sure to leave openings around electrical connections, thermostats, heating elements, and drain valves.

Go tankless. Tankless water heaters, also called instantaneous or demand water heaters, provide hot water only as it is needed. Traditional storage water heaters produce standby energy losses that cost you money. Tankless water heaters, on the other hand, heat water only when there is a need, saving you energy.

Appliances

When buying an appliance, remember that it has two price tags: what you pay to take it home and what you pay for the energy and water it uses. Energy Star certified appliances use 10 to 50 percent less energy and water than standard models. The money you save on your utility bills can more than make up for the cost of a more expensive but more efficient Energy Star model.

Put your fridge on a diet. If your refrigerator is equipped with a power-saving feature, use it. Set your refrigerator temperature at 38° to 42°F; your freezer should be set between 0° to 5°F. Keep an eye on the items in your refrigerator or freezer any time you change the temperature, to be sure that nothing spoils prematurely (especially if you have an older unit that may not be as precise on the temperature gauge, or as efficient as a newer model). If you have an extra refrigerator that you are not using, unplug it. Keep your refrigerator full but don't overfill it. Air needs room to circulate around food. Keep the freezer full as well to maximize efficiency.

ESSENTIAL

Test the gaskets around your fridge to make sure they are clean and tight to lock in cold air. Close a dollar bill in the refrigerator door with part of it sticking out. If it is difficult to pull out, the gaskets are sealing properly. If it pulls out easily, it is time to replace them.

Also, be sure to clean the vacuum the coils on the back of your refrigerator twice a year to maximize efficiency and make sure there is a space between your fridge and the wall behind it to allow air to circulate freely and eliminate the buildup of heat.

Cook up some energy savings. When cooking, use the right size pot for the job. The larger the pot, the more energy it will require to heat up. Use a pot with a flat bottom that completely covers the burner and put a lid on it to keep heat from escaping (this will also cook your food more quickly). Since your food may heat up quickly when covered, keep a close eye on your pots and pans during cooking. If you have a gas range, lower the flame if it is burning around the side of your pot or pan.

Take a few minutes to clean and maintain your oven and you can greatly improve its energy efficiency. A dirty oven does not reflect heat as well as a clean one. That means it will have to use more energy to heat up and stay warm. Also, check the seal on your oven door to make sure all of that heat is staying inside.

ALERT

Be on the lookout for phantom energy users! Even when appliances are off, they are still draining energy in standby mode. Use a power strip to turn off televisions, stereos, and computer systems when you are not using them and unplug appliances such as phone chargers, extra refrigerators, and printers until you need them.

When you are baking, skip the preheating step if possible. Only the most delicate recipes require that the oven be at a pre-set temperature before cooking begins. And resist the temptation to peek inside your oven any more than necessary, even opening the door just once can cause the temperature inside to drop considerably.

Green dishes? Don't run your dishwasher unless it is full. When you do run it, set it to the shortest setting for all but the dirtiest dishes. Avoid using energy sucking options such as heat-dry, rinse-hold, and pre-rinse features. If you have time, let your dishes air-dry to reduce your dishwasher's total energy use by as much as 20 percent.

FACT

For cooking or reheating small items, microwave foods instead of heating them in the stove or oven. This can reduce energy use by as much as 75 percent.

Green washing. Wash your clothes in cold water whenever practical and make sure your machine is set to always rinse in cold. Set your washer to the appropriate water level for the size of your load. When you are in the market for a new machine, consider a front loading washer that cuts hot water use by 60 to 70 percent.

Clean the lint filter in your dryer after each use to keep it running efficiently. Cut energy use by drying clothes under the *automatic*, instead of the *timed*, setting. Better yet, install a clothesline in your backyard and dry your clothes for free!

Compute the savings. Power down your computer any time you will be away from it for a period of an hour or more. For short breaks, use the *sleep* or *hibernate* modes to reduce energy use and save the time it takes to reboot.

Lighting

The types and amount of lighting in your home can significantly affect the amount of energy you use each month. Use these tips to save energy with the flick of a switch.

Install CFLs. Consider swapping out regular light bulbs for energy-saving, long-lasting compact fluorescents (CFLs) to save both energy and cash. CFLs cost a few cents more than standard bulbs, but they require about one-quarter of the energy to produce the same amount and quality of light, and they last ten times as long (saving you money down the road). They are also cooler to operate, making them safer for homes with little fingers. For lights you use regularly, install dimmers to save energy and extend the life of your bulbs.

The lights are on and nobody's home. Don't overlook the obvious: turn off lights when you leave a room. Use the minimum amount of outdoor security lights and be sure they are set on a timer or motion sensor so that they turn off during the day. Occupancy sensors are great indoors for rooms, like bathrooms, that see a lot of in and out traffic.

Clean and bright. Dirty bulbs don't give off as much light as clean ones. So get out that dust rag and clean them off. Your bulbs will give off more light and you will use less energy because you won't have to have as many lights on!

Energy-Saving Gadgets

There are a number of gadgets you can use to help you save energy around your home.

Power Strips

Even if you turn off appliances and computer equipment when you're not using them, they may be draining valuable energy just by being plugged in. If you have too many gadgets to unplug them all individually, plug them in to a power strip that will allow you unplug all of your gadgets with one shot.

Programmable Thermostats

If you have central air conditioning, a programmable thermostat can help you keep your home at a precise temperature control. It can also be used to automatically lower your air conditioning and/or heat use while you are not home. Just program it and forget about it; it will automatically adjust things for you so that you are not wasting electricity and money.

Electricity Monitor

Similar in appearance to your household thermostat, an energy monitor, like the Meter Reader from Energy Monitoring Technologies (*www.energy monitor.com*), can help you cut your energy use by giving you a visual, indoor display of the amount and cost of energy that you are using throughout your home.

An electricity usage monitor can give you a much better idea of which devices uses the most energy and which you don't need to be concerned about. This device is also useful for figuring out how much power various home devices are draining and, how much they are costing you to run.

Energy Star Products

Appliances and gadgets that carry the Energy Star label use less energy and water than comparable models. And you can find an Energy Star version of just about any product you need. Check out the Energy Star website (*www.energystar.gov*) for a complete list of products that can be certified with the Energy Star label.

Solar Powered Chargers

Consider purchasing a solar-powered battery charger to power up your camera, cell phone, iPod, or laptop. Sundance Solar (*http://store.sundance solarcorp.com*) makes a series of foldable solar battery chargers that are small enough to fit in a backpack. Solio (*www.solio.com*) and Solar Style (*www.solarstyle.com*) also make affordable options.

Renewable Energy

Once reserved only for the most ardent environmentalists, alternative energy from solar, wind, or water power is becoming easier and more cost efficient for average Americans to use. Solar energy is a good bet for those who have the space and live in the right climate. Solar water heaters, in particular, are a simple and cost-effective way to cut your energy bill without a lot of fuss. Small, family-style wind turbines are also increasing in popularity for those who live in windy areas.

Green Energy Suppliers

Depending on where you live, you may now have the option to choose your own energy supplier. If so, seek out a company that uses renewable sources of power such as solar, wind, low-impact hydroelectric, or geothermal. In some areas, you may also be able to purchase renewable energy credits (RECs) that offset your energy use by supporting renewable energy programs. Be sure to look for a reliable program like Green-e (*www.green-e.org*), a nonprofit group that verifies and certifies RECs.

CHAPTER 9

Put Your Trash Can on a Diet

According to the EPA, each American generates about four and a half pounds of garbage each day, adding up to more than 251 million tons of garbage across the United States each year. This is almost twice as much trash per person as in most other industrialized countries. As a consumer, you have the power to help alleviate America's mounting trash problem by making environmentally aware decisions in the way as you go about your daily activities.

What's in Your Trash Can?

Just what's in all of your garbage? The three major items in the waste stream are paper and cardboard (34 percent), yard trimmings (13 percent), and food scraps (12 percent). The good news is that these items are also some of the easiest to keep out of the trash can.

Another piece of good news is that reducing trash even by small amounts can make a huge difference. Each item you keep out of the garbage prevents emissions of greenhouse gases, reduces pollutants, saves energy, conserves resources, and reduces the need for new landfills and incinerators. It also saves you money in garbage removal costs.

Where Does All the Garbage Go?

You probably don't think twice about your garbage after it hits the trash can. On trash pickup day in your neighborhood, you push your can out to the curb, and a big truck comes to haul it all away. You don't have to think about it again. But have you ever wondered just where all of those takeout containers, milk cartons, baby diapers, and newspapers wind up after the trash truck carts them away? About 32.5 percent of the trash is recycled or composted and 12.5 percent is burned, but the majority (55 percent) is buried in landfills.

ESSENTIAL

The strategy for reducing trash is simple, and you've probably heard it a thousand times: reduce, reuse, and recycle, with recycling as the last resort. For example, you could buy water by the gallon and toss the plastic jugs in the recycle bin. But a better idea is to use a water filter and reusable containers to eliminate the waste altogether.

Landfills

Most people think that a landfill is a simple hole in the ground where trash is dumped and buried. If that's your idea of a landfill, you may wonder why it is important to compost food scraps or recycle paper. After all, these items will just break down in the landfill, right? Wrong.

Landfills are actually specifically designed to keep items from breaking down. In order to prevent ground, water, and air pollution, trash in landfills must be isolated from the environment, so landfills have a bottom liner made from either clay or plastic and they are covered daily with soil to prevent contact with air and moisture. The three necessary components for decomposition, sunlight, moisture, and oxygen, are purposefully kept out of a landfill to minimize leaks into the environment. Under these conditions, trash will not decompose much.

Breaking It Down

How long does it take for trash to decompose in a landfill? Longer than you think! Isolation from the environment makes it very difficult for most items to decompose in the landfill. According to rough estimates compiled from the U.S. National Park Service, United States Composting Council, New Hampshire Department of Environmental Sciences, and the New York City government, here's how long it takes these common trash items to breakdown:

- Aluminum cans: 80–200 years
- Cigarette butts: 1–5 years
- Food scraps: 2 months–20 years
- Glass: Unknown (too long to count!)
- Newspaper: 2–4 weeks
- Plastics: 500+ years

As you can see, just because you toss these items in the trash can does not mean that they are gone for good. In fact, most of these items will remain in the environment so long that your grandchildren may end up dealing with them!

Incinerators

A little over 12 percent of the nation's trash is sent to incinerator facilities to be burned rather than buried. Waste that takes a turn through an incinerator is burned down to ash that is then buried in a landfill. Incinerators do reduce the volume of waste left lying around, but they create a number of additional environmental concerns. In essence, they convert solid waste into hazardous ash and gas particles.

Incinerator facilities are required by law to use special gadgets called scrubbers and filters to remove tiny toxins from the incinerated before they are released into the air. A small number of incinerator facilities also recover recyclables before waste is tossed into the combustion chamber.

Reduce Your Trash

The very best thing you can do to save the planet and keep your baby from dealing with the environmental burden caused by garbage is to reduce the amount of trash you create each day. In today's disposable society that can be easier said than done. Here's how to minimize the amount of trash you create each day.

Leave it at the store. The best way to reduce waste is to keep it from coming home with you in the first place. Think twice before making a purchase to determine if you really, *really* need it. Try this old money-saving trick: Leave the item at the store and promise yourself that if you really need it, you will pick it up the next time you shop.

Make a waste-free lunch. Many American rely heavily on pre-packaged and disposable goods when packing lunches. Sure, they're convenient, but what is the cost of this convenience? Much of the trash generated in the average American home comes from the packaging on the food you buy.

FACT

According to the website *www.wastefreelunches.org*, the average school-age child generates about 67 pounds of waste each year in his school lunches alone. That works out to 18,760 pounds of lunch waste created annually for just one average-size elementary school!

Ditch those prepackaged goods and make a waste-free lunch by replacing disposable items with reusables. Use a reusable container instead of foil or baggies to wrap sandwiches and sides. Skip the bottled water or soda and fill a reusable bottle with your beverage of choice. Use cloth napkins and reusable utensils and toss it all together in a cloth tote or reusable cooler instead of a disposable bag.

Grasscycle. Bagging up leaves and other yard trimmings not only wastes your time and energy, it also puts a tremendous strain on the environment when it winds up in a landfill. Instead, try grasscycling. Leave grass clippings on your lawn where they will naturally decompose, hold in soil moisture, prevent freezing, and return nutrients to the soil.

Go paperless. Think twice before you hit that *print* button. Read documents, news, and magazines online. Request e-bills and pay bills over the web to save paper from bills and checks. Send out e-cards to save both paper and cash. At work, distribute memos and circulate documents by e-mail.

Be picky about packaging. If you have a choice between two products, go for the one with less packaging so that you will have less to throw away when you get it home. Also, seek out a product with packaging that can be reused for other purposes at home, such as a box that can later be used to ship a package or cardboard that will make an interesting art project.

Choose reusable over disposable. Steer clear of disposable products such as batteries, plates, cups, razors, and pens. Use reusable, rechargeable, or refillable products instead.

Consider pre-loved. When you need a new item, consider purchasing a gently used or pre-loved item to keep it out of the landfill and reduce the use of virgin materials.

Go back for seconds. At the dinner table, get in the habit of taking smaller portions and going back for seconds if you are still hungry. This strategy is not only good for minimizing nausea during pregnancy; it will also significantly reduce the amount of food wasted.

Don't buy it—borrow instead. Start a toy exchange with friends. As every parent knows, today's favorite toy is tomorrow's closet clutter. Instead of buying new toys every week, bring a box of your old toys to a friend's house and bring a box of their old toys home. Swap them back after a few weeks. Instead of buying books, movies, and magazines, exchange with your friends, utilize your local library, or visit a movie rental store.

Stop junk mail. Every time you order something online, fill out a warranty card, or join a club, your personal information is collected and sold to marketers who will flood your mailbox with offers that waste paper as well as your time. To stop junk mail, start by contacting the Direct Marketing Association's (DMA) Mail Preference Service to request that your contact information be removed from lists run by them (the DMA is a trade group of marketing companies). Removing your information from this mailing list will cost $1 but it will also help to stop junk mail for up to five years. This can be done online at *www.dmachoice .org*, or by sending a postcard or letter to:

Mail Preference Service
Direct Marketing Association
P.O. Box 643
Carmel, NY 15012-0643

Credit card offers are another big source of junk mail. Call 1-888-5 OPT-OUT (or 1-888-567-8688) twenty-four hours a day to stop any and all unsolicited credit card offers from coming your way.

Start Your Own Compost Pile

Food scraps make up over 12 percent of the U.S. waste stream. According to the EPA, Americans throw away more than 25 percent of the food they prepare, amounting to about 96 billion pounds of food waste each year! These food scraps can easily be converted into valuable nutrients for the soil.

Compost piles break down food scraps (like vegetable peels, bread crusts, and eggshells) into super-rich, super-usable fertilizer for your flower beds and garden. Find a suitable place in your yard to start your own compost pile. To get started you will need two types of ingredients:

- Carbon (shredded newspapers, cardboard, and straw)
- Nitrogen (lawn clippings, food scraps, and weeds)

Combine these two components together and before long you will have compost. If you are feeling lazy, you don't need to do anything else (but wait and wait). You will have usable compost by next year even if you never touch the pile again. If you'd like things to move along a little more quickly, you will need to turn the pile and add a few drops of water every few weeks.

ESSENTIAL

For in depth info about starting and maintaining a compost pile, read *Let It Rot: The Gardener's Guide to Composting* by Stu Campbell or *Compost: The Natural Way to Make Food for Your Garden* by Kenneth Thompson. Online you can check out How to Compost (*www.howto compost.org*) or Florida's Online Composting Center (*www.compost info.com*).

Enclosed compost bins can help keep your pile neat and organized. The size compost bin that you need will be determined by your expectations and dedication to the project, as there are bins in all shapes and sizes. You can build your own with a couple of boards or a wire cage. If you decide to purchase one, check out the Back Porch Compost Tumbler available through Planet Natural (*www.planetnatural.com*). It doesn't take up a lot of space, won't look unsightly in your yard, lets you roll the compost (rather than turn it with a shovel), and it can produce finished compost in four to six weeks.

Reuse

The next best way to keep garbage out of the landfill and eliminate the need to continually make new stuff is to look for ways to reuse the items you already own. Before you recycle or dispose of anything, consider whether it has life left in it.

Repurpose it. Keep those old toys or clothes out of the trash by finding a new life for them; repair, refill, rebuild, or otherwise repurpose things instead of tossing them. Get creative by using old items (such as broken toys, torn clothing, or plastic bottles) as art supplies, or turn one of your old T-shirts into a child's art smock.

Turn trash into cash. If they are worth something, you can make a tidy profit by selling toys, clothes, and books at yard sales, consignment shops, or on websites like eBay (*www.ebay.com*) or Craigslist (*www .craigslist.org*). If those don't work, donate items to your local thrift store or use Freecycle (*www.freecycle.org*) to find someone in your area who might need them. One person's junk is another's treasure.

Get crafty. There are a lot of creative ways that you and your baby can turn ordinary garbage into fun crafts. A plastic water bottle or milk jug makes an excellent bird feeder, baby food jars convert easily into paperweights or snow globes, and a toilet paper tube can be transformed into a pencil holder or a napkin ring. Check out *www.resourcefulschools.org* to learn how to make your own paper or find ten crafts to make with a paper bag.

See double. Whether you are at home or at work, get in the habit of using both sides of a piece of paper. Kids' art projects, grocery lists, and messages can give paper a second life. At the store, bring along your own shopping bags; either the plastic bags from your last trip or, better yet, a reusable tote bag to minimize waste.

Packing peanuts. Call the Plastic Loosefill Council at 1-800-828-2214 for a list of locations where you can drop off the plastic peanuts that protect shipped materials. Most UPS Store locations accept foam packaging peanuts for reuse. Check out *www.theupsstore.com* for a location near you.

Recycle

Okay, if you've already bought it and you can not reuse it, the next best thing is to recycle it. Recycling is a great idea, but when you are pressed for time, it may seem just so much easier to toss things in the trash. When you are trying to clean up the dinner dishes, feed a fussy baby, and put in a load of laundry, it can be a real drag to rinse out that empty jar of spaghetti sauce or can of soup. Just keep this little mantra in mind: Recycling creates jobs, saves energy, preserves natural resources, reduces greenhouse-gas emissions, and keeps toxins from leaking out of landfills. Recycling makes a difference to your environment and the world you will pass on to your children.

Know Your Plastics

Plastics are everywhere, especially when it comes to the products geared to helping you feed, clean, and care for your newborn baby. So it is important to get to know which plastics are safe and which are to be avoided. Fortunately, this information is listed on the product itself, in the form of the numbered recycling codes on the packaging of all plastic products. Look for these numbers before you buy a product and avoid those that are unsafe for your baby and the planet.

The safer plastics are those labeled one, two, and four, while plastics coded as three, six, and seven should be avoided. Also, keep in mind what types of plastics you will be able to recycle at your local recycling facility. Although many plastic products are labeled as *recyclable*, you may not be able to recycle them in your area. Here's a look at the meaning behind those mysterious number codes:

- **#1: PET or PETE (polyethylene terephthalate).** Found in most disposable drinking bottles, this type of plastic can be recycled in most recycle centers across the United States.
- **#2: HDPE (high-density polyethylene).** Found in many toys, milk jugs, detergents, and personal care product bottles. Can be recycled in many U.S. locations.
- **#3: PVC (polyvinyl chloride).** Found in pipes, cling wrap, and some food and detergent containers. Not easily recyclable.
- **#4: LDPE (low-density polyethylene).** Found in soft, flexible plastics such as some cling wraps and garbage bags.
- **#5: PP (polypropylene).** Found in yogurt containers, drinking straws, syrup bottles, and baby diapers.

- **#6: PS (polystyrene).** Found in stiff plastics such as disposable coffee cups, plastic utensils, and take out containers.
- **#7: Other (typically polycarbonate, nylon, or acrylic plastics).** Found in baby bottles, teething rings, and pacifiers. Number seven plastics that are made from polycarbonate are a source of the dangerous toxin BPA (or bisphenol-A). Avoid using them.

Make it a habit to check out the plastic recycling code on the bottom of food containers, toys, and household products and before long you will have a much better idea of which products are safe and which you should avoid.

What Items Should You Recycle

Recycling options vary by city or county. Most areas collect office paper, cardboard, magazines, newspaper, aluminum, plastics, glass (colored or clear), steel, yard trimmings, tires, batteries, and building materials. Contact your local recycling facility, or check out Earth911 (*www.earth911.org*) to find out what items are recycled in your area. According to the National Recycling Coalition, following are the top ten items you should try to recycle whenever possible.

Aluminum. Americans use 200 million aluminum beverage cans every day. There are no labels, covers or lids on these cans, so they are 100 percent recyclable. Making new aluminum cans from recycled cans uses 95 percent less energy than that needed to produce one from virgin ore.

PET plastic bottles (#1). PET (polyethylene terephthalate) is a form of polyester used to produce lightweight plastic bottles for items such as soft drinks, water, juice, liquor, cough syrup, tennis balls and cleaning products. These bottles make up 48 percent of the plastic bottles used in the United States. Once recycled, PET bottles can be used to make new plastic containers, sweaters, shoes, luggage, upholstery, carpeting, fiberfill for sleeping bags, coats, and fabric for T-shirts and tote bags.

Newspaper. Compared to the production of virgin newspaper, recycled newspaper saves trees, cuts energy use by over 50 percent, and creates

74 percent less air pollution. Newspapers are easily recycled back into newsprint or into other papers, such as boxboard or newsletter stock.

Corrugated cardboard. Over 90 percent of all products in the United States are shipped in corrugated cardboard boxes. These bulky boxes take up a lot of space in dumpsters. Recycled corrugated cardboard is used to make chipboard, boxboard (e.g., cereal boxes), paper towels, tissues, and printing paper.

Steel cans. According to the U.S. Energy Information Administration (EIA), the average family in the United States uses 90 pounds of steel cans a year. The EIA estimates that recycling that steel would save 144 kilowatt hours of electricity, 63 pounds of coal, 112 pounds of iron, and 5.4 pounds of limestone. Today, all steel products are made with at least some recycled steel.

HDPE plastic bottles (#2). HDPE (high density polyethylene) plastics account for 47 percent of all plastic bottles consumed in the United States. These stiff, impact resistant bottles are often used to hold products such as milk and laundry detergent. Once recycled, they are easily converted into new bottles or plastic pipe.

ALERT

Chemical or toxic products like cleaning agents, paints, pesticides, and batteries are considered hazardous waste and should never be thrown into a traditional landfill. Call your local environmental, health, or solid-waste agency for instructions on proper use and disposal and to learn about local hazardous waste–collection programs.

Glass containers. Glass is used to package many food products such as juices, jellies, baby food, and vegetable oils. It currently makes up about 5 percent of the trash that hits U.S. landfills. Recycled glass is easily made into new glass jars and bottles or into other glass products like fiberglass insulation. And, unlike paper, glass products can be recycled over and over again without wearing out. Using recycled glass to make new glass products requires 40 percent less energy than making it from virgin materials.

Magazines. Tons of outdated magazines and catalogs hit the landfills each year. Instead of tossing yours, donate them to local schools or day-care centers for craft projects. Hospitals and doctors' offices often accept donations of recent-edition magazines. Recycled magazines and catalogs can also be combined with old newspapers and wood chips to make newsprint, tissue, boxboard, and printing paper.

Mixed paper. Paper products such as office paper, envelopes, telephone books, and brown bags make up about 35 percent of the trash in the United States, the largest single sector of waste.

FACT

According to the World Resources Institute, in 2005, each person in the United States consumed 653.5 pounds of paper. That means it takes over 1 ton of paper and 4.3 cubic yards of landfill space to handle the yearly paper consumption for a family of four.

Recycled paper can be used to make products such as new paper, molded packaging, compost, and kitty litter. Recycling paper products reduces energy consumption, decreases combustion and landfill emissions, and decreases the amount of carbon dioxide in the atmosphere.

Computers. Old computers and electronics are a major contributor to the waste stream. That's no surprise considering how quickly these items become outdated and obsolete. They are also difficult to dispose of because they are made up of a number of components that are toxic to the environment. Fortunately, many computers can be repaired or upgraded, extending their life by a few years. They can also be donated (with a tax deduction) and refurbished for use in local schools, charities and nonprofit organizations. Earth 911 (*www.earth911.org*) maintains a list on their website of organizations that accept computer donations. As a last resort, computers can be recycled so that their components (plastics, glass, steel, gold, lead, mercury, and cadmium) can be recaptured and used again.

Closing the Loop

When you are talking trash, the final step in the process is to support the recycling industry by purchasing recycled products. You can find everything from printer paper to furniture to ski jackets that are made from recycled materials. This helps increase demand for recycling and reduces the use of virgin materials and the production of new wastes.

The Waste-Can Weigh-In

Pregnancy is no time for weight-loss diets, but that doesn't mean that your trash cannot go on a diet instead. Try this experiment at home. Every night for a week, collect your household garbage and weigh it on your bathroom scale. Record your results and compare your numbers from week to week. Set a goal to reduce the weight of your trash by two pounds each week. And be sure to celebrate your success as your trash slims down.

CHAPTER 10

Saving Water

You use water every day for drinking, cooking, cleaning, bathing, and even shopping (since water is used to produce every item on the store shelves, from milk to blue jeans). Yet there is only a limited supply to meet the global demand for this valuable resource. It is not likely that the planet will ever run out of water. But the amount of clean, fresh, water that you have access to each day may become limited as supplies dwindle.

Why Conserve Water?

Why is it necessary to conserve water when there is water everywhere? Contrary to appearances, fresh water is not really as plentiful as you might think. Ninety-seven percent of the water on the planet is actually salt water, not suitable for consumption. Only 3 percent of the Earth's water supply is fresh, and the majority of that is locked away in ice caps and glaciers. The reality is that just 1 percent of the water on Earth is available for all of the world's agricultural, manufacturing, sanitation, and personal household needs. So it is important to conserve what we have now.

How much water do you use each day? Would you believe that each American uses roughly 100 to 150 gallons of water on a daily basis? Find out where all of this water goes and how you can conserve it.

Inside the house, the bathroom is the biggest water drain, accounting for three-quarters of all indoor water use. Outside, it's lawn care and car washing that suck up most of the water.

Remember, you pay for water three times: to buy it, to heat it (for hot water), and to take it away. So, reducing water consumption can save you a bundle on your water, energy, and sewer bills. It also eases the burden on water treatment facilities, curbing pollution and conserving energy.

Conserve Water at Home

Most Americans use about fifty to seventy-five gallons of water each day in their homes. You use it to flush your toilets, cook your food, wash your face, and of course, to quench your thirst. Most households use less water in the early morning, while most people are sleeping, and during the winter. Peak consumption is in the spring and summer and when the family gets home in the late afternoon. Taking a closer look at your consumption patterns will give you a better idea of how you and your family can conserve water.

It is easy to waste water when you are not thinking about it and just as easy to conserve it by paying closer attention to how and when you turn on the tap. Make a conscious effort to track how much water you use when you brush your teeth, shower, cook, do your dishes, or clean your home, and look for ways to minimize water use at each step.

Don't Be a Drip

Even a small leak can waste a ton of water. A leak of just one drop per second wastes 2,700 gallons of water a year. Get out a wrench and put a stop to those drips. Toilets are the leading cause of household water leaks, and even a small toilet leak can cost you fifty dollars or more each year in increased water and sewer bills. Not sure if your toilet is leaking? Drop a little food coloring in your toilet tank. If the color seeps into the toilet bowl without flushing, you have a leak.

In an Emergency

Make sure you know how and where to turn off your water quickly if a pipe were to burst. This could save thousands of gallons of water and thousands of dollars in damage to your home.

Do Double Duty

Get more out of your water use by multitasking. Think of ways to use the same water more than once while grooming, cleaning, washing dishes, and playing. For example, allow cooking water to cool and use it to water plants both indoors and out.

Bathroom

The vast majority of the water flowing through your house is going in and out of your bathroom. So this is by far the best place to focus your energy when it comes to conserving water.

Go low flow. Water-saving shower heads or flow restrictors can save as much as 500 to 800 gallons of water per month. Installing one takes only a few minutes, and for a small investment of ten to twenty dollars, you could save fifty to seventy-five dollars per year on water bills and twenty to fifty dollars or more per year on energy bills. Some municipalities even give low-flow gadgets away for free, so check with your county or other local resources before you buy.

New low-flow models do more than just block the flow of water. They are designed to aerate water, giving you a robust shower that is comparable to standard models. If you are building a new house or remodeling, consider installing a low-flow toilet that can reduce indoor water use by 20 percent.

Save water while you groom. Old habits are hard to break, but letting the water run while you are grooming is a good one to change. Turn the water off while you brush your teeth and you will save four gallons a minute. That's 200 gallons a week for a family of four! Save three gallons of water each day by turning off the water while shaving. Instead, fill the bottom of the sink with a few inches of water to rinse your razor. In the shower, turn off the water while you shampoo and condition your hair and you can save more than fifty gallons a week. Do double duty by brushing your teeth in the shower.

Waiting for hot water? Do you have a faucet or shower that takes forever to produce hot water? This is often the case when water has to travel a distance through plumbing to reach its destination. But a lot of water gets wasted while you are waiting for your shower to heat up. Don't let the cold water go down the drain. Instead, capture it with a cup or watering can to use later on house plants or your garden. This can save anywhere from 200 to 300 gallons of water each month.

For baths, plug the drain before turning the water on and adjust the temperature as the tub fills up.

ESSENTIAL

Consider installing a point-of-use (tankless) water heater to produce instant hot water right where and when you need it. This can significantly minimize the amount of water you waste while waiting for your next hot shower. Some states and localities offer rebates and tax incentives for installing these devices.

Double up. You may not have the option to share a shower once your baby is born. But until then, it makes sense to take advantage of this water saving trick! You and your partner can also shower one right after another so that you don't have to wait for the water to heat up.

Toilet dams. You only need about 2 gallons of water to successfully flush your toilet (older model toilets use seven to 10 gallons while newer models use three to five). You can minimize this water waste by making a toilet dam that cuts down on the amount of water used for each flush. Fill a plastic water bottle with pebbles or water and place it in your toilet tank. If you have an active toilet, this can save you roughly 300 gallons of water each month.

Use your trash can. Your toilet uses more water than anything else in your home (up to 28 percent). So conserve flushes by tossing dead bugs, tissues, and baby wipes (even the flushable ones) in the trash can instead of the toilet to avoid unnecessary flushes.

Kitchen

About 10 percent of all the water used in your home is used in the kitchen, primarily for dishwashing, cooking, drinking, and cleaning. Here's how to save water in each of those areas.

The dirt on dishes. A recent study conducted by researchers at the University of Bonn in Germany found that washing dishes with a dishwasher uses half the energy, one-sixth the water, and much less soap than washing dishes by hand. They even accounted for washing half loads and particularly dirty loads. Of course, your best bet is to run the dishwasher with a full load to maximize water and energy efficiency.

If you don't have a dishwasher, or if you just like to wash your dishes by hand, minimize running water by filling one sink with soapy water and one with rinse water. If you only have one sink, use a spray device or short blasts from the tap to rinse.

Thirsty? It is important to drink a lot of water during your pregnancy. Keep a bottle or a pitcher of drinking water in the refrigerator. This way you won't have to run the tap to get a cool drink. Water carries nutrients through your blood to your baby, and helps support the production of amniotic fluid in the womb. Water also helps flush toxins from the body.

Think again before purchasing bottled water. Bottled water uses more energy and resources in its production and shipping than tap water, and it is often of similar or lesser quality. Americans throw away roughly twenty-two million water bottles each year, clogging up landfill as well as resources. And according to the Natural Resource Defense Council's four-year study on the bottled water industry, water that comes from a bottle is no cleaner or safer than water that comes from the tap. In fact, their study found that at least 25 percent of bottled water is actually just bottled tap water. Save money and resources by carrying your own reusable bottle filled with tap water, instead.

ALERT

One place you don't want to skimp on water is the amount of water you drink each day. Women who are pregnant or nursing need lots of water to stay hydrated. The Institute of Medicine recommends that pregnant women drink about ten cups of water each day and women who breastfeed consume about thirteen cups per day.

The big chill. Defrosting your meat or veggies with tap water can waste 100 gallons of water each month. Plan ahead and defrost food in the fridge or use the microwave when time is short.

Clean those veggies. Wash your fruits and veggies in a small pot rather than a stream of running water. When you finish, toss the rinse water on a houseplant.

Get more from your garbage. Skip the garbage disposal (which needs a lot of water to operate properly). Instead, consider starting a compost pile to get rid of food waste.

Laundry

Your laundry machine is the second biggest user of water in your home, so it has a big impact on your water, sewer, and energy bills. Reduce water consumption with these tricks for greening your laundry pile.

Depending on the make and model of machine that you own, each load of laundry you wash will use between 27 and 54 gallons of water. Get the most out of that water by washing full loads of laundry whenever possible.

If you do need to wash a small load, set the water on the lowest fill-setting possible.

ESSENTIAL

In the market for a new laundry machine? Make it green. When it's time to replace your washing machine, look for a water efficient model, such as a front loading washer that carries the Energy Star rating. Energy Star washing machines can save as much as 7,000 gallons per year.

When washing clothes by hand, put a stopper in the sink or tub for both wash and rinse. Don't just let all of that precious water run down the drain.

Air Conditioners

If you already have an evaporative air conditioner, direct the water run-off to a flower bed or the base of a tree. Or, consider installing an air-to-air heat pump on your air conditioning system to stay cool without wasting water.

Outdoors

Typically, outdoor water use accounts for up to 50 percent of water consumed by households. You can reduce your outdoor water consumption by taking a few simple steps to tighten those taps, eliminate those leaks and use water wisely.

From the hose. Attach an adjustable nozzle to the end of your garden hose so that you can control water volume and flow. Winterize outdoor spigots when temperatures dip below freezing to prevent leaks or burst pipes.

A clean ride. When it comes time to wash you car, you will actually use less water at a car wash than you would at home. Commercial car washes use high-powered hoses and recycled wash water to maximize water conservation. If you want to do the job at home, use a bucket of water to soap up the car followed by a quick rinse with the hose. If you can, make the water do double duty by washing the car on your lawn so that your grass gets a drink as well.

For the pool. If you have a pool, use a pool cover to cut down on evaporation. An uncovered standard-sized (16 ft. × 32 ft.) pool loses approximately one inch of water each week to evaporation. Mark the water level with a grease pencil, so that you can closely monitor for leaks. Also, consider installing a water-saving pool filter.

Conserve Water at the Store

Did you know that it takes 1,800 gallons to make a pair of jeans, 1,000 gallons of water to make a loaf of bread, 400 gallons of water to make one cotton T-shirt, and 48 gallons of water to produce 8 fluid ounces of milk? Water is a primary ingredient in the manufacturing of almost all of your favorite stuff, so reducing your overall consumption can help to conserve water as effectively as shutting off your household tap.

Water-Saving Gadgets

Invest in some water-saving gadgets to minimize the amount of water you use in your home. Faucet aerators and low-flow shower heads payback their investment quickly by reducing water, energy and sewer bills.

Toilets

If you have an older toilet, consider purchasing Athena's Controllable Flush Replacement Handle (*www.athenacfc.com*). This water-saving gadget turns into a dual flush system. Just pull the handle up to flush with your tank's full capacity; pull down to use only one and a half gallons. Athena estimates that a family of four can save over 30,000 gallons of water with this device.

Low-Flow Shower Heads

A low-flow shower head installs easily onto your shower to minimize the amount of water you use each time you bathe. Gaiam's Lowest Flow Shower

Head (*www.gaiam.com*) uses 2¼ gallons of water per minute. Bricor (*www .bricor.com*) makes a shower head that uses one gallon of water per minute and features a pause button that can be used while shaving or lathering to reduce flow further. The Aqua Helix (*www.aquahelix.net*) shower head squeezes out only ½ gallon per minute.

Faucet Aerators

Faucet aerators are inexpensive gadgets that often cost less than one dollar while reducing your water consumption at the sink by as much as 50 percent. If your faucet already has an aerator installed, it will have its flow rate imprinted on the side. Look for faucets with a rate of two and three-quarter gallons per minute or lower. If your faucet doesn't already have an aerator, you can install your own as long as the inside tip of the faucet is threaded. You can find faucet aerators at any local plumbing or hardware store, but call your water utility company first as they may give them out for free. Online, check out Niagara Conservation (*www.niagaraconservation.com*).

Energy Star Appliances

Energy Star appliances do more than just cut down your energy bill. Dishwashers and clothes washers that meet the Energy Star criteria also help you reduce your water and sewer bills. For instance, most qualified washing machines use only 18 to 25 gallons of water per load, compared to the forty gallons used by a standard model.

Point of Use Water Heaters

If it takes a long time for the hot water to reach your bathroom or kitchen, consider installing a point of use water heater such as the one from Ariston (*www.boschhotwater.com*). Point-of-use water heaters produce instant hot water right where you need it and eliminate the need to run water until it is hot.

Water Savers

The AQUS Water System from Water Saver Technologies (*www.water savertech.com*) is a cool new gadget that collects the grey water from your sink and sends it over to your toilet tank to be used in the next flush. It fits directly under your vanity and can hold up to 5½ gallons of water.

Water Filters

Water filters not only take the toxins out of your water supply, they may also help you conserve water as well. In-home filters soften hard water, which can clog pipes and appliances, reduce clothing longevity, leave a film (meaning more cleaning) on bathtubs and shower tiles, and increase the cost to heat water by up to 30 percent. These clogs also shorten the overall life of your water heater. Install a filter to keep your water system running smoothly.

Collecting Rain Water

If you do a lot of gardening, it might make sense to try collecting rain water to water your plants and minimize the amount of water you use from the tap. With a little ingenuity, you can collect rain water for watering your plants in any container that will hold water. The only major criteria is that your container has a mesh screen on top to prevent the breeding of mosquitoes.

In the simplest set-up, a rain barrel with an open top is placed underneath a gutter downspout, catching rainwater runoff from the roof. Commercial containers typically hold about 50 to 80 gallons of water and many come pre-equipped with a valve that allows for easy hose attachment.

ESSENTIAL

Natural rain water is not processed like the water that comes out of the tap. It doesn't contain the minerals found in wells or the chlorine in municipal supplies, so it is ideal for watering the lawn, washing the car, doing the laundry, and even taking a shower.

If you want to get technical, surf over to the Center for Watershed Protection (*www.cwp.org*) and search for rain barrel for instructions on building and installing a rain barrel using a 55-gallon drum. For the premade variety, browse your local garden supply store, or try Clean Air Gardening (*www .cleanairgardening.com*).

CHAPTER 11

Make Your Grass a Little Greener

How green is your grass—not just green as in color, but green as in healthy and environmentally friendly? A natural lawn is safer for your growing family and for the plants, birds, mammals, and insects that rely on it for food and shelter. Healthy grass also prevents soil erosion, filters contaminants before they make their way into your waterways, and absorbs many types of air pollution like dust and soot. You don't have to be an expert to make your grass greener. This chapter will show you how it is done.

Is Your Yard Green?

Every year Americans use 1,000 gallons of water, 70 million pounds of pesticides, and over 5 billion dollars worth of fertilizers in an effort to create natural looking lawns. According to the U.S. Fish and Wildlife Service, homeowners use up to ten times more chemical pesticides per acre on their lawns than farmers use on their crops. These chemicals wreak havoc on the environment and leave a chemical residue on your lawn that is anything but safe for children.

And kids don't even have to play outside to be affected. Lawn-care chemicals that are tracked indoors on people's shoes and pet's paws can migrate all around the house. In a 2001 study published in the journal *Environmental Health Perspectives*, researchers tested indoor surfaces after the popular herbicide 2,4-D (a known hormone disruptor) was applied to lawns. Their study found the pesticide "in indoor air and on all surfaces throughout all homes," including kitchen tables, windowsills, and floors.

Making your yard more eco-friendly will have a bigger impact than you might think. Yes, your yard may only be one small chunk of land, but all across the country, American yards make up a good portion of the environment. Make a difference by going green, starting in your own backyard.

ALERT

According to the EPA, even short-term exposure to high levels of the popular herbicide 2,4-D can cause nervous-system damage. Long-term exposure to this chemical has been linked to kidney and liver damage. Keep your baby safe and avoid using chemical pesticides on your lawn.

Planting

You can significantly reduce the amount of water and chemicals you need to use on your lawn by planning ahead with your landscaping. Plants that are well suited to your growing environment and cared for regularly will be able to out-compete most weeds and fend off most insect attacks, without the use of harsh chemicals.

Xeriscaping

Xeriscaping is a scary-sounding term, but it simply means choosing plants that are suited to the fuel moisture and soil conditions of your yard. Plants that are native to your area will survive and even thrive in your particular climate without extra effort on your part.

Plant in Groups

Group plants together based on similar water needs to save time and avoid wasting water. For example, vegetables and bedding plants tend to have relatively shallow roots and require more frequent watering than, say, cacti or drought-tolerant shrubs like California Lilacs.

ESSENTIAL

After your baby is born, consider planting a tree or flower garden to commemorate the event. Plants absorb air pollutants and the greenhouse gases that contribute to global warming. They can also provide food and shelter for birds and other wildlife. And planting a tree to commemorate the birth of your baby will create a memory that will last year after year.

Get Your Timing Right

Timing is everything when it comes to getting a great looking yard. Plant in the spring or fall when temperatures are cooler and the water requirements for plants are lower. Your plants will have a greater chance of thriving with less work on your part.

Reduce Your Yard

According to *Consumer Reports*, it costs about $700 per acre to maintain your yard each year. Walkways and patios can help you get better use out of your yard while adding value to your property and reducing the amount of yard that needs to be maintained and watered. Also, heavy mulching around trees, shrubs, and flower beds helps to control weeds, reduce evaporation, and maintain more consistent soil temperature.

Mowing

If mowing your lawn is the bane of your existence you will be happy to know that less is more when it comes to green lawn care. So give your mower and yourself a break as you work toward growing a greener, healthier lawn.

Buying a Green Lawn Mower

Why buy a green lawn mower? Just like cars and trucks, lawn mowers create emissions that cause pollution and contribute to global warming. Sure, their contribution is much smaller than that of automobiles, but collectively, the 35 million lawn mowers in use in the United States have one large impact. Gas mowers generate emissions directly; electric mowers, indirectly in the form of power-plant emissions.

Don't buy more mower than you need. If you have a small, flat yard, consider purchasing a manual-reel mower. They're quiet, inexpensive, and non-polluting. If you need a little more power, try a self-propelled walk-behind mower. This type of mower is fine for most lawns and uses less fuel than a larger tractor.

ALERT

The plastic gas can that you use to fill-up your mower is another potential source of pollution. In California alone, gasoline containers account for about 87 tons a day of smog-forming pollution, equal to the emissions from about 1 million cars. Look for a newer no-spill gas can to eliminate spills and reduce evaporation.

Mow Less

Longer grass grows deeper roots that make it stronger, healthier, and less susceptible to weed and pest infiltration. Mow your lawn less and you will not only save yourself time and sweat, you will also save the planet by reducing the need for water, fertilizers, and pesticides.

Grasscycle

A 1,000-square-foot lawn can generate about 300 pounds of clippings a year. Multiply that by a typical suburban neighborhood and you can quickly see the impact on your local landfill. Compost grass clippings or use a mulching lawn mower that returns them to your yard, and you will not only minimize waste, you will also fertilize your yard naturally.

FACT

If you hire out your lawn care, you can still keep it green by making sure the company or individual you choose understands organic yard care. Check out the websites for Beyond Pesticides (*www.beyond pesticides.org*) or the Northeast Organic Farming Association (*www .nofa.org*) to find an accredited green specialist in your area.

Maintain Your Mower

Save energy by making sure your lawn mower is in good working order. A tuned engine runs more efficiently and releases fewer pollutants. Use this checklist as your guide to make sure that your mower is properly maintained, to extend the life of your mower, and to save energy and money in annual repairs.

AT THE BEGINNING OF EACH MOWING SEASON:

- ❏ Sharpen the blades. This is important for your lawn's health. Dull blades tear grass, leaving a larger area of tissue vulnerable to disease.
- ❏ Set blades one notch higher. This will allow grass to grow just a smidge taller to shade out weeds and hold onto moisture.
- ❏ Change the oil, draining the crankcase and refilling with manufacturer-recommended oil.
- ❏ Replace any worn spark plugs.
- ❏ Clean or replace the air filter.

AFTER YOU MOW:

❑ To maintain proper airflow and foster better performance, use a plastic trowel to keep the deck clear of clippings (disconnect the spark-plug wire if the clippings are damp).

❑ Recharge cordless electric models correctly. Don't drain your battery completely as this can shorten its life. Stop mowing and plug in the charger when the battery starts running down. Manufacturers also suggest leaving the battery on *charge* when you are not using the mower.

AT THE END OF EACH MOWING SEASON:

❑ Prepare your gas mower for the off-season by adding a stabilizer to prevent deposits that can clog the fuel passages. Briefly run the engine to circulate the mixture. This eliminates the wasteful and polluting practice of draining the tank at the end of the season.

Watering

Ideally, if your plants are well-suited to your environment, they will get all the moisture they need from your local weather conditions. But even in ideal situations some plants may need a little help. Get the most out of your watering with these eco-savvy tips.

Water Less

Did you know that more plants die from over-watering than from under-watering? Keep that in mind the next time you reach for a hose. Only water your lawn when it needs it. How can you tell if you lawn needs a drink? Step on it. If it doesn't spring back, give it some water.

Less but More

As a rule of thumb, it is best to water your plants deeply but less frequently to encourage strong, healthy plants. When plants receive frequent bursts of water, they focus on top growth rather than driving down roots. Deep watering promotes deep root growth and develops healthier plants that look great with less attention from you.

Maximize Your Efforts

Water in the cool, early morning hours to prevent evaporation and maximize your watering efforts. Watering in the evening is fine, too, but may lead to the development of fungus. Skip watering on windy days when you are more likely to water your fence than your yard. Water hanging baskets and potted plants by placing an ice cube under the dirt. For gardens and flower beds, consider using soaker hoses or drip irrigation systems to make water conservation easy.

Give It a Sprinkle

If you use a sprinkler, look for one that delivers large drops of water close to the ground, as mist sprays are more likely to evaporate. Set a kitchen timer so that you don't forget to turn off the water. Turn off sprinklers when it is raining or install a rain shut-off device to do it automatically. Also, check your sprinklers regularly to make sure they are watering your lawn and not your driveway or sidewalk. For steep slopes, use a soaker hose or water in timed intervals to prevent wasteful runoff.

Weeding

Weeds and pests compete with your plants for food and water, so you will need to get rid of them to keep your plants healthy. But there is no need to reach for chemicals that are harmful to your children, pets, and the environment when natural alternatives are just as effective.

Skip the Chemicals

Replace your toxic chemical pesticides, herbicides, and fertilizers with these greener solutions.

Liquid soap. Soap works wonders at eliminating aphids, sawflies, spider mites, scale, whiteflies, and wasps. Mix two tablespoons of liquid soap with one gallon of water in a spray bottle. Alternatively, mix one cup vegetable oil (such as corn or safflower) with one tablespoon dish soap and one gallon of water and spray on plants.

Vinegar. Regular, household vinegar is an effective herbicide that can kill weeds without harming the environment. However, be sure to use it sparingly and only in areas where you don't want anything to grow as it will kill any plant in its path (from dandelions to your prized roses).

Hot pepper. Combine one-half cup hot pepper with two cups of water in your blender and spray on garden plants to detract pests such as cucumber beetles, tomato hornworms, and caterpillars.

Corn gluten. Corn gluten is a nontoxic byproduct of milling corn that kills weed seedlings and adds nitrogen to the soil. It only works on plants before they sprout, so it is safe to use on existing grass. It is especially effective against crabgrass.

Bacillus Thuringiensis. This bacterium, also known as Bt, can be added to your garden in powder or spray form to attack garden pests.

Beer. To get rid of slugs and snails, fill a small dish with beer to attract the pests and drown them.

Plants. Check with your local garden center to learn more about plants that you can use to naturally protect your garden. For instance, daisies will attract wasps that eat beetles.

Natural Fertilizers

Rather than raking up grass clippings after you mow, leave them on your yard to return nutrients to the soil. This is especially useful if you have clover in your yard as this legume adds rich nitrogen to the soil (so you don't need to use a chemical fertilizer). In the fall, ditch the rake and mow leaves into usable compost to feed your lawn. If you have a fish tank, pour the nutrient-rich water into your garden every time you clean it out.

Compost

One of the best all-natural fertilizers is organic compost. You can purchase it at the store or make your own from yard trimmings and kitchen waste. Keep your food scraps, yard waste, and newspapers out of the garbage by turning them into usable compost instead.

ESSENTIAL

Vermi-composting is a fun way to learn about nature while turning your food scraps into usable compost. Using red wiggler worms, vermi-composting processes organic food into nutrient-rich soil. You can start with a small bin (such as a twelve-gallon plastic tub) and a pound of worms, or go larger if you have a big family (and lots of scraps).

Commercial Fertilizers

Check out Planet Natural (*www.planetnatural.com*) and Gardener's Supply Company (*www.gardeners.com*) to find gardening supplies such as organic compost and other all-natural fertilizers.

Start Your Own Garden

Starting a baby garden is a great way to introduce your baby to nature and ensure that her first foods are fresh and chemical free. Even if you don't have a big yard, many common plants do very well in pots on sunny decks or porches. Summer squash, green beans, peas, pumpkin, sweet potato, and zucchini are all easy to grow in an outdoor or indoor garden. Berry plants like strawberries and blueberries, are also easy to grow, but your baby probably won't be able to enjoy them until she is at least twelve months old.

For more information about starting your own garden, pick up a gardening guide like *The Gardener's A-Z Guide to Growing Organic Food* by Tanya L.K. Denckla or *Fresh Food from Small Spaces: The Square-Inch Gardener's Guide to Year Round Growing, Fermenting, and Sprouting*, by R.J. Ruppenthal. Online, check out Garden Web (*www.gardenweb.com*) or the National Gardening Association (*www.garden.org*).

CHAPTER 12

Green on the Go

With gas prices on the rise and global warming and pollution increasing in severity, there is no better time than now to reconsider your transportation options. Obviously, the very best way to maximize your fuel economy is to leave the car at home in the first place. Take public transportation, walk, or bike whenever possible. Even if you only do it once in a while, you will save money, decrease the wear and tear on your car, and reduce your impact on the planet.

Planes, Trains, and Automobiles

America is a nation on the go! According to the Center for the New American Dream, the number of miles that Americans travel each year has more than tripled since 1960. About 28 percent of the energy this country uses each year goes to transporting people and stuff from one place to another. Personal vehicles, such as cars, SUVs, and light trucks, consume 63 percent of the total energy used for transportation while mass transit (like airplanes, trains, and buses) accounts for the rest.

Most means of transportation produce greenhouse gases that cause climate change.

ALERT

Planes emit more carbon dioxide per traveler than any other means of transportation, followed by cars and trains. In addition, airports and their aircraft produce large quantities of noise pollution and toxic emissions, both of which are a threat to human health. In particular, they produce very large quantities of nitrogen oxides and VOCs.

If you are traveling in the United States, consider taking a family-friendly train ride to your destination. Try to reduce the number of plane trips you take and try not to use a plane for any trip under 600 miles.

Use Your Legs

Isn't it great that the most eco-friendly ways to get around are also the healthiest for you and your family? Walk or ride your bike whenever possible and you will save money, decrease the wear and tear on your car, reduce pollution, and get lots of great exercise.

If you are pregnant, talk to your health care provider first before you start adding a lot of walking or biking to your exercise regimen. And be careful biking, as your center of gravity will shift throughout your pregnancy. If you are new to biking, try sharing a bike with your partner until you get the hang of it, or pairing up with a more experienced cyclist as a mentor.

Another great way to get exercise is to use the stairs instead of elevators and escalators whenever possible.

Public Transportation

Did you know that if one out of every ten Americans used public transportation on a daily basis, this country could reduce its dependence on foreign oil by roughly 40 percent? According to the Center for Transportation Excellence, riding a bus is 79 percent safer than riding in a car. Public transportation, or the buses, trains, subways, and ferries that you can ride just to get around or as part of your daily commute, often get a bad rap. But the fact of the matter is that they do ease congestion, reduce emissions, and give you time to unwind from a busy day or get your mind ready to start another one.

ESSENTIAL

According to the Center for Transportation Excellence, public transportation saves 855 million gallons of oil each year. This is equivalent to 45 million barrels of oil, or roughly the equivalent of the energy needed to power one-quarter of all American homes for a year.

If the public transportation options in your area don't suit your needs, write to your city representatives to request that changes are made. If the buses are dirty or unsafe, tell your local officials to do something about it.

Driving Green

Despite recent advances, car manufacturers have been painfully slow to produce eco-savvy cars that get the most mileage for their fuel. In 1987, the average fuel economy of cars and light trucks peaked at twenty-two and one-tenth miles per gallon (mpg); twenty years later (in 2006), the average fuel economy for passenger cars hit twenty-one mpg. Surely twenty years of technological advancement could do better than that?

But with gas prices continuing to soar, the American addiction to oil is not just painful financially; it is also painful to the environment, polluting the air, water, and soils. Car manufacturers are finally getting the message that Americans want greener cars that save money and save the planet. But even if you don't yet have one of these eco-cars, you can make better decisions about what and how you drive to minimize your impact on the Earth.

- **Slow down:** One of the best ways to improve your fuel efficiency is to stay at or below a speed limit of fifty-five miles per hour when you drive. For every five miles per hour above fifty-five that you drive you reduce your fuel efficiency by 10 percent.
- **Carpool:** Pair up with a friend or a colleague (or two) and share rides to work, school, and even the grocery store. You will save money at the pump and at the parking lot, and significantly cut back on polluting vehicle emissions.
- **Be a smooth driver:** Drive smoothly to get the most out of your fuel economy. Avoid jack-rabbit starts, aggressive driving, and hard breaking. Also, resist the temptation to speed.
- **Plan ahead:** Planning ahead to combine trips when possible will save you time, money, and energy. A cold engine pollutes up to five times more than one that is warmed up. So combining several short trips into one can make a big difference for the planet.
- **Lighten up:** Is your car a rolling closet, housing everything from spare clothes to sports equipment to groceries? All of that excess weight could be affecting your fuel economy. It takes about 100 extra pounds to reduce your fuel economy by 1 percent. So, if you just have a few extra pairs of shoes rolling around, don't sweat it. But if you are carting a load of heavy recycling, it might be time to clean it out.
- **No American "idles":** Newer cars do not have to be warmed up like older models, so there is no need to allow you car to idle in the driveway anymore. Turn off your ignition any time you will be stopped or parked for more than a few minutes. In the winter, use a reflective windshield shade to help reduce frost and save you elbow grease with the scraper.
- **Cruise:** If your car has a cruise control feature, use it to maximize your fuel economy. At highway speeds, using cruise control can reduce your fuel consumption by as much as 7 percent.
- **Park it:** When you park, protect your car from the elements and it won't have to work as hard to heat up or cool down. In the summer,

park in the shade or use a reflective windshield shade to keep your car cool and reduce fuel evaporation. If you have access to a garage, use it to keep your car cool in the summer and warm in the winter.

Green Car Guide

You don't need to run out and buy the latest-model eco-car just to go green. But if you are in the market for a new vehicle, consider making it a clean one. The market for environmentally friendly cars has exploded over the past few years, so there is now an eco-savvy option for every family. Eco-savvy cars release fewer emissions into the air and help you go further on each tank of gas.

Gasoline-Powered Eco-Cars

The majority of eco-cars on the road today are called partial-zero-emissions vehicles (PZEVs) that run on gasoline but use advanced technology to improve gas mileage and reduce pollutants. Hybrid cars also use gasoline but minimize its consumption with electric power. Hybrid cars emit fewer pollutants and use less fuel than their traditional counterparts, but these models will also be more costly than their gas-guzzling cousins.

Flexible Fuel Vehicles (FFV)

According to the U.S. Department of Energy (DOE), all gasoline vehicles are capable of operating on gasoline/ethanol blends with up to 10 percent ethanol. However, there are also millions of cars on the road today known as Flexible Fuel Vehicles (FFVs) that can run on E85 (85 percent denatured ethanol and 15 percent gasoline.)

FACT

You may even be driving an FFV without knowing it. Current models of the Cadillac Escalade, Chevy Avalanche, Chevy Tahoe, Chevy Silverado, DaimlerChrysler Sebring, Dodge Stratus, Ford F-150, Ford Taurus, GMC Silverado, GMC Savana, GMC Yukon, Mercedes-Benz: C 320, Mercedes Benz 240, and Mercury Sable are all FFVs.

Check your owners' manual or talk to your dealer if you think your car might be able to run on ethanol. Check the U.S. DOE website (*http://afdc map2.nrel.gov/locator*) to find an ethanol fuel station near you.

Biodiesel

Biodiesel is another great eco-friendly option. Biodiesel is a combination of diesel and refined vegetable oil. It burns cleaner than straight diesel and produces fewer emissions. Biodiesel fuel can now be purchased in almost every state in the country. The National Biodiesel Board maintains a list of biodiesel retail locations (*www.biodiesel.org/buyingbiodiesel/retail fuelingsites/default.shtm*). Or, if you'd like to run on straight vegetable oil, check out Golden Fuel Systems (*www.goldenfuelsystems.com*) or Greasecar (*www.greasecar.com*) to purchase a DIY conversion kit.

Car Maintenance

Take care of your car, and it will take care of you. Regular maintenance and tune-ups, changing the oil, and checking tire inflation extend the life of your car, reduce the incidence of break-downs, and improve gas mileage.

Get a Tune Up

A tune-up will keep your car operating at its maximum efficiency, emitting fewer pollutants and sucking down less fuel. Whether you do it yourself or go to a mechanic, be sure your car is checked for worn spark plugs, dragging brakes, and low transmission fluid. Replace your air filter as necessary and be sure your wheels are properly aligned and rotated.

ESSENTIAL

For the same money as traditional automobile clubs you can get a membership to Better World Club (*http://betterworldclub.com*) that includes all of the standard auto club privileges as well as eco-travel assistance, discounts on hybrid cars, and bicycle roadside assistance. The company also donates a portion of their annual revenues toward environmental cleanup and advocacy.

Inflate Your Tires

Keep tires properly inflated to reduce wear and tear on the tread and save fuel over the long run. Check your owner's manual for the recommended inflation level (this number is also usually printed inside the door frame of your car).

Change Your Oil

Changing your car's oil and oil filters is another good way to improve its fuel efficiency. If you do it yourself, be sure to recycle the oil properly and fill up your engine with clean recycled motor oil. Plug your zip code into the Earth 911 website (*www.earth911.org*) to find a used motor oil drop-off location near you. If you take it in to a service station, make sure that they will do the same.

Clean Car Washing

According to the International Carwash Association, washing your car at home uses between 80 and 140 gallons of water, while a commercial car wash averages less than 45 gallons per car. Commercial car washes use high-pressure, low-flow nozzles to minimize water usage. Washing your car at home also sends a bucket load of soap suds, gasoline, and exhaust residue directly into storm drains and waterways. Carwashes, on the other hand, are required by law to drain their wastewater into sewer systems for treatment. Some even recycle their greywater to further reduce water consumption.

Fueling

Avoid "topping-off" your gas tank when filling up at the pump. Overfilling your car by even a little bit can lead to pollution caused by gasoline spills. When possible, get fuel when the weather is cool to minimize evaporation and prevent gas fumes from heating up and creating ozone. And seek out gas stations that use pollution-reducing vapor-recovery nozzles (those thick, accordion-looking plastic devices covering the gas nozzle).

Eco-Vacations

American vacations are as unique as the Americans themselves; some offer the peace and tranquility of wilderness camping while others bring the fun, action, and excitement of a major city. But no matter what kind of vacation suits you and your family, it is likely to cause an impact on the environment.

You can green your vacation by simply reducing waste on your trip or making a few adjustments to your itinerary. Whether you are headed to your local state park or a luxury foreign resort, here's how you can go green and relax with a clear conscience.

Go Local

Chances are there are attractions in your local area that you have not seen or visited in years. Instead of stressing out about travel, accommodations, and logistics, take a relaxed vacation at home. Visit the newest exhibits at the local art and science museums, aquariums, zoos, or botanical gardens. Grab some adventure by taking a canoe trip down your local waterway or see the wildlife at a nearby state park. Mark your calendar for special events like children's theater, art shows, food-and-music festivals, book readings, and more.

Line up Green Lodging

Check out the Green Hotels Association (*http://greenhotels.com*) or Environmentally Friendly Hotels (*www.environmentallyfriendlyhotels.com*) to find an eco-savvy hotel, motel, or B&B at your destination.

Minimize Waste

Reuse your towels at the hotel to save energy and water. Turn off the television and lights, and adjust heat or air conditioning settings if you are going to be gone for the day. Pack a reusable drink bottle to refill with clean water. And pack your own toiletries rather than using the hotel's mini bottles.

Buy Sustainable Souvenirs

If you want to bring some souvenirs home from your trip, look for locally produced foods, crafts, art, or jewelry that support the community and reduce the pollution and transportation costs associated with importing goods. Do not buy souvenirs made from endangered species, hardwoods, or ancient relics.

At Home

Save money on your electric bill by taking a few minutes to unplug appliances, computers, power strips, and televisions before you head out. Adjust your thermostat so that you are not heating or cooling an empty house (but be mindful to leave the house a comfortable temperature if pets are staying behind).

Rent Your Gear

If you are going on a gear-intensive vacation (like a camping or scuba diving trip), save money by borrowing or renting equipment instead of buying it. Check out the directory of REI rental locations (*www.rei.com/stores/rentals.html*) or look for a local outfitter to rent your gear and support local businesses.

Go Digital

Invest in a digital camera to capture your vacation's highlights. If you take a lot of pictures, you will easily recoup the costs of the camera in the saved film and processing fees. The latest camera models come equipped with rechargeable batteries, but if you have an older model, be sure to load your camera with rechargeable batteries and bring your charger along.

FACT

Purchasing a guidebook is a great way to learn more about the highlights of your destination. Lonely Planet (*www.lonelyplanet.com*), Rough Guides (*www.roughguides.com*), and Moon (*www.moon.com*) offer guidebooks that include a wealth of travel information as well as facts about the environmental, social, and political issues of your destination.

Support Conservation

If you visit a natural area on your vacation, respect the environment by following designated trails, paying entrance fees, disposing of your trash properly, and not harassing the wildlife. Take only pictures and leave nothing but footprints.

Get Cultural

If you are traveling to another country, minimize your global impact by showing your respect for the local culture. Read up on the environmental, economic, and social issues of your destination. Learn a few words of the local language and be sure you understand and adhere to cultural norms.

Carbon Offsets

If you really want to negate the carbon emissions of your transportation, consider purchasing carbon offsets, or greentags, for your trip. The money you spend on carbon offsets will be used to plant trees or support a renewable energy project, thereby *offsetting* the carbon emissions generated during your travel.

The important thing to remember about carbon credits is that you need to purchase them from a trustworthy company to ensure that they will actually be used to support a green project. So do your homework. Before you spend your hard earned dollars on carbon offsets, check out a carbon credit buying guide such as Clean Air-Cool Planet (*www.cleanair-coolplanet.org*) to get a better idea of what to look for in a carbon-credit company.

Look for carbon credits that are certified and audited by a third-party such as Environmental Resources Trust or the Climate, Community, and Biodiversity Alliance.

Good companies to choose from include Carbon Neutral (*www.carbon neutral.com*), Carbon Fund (*www.carbonfund.org*), Green-e (*www.green-e .org*), or Green Tags USA (*www.greentagsusa.org*).

CHAPTER 13

Green Your Pets

Does your home accommodate critters of the hairy, feathered, or scaled variety? According to the Humane Society, there are currently 73 million dogs and 90 million cats in homes across the United States. Birds, bunnies, ferrets, and lizards are other popular pets for children. The food, toys, and bedding for these pets (and even the pets themselves) have a significant impact on the environment. Here's how to reduce your pet's ecological paw print.

Greening Your Pet

Pets are part of the family too, so they deserve the very best when it comes to their health and well-being. The chemicals and toxins that accompany many pet products serve as another avenue of exposure for the rest of your family. So keep Fido, FeFe, Spot, and the rest of the gang happy by taking the steps to reduce the impact that they and their gear have on the planet.

Adopt

There are over 5,500 puppies and kittens (compared with 415 human babies) born every hour in the United States. According to the Humane Society of the United States (*www.hsus.org*), animal shelters take in between 6 and 8 million dogs and cats every year, of which 3 to 4 million are euthanized. Why buy a dog or cat when you can adopt one from your local animal shelter for a fraction of the cost? Check out *www.petfinder.com* to find your next dog, cat, bird, rabbit or reptile friend. If you are looking for a specific breed, contact the Human Society (*www.hsus.org*) to locate a breed-specific rescue group in your area.

ALERT

Animal cruelty is a crime and one that often goes unreported. Yet law enforcement officers depend upon the reports from everyday citizens to protect the country's animals. Call your local law enforcement office if you think an animal is being abused. If the abuse is occurring at a pet store or animal breeding facility, contact the USDA at 1-301-734-7833.

Spay or Neuter

Spaying and neutering your pet can help to reduce the overpopulation of animals around the country. It also helps dogs and cats live longer by eliminating the possibility of uterine, ovarian, and testicular cancer, and decreasing the incidence of prostate disease. Check with your local animal shelter to see if they offer a free or low-cost spay or neutering service.

Give Kitty Some Jingle Bells

Keep your kitty indoors to protect her overall health and that of the environment. Cats are keen hunters and are a leading cause of death for birds, second only to habitat destruction. If your feline loves to roam, put a bell on her collar to keep her out of mischief and give the birds a flying chance.

Feeding Fido

Many conventional pet-food brands are made from the inedible waste from beef and poultry farms that is produced using *4-D* meat (in other words, the animals that are Dead, Dying, Diseased, or Down—unable to stand—when they are prepared for slaughter). How healthy would you be if you ate diseased food at every meal?

Natural and organic pet foods use higher quality meats that are raised humanely without added drugs or hormones. The foods are minimally processed and preserved with natural substances. Certified-organic pet foods must adhere to strict USDA standards that ban pesticides, hormones, antibiotics, and artificial or genetically engineered ingredients.

If protecting the health of your pet is not enough to convince you to switch, just remember that no matter how closely you supervise, it is almost guaranteed that at some point in the future, your precious baby will wind up with that pet food in his mouth.

Go Organic

It may seem pretentious to purchase organic pet food for your furry friend (who is content to lick himself clean and drink from curbside puddles), but the crops and livestock raised to produce Fido's food can be just as harsh on the environment and on your pet as the food humans eat.

Cats and dogs can enjoy a feast of natural and organic ingredients in Newman's Own Organic Pet Food (*www.newmansownorganics.com*). If you want to go for the gold, try Castor & Pollux's Organix line of organic cat and dog foods (*www.castorpolluxpet.com*) or the dog food from Karma Organics (*www.karmaorganicpet.com*) that carries the 95-percent-Certified-Organic label.

Making Your Own Pet Food

One inexpensive way to ensure that your pet is eating healthy, all-natural food, is to make the pet food yourself. Talk to your veterinarian about the vitamins, minerals, supplements, and proteins your pet needs in its diet each day. For dogs, you can also check out the list of homemade dog food references compiled at *www.dogaware.com/dogfeeding.html#references.*

ALERT

Early in 2008, 1,950 dogs and 2,200 cats were killed by exposure to melamine-laced pet food. The contaminated products were subsequently recalled, but the incident left many pet owners shaken. Organic pet foods are not exposed to any of the contaminants found in conventional pet foods.

Recycle

No matter what brand or type of food you choose to buy for your pet, it is likely that it comes in some type of can, bottle, or bag that can be recycled. Contact your local recycling center if you have any questions about the resources that can be recycled in your area.

Green Pet Gear

A recent study by the Environmental Working Group found that cats and dogs are carrying around as many forty-eight different industrial chemicals in their bodies; and many of them at much higher levels than the dangerous levels found in humans. Some of the most harmful chemicals found in pets are flame retardants from beds, furniture, and polluted food; stain and grease-proofing chemicals from carpets, beds, and food packaging; and plastic softeners known as phthalates, which are found in products ranging from shampoos to toys to medicines. These chemicals have been linked to thyroid problems, birth defects, and cancer, among other conditions.

The boom in green design and marketing means that you can now find all kinds of eco-friendly toys, bedding, and grooming products for your pet.

You can also find pet beds and toys made from organic cotton or recycled plastic bottles as well all-natural grooming supplies.

Planet Dog (*www.planetdog.com*) is a great source for eco-friendly pet supplies such as hemp collars and toys made from recycled materials. And give your pet a safe, clean place to snooze with a pet bed from Worldwise (*www.worldwise.com*) that is made from recycled plastic bottles.

According to *The Green Book* by Elizabeth Rogers and Thomas Kostigen, if every pet toy sold each year were made of 100 percent recycled materials, it would save enough virgin materials to make a Frisbee more than two miles in diameter. Look for recycled toys whenever you purchase something new for your pet.

Like children, pets rarely need elaborate toys to make them happy so look for simple, eco-friendly toys for your pet. Dogs love to chase and chew sticks of any kind. Cats and rabbits might enjoy leftover boxes and bags (not plastic) from your holiday wrapping, pine cones from the backyard, or a paper bag.

Bathing

Most pets, like cats, ferrets, and bunnies, do a pretty good job of keeping themselves clean without any help from their human friends. Dogs, on the other hand, usually need a little help in the grooming department. It is important to keep your dog clean and regularly groomed so that you can check for burrs, ticks, fleas, parasites or any matting.

Many conventional pet shampoos contain a cocktail of toxic chemicals that are just as dangerous to humans as they are to your pets. After a bath, these chemicals wash off of your pet and make their way into the environment.

Why not instead buy a green doggie shampoo? Castor & Pollux (*www.castorpolluxpet.com*) makes a Head to Tail line of all-natural pet shampoos that contain ingredients such as aloe vera, shea butter, lavender, and peppermint oil.

Homemade Doggie Shampoo

Here's a quick and easy pet shampoo you can use to keep your dog clean and healthy:

INGREDIENTS
2 cups nontoxic dishwashing liquid
2 cups water
2 cups apple cider vinegar
4 ounces glycerin

Combine all ingredients in an airtight container (an old dishwashing or shampoo bottle will be perfect). Make sure the container is clearly labeled and stored out of reach of children. Shake well before using.

Fleas

Nothing can send a pet owner reaching for the chemicals faster than the sight of fleas in her home. That's especially true of parents who want to keep these disease-carrying bugs away from their new babies.

Groom your pet frequently to remove dirt and matting and to check for fleas. To check for fleas, place a piece of white paper under your pet while brushing. Some of the fleas will drop off during grooming and the white paper will make them easy to see. To check your dog for fleas when bathing, place a large white towel underneath him while you dry him off. Fleas will fall off and be easier to spot on the towel.

If fleas are a problem in your area, add a little fresh garlic to your pet's food each day. Small quantities of garlic can help repel fleas by making the animal taste unpleasant to fleas. Rinsing your pet's fur with apple cider vinegar will also help keep fleas at bay. Or you can dab essential oils like lavender, lemongrass, peppermint and citronella between your pet's shoulder blades to act as a natural bug repellent. If you prefer to use a commercial product, check out the natural, nontoxic flea repellant and control products from Precious Pets (*www.preciouspets.org/fleafree.htm*).

Pet Poo

If you've got a pet, then you also have pet poo to deal with. And how you choose to deal with that poop can actually have a rather large impact on the environment because pet waste contains bacteria that can become a problem if it is allowed to contaminate local waterways. In general, you can green pet poo by dealing with it in one of the following ways:

- Flush it.
- Compost it.
- Use biodegradable and/or recycled products to handle it.

Your best bet is to keep pet waste out of the landfill by flushing or composting it whenever possible. If you do need to toss it, just make sure you use eco-friendly gear (like biodegradable pet waste bags or shredded, recycled paper) to deal with it.

QUESTION

Can I add pet poop to my compost pile?
Yes and no. Pet waste can be composted, but it must be done carefully. Raw pet poop contains toxic organisms and bacteria (like E. Coli, salmonella, and streptococcus) as well as parasites that can be toxic to humans. Purchase an additional compost bin to keep pet waste compost separated from other compost and never use pet waste compost on food crops.

Kitty Litter

Conventional cat litter is nonbiodegradable, made from strip-mined clay, and infused with carcinogenic silica dust and sodium bentonite. These chemicals are harmful for the health of your cat as well as your children. There are several eco-friendly, nontoxic, biodegradable kitty litter options available for kitty to take care of business. Sweat Scoop (*www.swheat scoop.com*) is a natural, biodegradable wheat litter. Most major retailers will also have several earth-friendly options available in-store. The best part about these eco-savvy options? Many of them can be flushed or composted (for non-food plants) rather than tossed. Your best bet will be to try a few different options until you find one that works for both you and kitty.

Doggie Bags

Why place biodegradable doggie doo in a plastic bag that will keep it locked up for hundreds (if not thousands) of years? Look for biodegradable poop bags to clean up doggie doo rather than plastic bags that will prevent any decomposition over the years. A biodegradable waste bag can be thrown in the compost bin (for use on non-food plants) or collected at your curb with other biodegradable yard waste. EcoChoices (*www.ecoanimal .com*) makes reasonably priced bags that are 100 pecrent biodegradable and made from non-genetically modified corn. Biobag (*www.biobagusa .com*) dog waste bags are also biodegradable and are found in many parks and dog run facilities.

Can't Have a Pet?

Many children light up at the mere site of an animal, whether it is a family-friendly dog or a giraffe. But resist the temptation to buy your child a pet as a toy. Keep in mind that pets become members of your family, requiring almost as much attention and care as your new baby. They also create their own ecological paw prints in the food, toys, bedding, and care they will require. So, if you are not ready to spend the time, energy, and money involved in feeding, walking, training, bathing, amusing, and loving a pet, consider one of these options instead.

Stuff It

Buy your little one a stuffed animal instead. If he has his heart set on a furry new pal, maybe he'd like a Build-A-Bear (*www.buildabear.com*) pet? Pet choices range from the traditional bear to dogs, cats, and bunnies, as well as dinosaurs and wild animals. And if you purchase one of their special wild animals, such as a cheetah or a panda bear, a portion of the proceeds will benefit the conservation efforts of the World Wildlife Fund (*www.wwf.org*).

Adopt-a-Shelter

Animal-loving kids can show their love for pets by helping out at their local animal shelter. Talk to your local organization to learn how you and your child can help. Even just bringing your child along to pet or play with the animals may put a smile on her face while showing the animals some love.

ESSENTIAL

Make an eco-treat for your feathered friends by generously coating a pinecone with peanut butter and rolling in oatmeal or sunflower seeds. Tie a string that is three to four feet in length around the stem of your feeder and hang it from a nearby tree branch.

Just be sure to use caution and never expose your child to pets that have not been evaluated by an animal-training expert and certified as safe for contact with children. And never leave your baby alone with a pet regardless of its disposition. Other animals or loud noises could combine to make an animal act differently than it would under normal conditions.

Pet Sit

If you and your baby love pets, but cannot have a pet of your own, try pet sitting for a friend or fostering a pet from your local shelter. It will give you both a chance to love and care for an animal without the commitment of a full-time pet.

part three

Planning for Baby

CHAPTER 14

Green Baby Essentials

From the moment you first find out you are expecting a baby, you will find yourself flooded with advertisements for all kinds of baby products. And of course, each and every product will market itself as essential to your new baby's health and happiness. But what does your baby really need? This chapter will help you sort through the marketing to choose the essential green items necessary to help feed, clean, and carry your new baby.

What Does Your Baby Really Need?

It is so easy to get caught up in all of the hoopla and stuff that engulfs a new baby. Teething rings, sleep petitioners, car seats, swinging seats, bouncers, stationary play areas, onesies, rompers. But what does your baby really need? And how can you make sure that the products you buy to protect and care for your baby are the safest ones for her and her environment?

All You Need Is Love

So many of the products produced for babies are marketed to parents by pulling at their utmost fears and concerns—the health and safety of their babies. If this is your first baby, it may be hard to imagine not using all of the products that claim to keep you child entertained for hours or increase her safety.

It is important to remember that the only things a baby truly needs are food, shelter, and love. Everything else is just a bonus. Keep that in mind the next time you feel overwhelmed by advertisements or product claims. Along those same lines, you should remember that items that are essential for one family may not be necessary for another. So keep the needs of your family in mind when putting together your baby essentials.

The Essential Item Checklist

Pretty colors and soft fabrics are nice, but they won't help you decide if you really need any item or not. As you are evaluating products to add to your new baby wish list, check to make sure they meet the following requirements:

- **Utility:** Before you purchase or borrow a new item for your nursery, ask yourself if you and your baby really need it. Does this item fill a need? Will it be a useful addition to your home or will it get in the way and become one more thing that collects dust in your closet or takes up space in a landfill?
- **Safety:** First and foremost any baby item that comes into your home should be safe for your baby; and also for the planet. Has this product been tested for safety by an independent third-party agency? How

do its safety ratings compare to comparable models? What materials and/or chemicals were used to make this product?

- **Cost:** Does this item fit within your budget? If not, is there a way you could borrow or rent the item rather than purchase it?
- **Ease of use:** Are you able to operate the item easily? Remember, you may be required to use this in a sleep-deprived stupor. Is it easy to clean? Store? Take apart?

If an item meets all of these requirements than it is safe to assume that it will be a useful and essential addition to your home.

Car Seats

If you ever plan to drive or ride in a car with your new baby, you absolutely must have a car seat. It is the law. A car seat is one of the most important pieces of equipment you will get to protect your baby in her first few months of life. Gone are the days of children sliding around in the back of mom and dad's station wagon. Today's babies are strapped down into a five-point harness piece of equipment that rivals the safety gear found in the military.

Types of Car Seats

There are several different options when it comes to finding a car seat for your baby. Infant car seats are made specifically for a new baby's first year of life. They are designed to be used in the rear-facing position only. They also typically have a handle, making them easy to carry around, and some models are even compatible with strollers so that a baby can be transported easily from car to stroller without removing, or waking, him.

FACT

The American Academy of Pediatrics (AAP) recommends that all infants should ride in rear-facing car seats starting with their first ride home from the hospital until they have reached at least one year of age *and* weigh at least twenty pounds. It is even better for them to ride in rear-facing car sets until they reach the highest weight or height allowed by their car safety seat's manufacturer.

Infant car seats are tremendously useful for the baby's first year, but cannot be used after a baby meets the age and weight requirements (twenty pounds and one year) to be turned around in her seat.

As their name implies, convertible car seats can be converted from a rear-facing infant seat to a forward-facing toddler seat. These seats can be used from infancy until well into a child's toddler years. However, without the handle and stroller compatibility, they are not nearly as convenient to use as other infant seats.

ALERT

According to the National Highway Traffic Safety Administration, (*www.nhtsa.dot.gov*) as many as 80 percent of all car seats are improperly installed and used. Follow the installation instructions for your car seat carefully, and for an extra measure of precaution, have the installation inspected at your local fire station.

Going for the Green

Most conventional car seats are made with plastics and fabrics that have been bathed in chemicals throughout the manufacturing process. So if your car seat is new, it is very important to make sure that it has an opportunity to air out for as long as possible before the baby is born.

Another way to avoid the off-gassing of chemicals is to purchase or borrow a gently used car seat that has already had the opportunity to air out. But be careful here. A gently used car seat is a wonderful thing for the planet and the baby, but only if it comes from a trusted source. A used car seat that has been involved in a car accident may have suffered structural damage that weakened the safety of the equipment. Only accept or purchase a used car seat from a close friend or family member who can assure you that the seat is accident-free. It is also a good idea to check with the U.S. Consumer Product Commission (*www.cpsc.gov*) to make sure the car seat has not been recalled since it was first purchased.

Strollers

While it is not 100 percent necessary to the health and safety of your baby, a stroller is one handy item that you probably won't want to be without. A stroller will allow you to go for walks with your baby and transport him from place to place more easily than carrying him.

Greening Your Baby's Ride

A stroller can be a great green addition to your baby gear, especially if it helps you get around without getting in your car. Taking your baby for a walk in a stroller is also a relaxing way for you and him to get fresh air and exercise and enjoy the natural world.

However, strollers tend to be less green in terms of their disposal. As recycling is limited, most strollers tend to end out their days in a landfill. The best way to avoid this is to purchase or borrow a gently used stroller and to see that it gets passed down again when you and your baby are finished with it.

QUESTION

What kind of features should I look for in a stroller?
Comfort and safety are the most important features you should look for when choosing a stroller. Make sure the stroller's safety belt is easy to use and is in good condition. Walk with the stroller and check the height of the handles and the alignment of the wheels to be sure they are comfortable for you.

If you do need to buy a new stroller, look for one that is made from sturdy content that can be recycled again at the end of its life cycle. Baby Planet (*www.baby-planet.com*) strollers are made from aluminum instead of plastic and the company offers a free recycling program through which they ensure that broken down strollers will be disassembled so that their components can be recycled appropriately.

Changing Tables

It is debatable whether or not you should consider a changing table to be an absolute necessity for you and your baby. The dilemma comes down to you and how and where you will want to change all of those 8,000 diapers that your baby will need before he is potty trained. Some parents simply use a clean blanket or pad laid out on a floor or secure table to change diapers. Others swear by the convenience and safety of having a dedicated, clean, secure place to change diapers and store their diaper-changing gear.

The Green Change

Don't limit yourself by looking for a product that is specifically labeled as a changing table. More often than not, a small, gently used dresser will do the trick. When purchasing new, look for a changing table that can be easily converted to a dresser or desk once your child outgrows diapers. You will also want to make sure that your changing table is constructed from sustainably harvested wood and finished without the use of toxic chemicals. If you use a changing pad, look for one with a nontoxic, organic cover that will be easy to remove and clean.

High Chairs and Boosters

For the first few months of your baby's life, she will need nothing but breast milk or formula to meet all of her dietary needs. But around the time she starts eating solid foods (usually four to six months), you will need to make sure she has her own safe, secure place at the table.

ALERT

According to Consumer Product Safety Commission, more than 7,000 children suffered injuries related to high chairs in 2005. The majority of these injuries occurred when children were not buckled properly into the high chair's safety harness. Make sure your baby is safely buckled up in her high chair, even if you will be sitting right next to her.

Greener Chairs

Most conventional high chairs are made from vinyl, PVC, and other harmful petroleum-based ingredients that will off-gas into your home. The typical high chair also tends to be awkward to store and transport, which is why it usually ends up in a landfill rather than stored once a baby has outgrown it. If possible, seek out a pre-loved high chair instead of a newer model and make sure it gets passed on to friends, family members, or to your local thrift store when your baby no longer needs it.

If second hand is not an option and you need to purchase a new chair, look for one made from sustainably harvested wood instead of plastic or PVC. Stokke (*www.stokkeusa.com*) and Safety 1st (*www.safety1st.com*) both make great green high chairs from sustainably sourced wood.

Slings and Babywearers

There is nothing quite like the feel of a new baby in your arms. And from the first moment that you feel him in your arms, it will be hard to imagine a time when you will ever want to put him down. Still, there will come a time when the need to fold laundry, or eat a meal will require that you do in fact put your baby down.

The Benefits of Babywearing

Many new parents use a sling or other babywearing device to combine the joy of holding their babies with the reality of needing their hands free to accomplish tasks throughout the day.

BABYWEARING:
- Aids in bonding between parent and baby
- Provides a safe and secure environment for baby
- Offers a convenient way for parents to hold baby
- Helps to soothe and comfort a fussy baby
- Helps new moms shed baby weight

Studies show that babies who are carried cry an average of 43 percent less overall and 54 percent less during the evening hours than those who are not.

Types of Babywearers

A few things to keep in mind when looking for a babywearer are the product's ease of use and adaptability to differing situations and positions. A traditional sling is nothing more than a long piece of fabric that can be worn around the body and tied in such a way that it provides a safe, snuggly cocoon for the baby. Depending upon the situation and the baby's preferences, slings can be worn on the front, back, or side, with the baby laying down or sitting in an upright position.

ESSENTIAL

If you've never worn a sling before, it may seem cumbersome or confusing to use. Talk to friends, family, or your midwife about the best ways to secure a sling properly and safely. Online, check out The Babywearer (*www.thebabywearer.com*) to learn about diagnosing and solving common sling-wearing problems.

Other popular babywearers are the front packs that can be worn across the chest and allow babies to sit upright in either a forward or backward position.

Going for the Green

Once you've decided on the style of babywearer you'd like to use to carry your baby, go for the green by lessening the impact of the item on the planet. Look for a gently used babywearer from friends, family members, the local thrift store, or a yard sale. You could also try posting a request on Freecycle (*www.freecycle.com*) to see if anyone in your local area is interested in giving one a way.

If you do decide to purchase new, look for a babywearer made from 100 percent natural fibers such as cotton or hemp, which are certified organic. Check out Pretty Momma Sling (*www.prettymommasling.com*), the Sling Station (*www.theslingstation.com*), or ERGObaby (*www.ergobabycarrier.com*), for slings and baby carriers made from organic fibers.

Baby Tubs

A bath is a great way to get your baby clean and help him relax and play. But until your baby is able to sit up on his own (at about six months) you will need to make sure his bathing environment is one that allows him to relax in the tub safely while laying down. To do this, you will have a few options. You can get in the tub with your baby. This can be a fun bonding experience for both you and your baby; however it may not be practical for you to hop in the tub whenever your baby needs a quick wash.

Another option is to hold your baby securely in your arms while you bath him. While this sounds ideal, it can be stressful and dangerous to hold a wiggly, wet, slippery baby in one arm while trying to wash him with the other. Not to mention the strain this positioning will place on your back.

A better bet is to get an infant bath tub that is designed to help you wash and play with your baby safely in the bath tub.

One green perk of the infant bath tub is that is allows you to use less water to bathe your baby than you would if you had to fill up your adult-sized tub. As with other types of baby gear it is best to look for a used infant bath tub from a friend or family member. If all else fails, baby tubs are usually plentiful (and inexpensive) at thrift stores and yard sales.

CHAPTER 15

Baby Clothes

What could be sweeter than dressing your baby in an adorable new baby outfit? Unfortunately, many of the clothes that look so cute in the store may introduce chemicals and other toxins into your home and the environment. Babies look beautiful no matter what they wear (or even if they wear nothing at all). So put fashion aside and keep the planet in mind as you look for clothes to cover your baby.

The Green Layette

A *layette* is a fancy word that describes a baby's first wardrobe—the clothes that he'll wear round the clock for the first few weeks of his life. Take a look in any baby store, and you will find long lists of clothing recommended for a baby's layette. But the truth of the matter is that for those first few weeks, your baby doesn't need fancy and uncomfortable outfits and you certainly won't want to deal with the hassle of trying to dress your baby in complicated garments.

So what does a baby really need in the first weeks at home? Not much. Simple clothing that is easy to put on and take off is best (as you will be doing this many times each day!). Here's what you will need for your baby's green layette.

- 2–3 organic cotton T-shirts
- 5–10 organic cotton onesies or rompers
- 5–7 baby sleepers or nightgowns
- 5–7 pairs of baby socks
- 1–2 newborn hats, depending on climate

The amounts vary depending on how often you want to do laundry. Some days, your baby may stay in one cotton T-shirt and a diaper all day. On others, he may go through every item in his wardrobe before lunch!

Natural versus Synthetic Fabrics

When you are looking at baby clothes, you will find items in all shapes, sizes, and colors. But what's most important about each garment is the type of fabric it is made from. Organic clothing is made from natural fibers grown without the use of pesticides, herbicides, and other toxic chemicals. It may also be manufactured without the use of chemicals. Look for organic baby clothing made from natural fibers such as cotton, wool, bamboo, and hemp.

The Dangers of Fabric Finishes

One of the great benefits of organic clothing is that it minimizes the amount of chemicals and pollutants that are poured into the environment in the growth and production of the fabric. But even more importantly for your baby's health, organic clothing minimizes the amount of chemicals that your baby is exposed to on a daily basis.

Almost all of the toxic and carcinogenic pesticide, herbicide, and insecticide chemicals used during the growing and production of conventional fibers (like cotton and wool) are removed during the fabric manufacturing process. It is during the finishing processes that conventional fabrics and garments are literally drenched with toxic and hazardous chemicals to give them special properties.

For instance, polyvinyl alcohol is often used as a sizing agent so that the fabric can be woven into a garment. Harsh chlorine is used to bleach and whiten. Conventional fabrics are scoured, cleaned, and depigmented with sodium hydroxide, heavy-metal salts, and cerium compounds in preparation for dying. Even the dyes themselves used to color conventional fabrics are toxic as they contain heavy metals and use formaldehyde as a fixing agent. Finally, the fabrics are drenched with a urea-formaldehyde product to lock in many of the easy-care finishes that are used to reduce shrinking and make clothing anti-microbial, anti-static, flame retardant, anti-wrinkle, and stain resistant.

FACT

According to Michael Lackman, organic clothing expert and the blogger behind OrganicClothing.blogs.com, you should avoiding all clothing that is labeled, *easy care*, *wrinkle-free*, *anti-static*, or *anti-bacterial*, as these garments have been finished with extremely toxic chemicals. Lackman recommends buying organic for the sake of the earth; and wearing organic clothing for the sake of your health.

Just how can all of these chemicals affect your baby? Our skin acts as a protective barrier against environmental elements, but it is also very absorbent, especially the fragile skin of a newborn baby. Chemicals and toxins applied to the skin are easily absorbed and can quickly enter a baby's blood stream. Your baby's clothing will be the closet thing to her delicate and developing body, so it is important to make sure that her clothing is not overloaded with chemicals.

Green Baby Clothing

When it comes time to dress your baby, you will want to make sure that the clothes you choose for her are as gentle and pure as she is. Fortunately, there are green, natural alternatives for every item you will need to dress your precious baby.

Seek out Hand-Me-Downs

Ask around to find friends or relatives who may be ready to pass on their baby clothes. More often than not, gently used baby clothes have only been worn a time or two. Some may even still have the tags on, as babies often grow so quickly in their first years that they may simply bypass many of the clothes their parents had prepared.

ALERT

Be sure to check baby clothes for loose buttons, long strings that could catch, zipper pulls that could detach, and appliqués or embellishments that could be chewed or pulled off. Current federal safety regulations prohibit drawstrings on children's clothing to prevent strangling, but hand-me-down clothing may have been made before these regulations went into effect.

Seeking out hand-me-downs and second-hand baby clothes is a great way to fill out your baby's wardrobe, especially in her first year. Because babies grow so quickly, the wear on the clothing tends to be minimal. And you are likely to get a whole closet full of clothes for free or for a fraction of the cost of new.

Buy It Big

When you do buy baby clothes, always buy a larger size than you think your baby will need. Babies grow so fast in the first few years that it would be a waste of money to buy an outfit that only fits them for one day. Buy a larger size to ensure a longer life for the clothes.

Remember the Weather

As you stock up on baby clothes for the next few months, remember to take the weather into consideration. If your baby is due in winter, look for newborn to six month clothing in heavy fabrics and designs. Stock up on sweaters, heavy pants, and jackets. If your baby is due in the summer, you will need lightweight T-shirts and rompers in these first sizes.

ESSENTIAL

As a general rule of thumb, infants usually need one additional layer of clothing over what adults need, to stay warm. If you are comfortable in a T-shirt and sweater, dress your baby in the same with a onesie underneath. Don't overdress your baby by bundling her in clothes that will just make her sweat.

Keep It Simple

The most important factor in choosing clothing for your baby is ease of use. It doesn't matter how eco-friendly a garment is, if it is difficult to take off or put on, you might as well just toss it in the pile to give away.

ALERT

You may want to get a winter coat to keep your baby warm on cold days. But if you plan to keep baby's coat on while traveling, choose a thin coat that will not interfere with her car seat harness. Thick winter coats do not allow for tight buckling and could leave your baby unsafe in her seat. Look for a winter coat that provides warmth without bulk.

One-piece jumpsuits, or rompers are usually more comfortable for a baby than two piece outfits. And remember that you will need to be able to change the baby's clothes and diapers easily several times throughout the day. So look for clothing with snap crotches and stretchy necklines for easy on and off. Try to avoid buying clothes with lots buttons or complicated clasps. Do not buy scratchy materials or seams or those that will be otherwise uncomfortable for your baby.

Seek out Greens

Look for clothing made from natural untreated fibers that are certified as 100 percent organic. Many online and storefront retailers now stock such clothing. Try BoodaBellie, (*www.boodabellie.com*), Sage Creek Organics (*http://sagecreekorganics.com*), Sckoon (*www.sckoon.com*), Better For Babies (*www.betterforbabies.com*), Under the Canopy (*www.underthecanopy.com*), and Pur Bébé (*www.purbebe.com*) for great selections of organic cotton, wool, and hemp baby clothing. You can even find organic baby clothing at mass retailers like Wal-Mart (*www.walmart.com*) and Target (*www.target.com*).

Beware of Tagless Labels

One of the latest trends in children's clothing is to use tagless labels that imprint the products materials and safety information directly on the garment rather than on a separate clothing tag. These tagless labels were intended to reduce irritation on children's clothing. However, many infants and young children have reported reactions to chemicals in the ink used to produce these tags. Reactions range from minor irritations to severe chemical burns. Government officials and clothing manufacturers have begun to look into this problem, but until the issue is resolved, it makes sense to steer clear of tagless clothing.

For the Feet

Don't forget your baby's feet when you gather clothes for his wardrobe. Onesies and footed rompers are perfect for keeping warm from head to toe. If you do need to get baby socks, be sure to have several pairs on hand for replacements, as they tend to fall off frequently. And look for socks made from organic cotton or other organic natural fibers. Newborns and pre-walkers don't need shoes, but slippers, like the Weebit from Simple Shoes (*www.simpleshoes.com*) that are made from organic and recycled-content materials, may help to keep socks on and baby-feet toasty.

When your baby does start walking, you can still let her go barefoot most of the time to help her figure out how her feet work. But if she is walking outdoors, you may want to put shoes on for protection. Look for baby shoes that are soft and flexible, so that baby can use his or her feet properly for balance, with a non-slip sole to provide traction.

Safer Sleepwear

During your baby's first few months, she will spend so much of her time sleeping that you may decide to keep her in sleepwear during the day and at night. Fabric and fit are important safety considerations for clothing you will dress your baby in to sleep. The current Consumer Product Safety Commission regulations state that infants' and children's sleepwear must either be made of flame-resistant fabric, or fit snugly.

Flame-resistant fabrics will not ignite easily and will self-extinguish quickly in the event of a fire. Flame-resistant fabrics may be worn either loose or snug-fitting. More often than not, they are made from treated polyester, but cotton garments can also be treated for flame resistance. Most fabrics must be treated with a formaldehyde finish in order to achieve this flame resistant status.

ALERT

To prevent suffocation, the American Academy of Pediatrics recommends that you keep blankets out of your baby's crib until he is at least twelve months old. To keep your baby warm at night, try a wearable blanket, or sleep sack, to replace loose blankets in your baby's crib. The Halo SleepSack (*www.halosleep.com*) is made from 100 percent organic cotton.

Sleepwear that fits snugly does not trap the air needed for fabric to burn and reduces the chances of contact with a flame. It is healthier and safer to choose snug-fitting organic cotton sleepers that have not been treated with formaldehyde.

Finding Green Baby Clothes on a Budget

Babies grow so quickly that many clothes that fit them one day will be too small the next. So it makes good financial sense to look for bargains when it comes to your baby's wardrobe. Fortunately, what's good for your wallet can also be what's best for the planet. Gently used, or pre-loved baby clothes can save you a fortune while also helping to reduce waste and minimize the consumption of new materials. Another great benefit is that most of the chemical finishes used on conventional fabrics wash away over time, so used conventional clothing is actually healthier for your baby than new! Here are some of the best ways to find green baby clothes on a budget.

Swapping

Let your friends and family members know that you are on the lookout for lightly used baby clothes. You may not know someone directly but someone else in your circle of friends who are willing (and often thrilled) to clean out their closets and put their old child's old baby cloths to good use.

Another alternative is to look for clothing swaps in your area that allow you to bring in a bag of gently used clothing to exchange for another. This is especially useful as your child gets older, since you can bring in a bag of clothing that she has outgrown and replace it with new stuff.

eBay, Thrift Stores, and Yard Sales

If you are looking for specific styles, colors, or sizes of baby clothing, you can find great bargains by shopping for pre-loved duds online or at your local thrift stores and yard sales. Check out eBay (*www.ebay.com*) for great selections and deals on new and gently used organic baby clothing. Browse the selections at your local thrift store and be sure to check your local newspaper listings for any upcoming yard sales that will feature baby clothing.

Easy Homemade Baby Clothes

If you are handy with a needle and thread, you be able to make some organic clothing for your baby at a fraction of the price of new, store-bought clothes. Check out your local fabric store or retailer to find easy, affordable patterns that can help you make everything from onesies to jackets. If you are new to sewing, start by making simple pieces like a pair of pants or leggings and build from there as you get the hang of it. You can also crochet or knit a lot of fun, simple pieces for your baby such as baby caps, booties, and sweaters. Another alternative is to purchase plain, organic clothing and embellish it with iron-ons, bows, appliqués, or even nontoxic fabric paint. Avoid any small items that your baby could swallow if they came loose from the garment. When you make your own baby clothing, you get unique, bou-tique-style clothing at about a quarter of the price that you'd pay in a store.

For more information and ideas about making homemade baby clothes, check out Make Your Own Baby Stuff (*www.make-your-own-baby-stuff.com/baby-clothes-pattern.html*). Or check out the free knitting and sewing patterns at Knitting Pattern Central (*www.knittingpatterncentral.com*) or Unique Baby Gear Ideas (*www.unique-baby-gear-ideas.com*).

Washing Baby's Clothes

The first thing you will need to do before you put your baby clothes away is to wash them. Whether you bought your clothes at a yard sale or in a store, the clothes may contain dust or toxins that will irritate you baby. Washing will not only clean them but also make the clothes softer.

Take special care when washing baby's clothing. Most conventional laun-dry detergents are made from synthetic, petroleum-based chemicals that are loaded with artificial dyes, fragrances, and optical brighteners. These chemicals not only wash off into the environment, they also leave a residue on clothing that can irritate and damage your baby's delicate skin. Look for green laundry detergents made from vegetable-based cleaning agents that do not contain artificial dyes or fragrances, are more effective at removing dirt, stains, and odors from clothing, and are gentler for your baby.

Avoid commercial fabric softeners on all of your clothes and especially when you are cleaning your baby's garments. Fabric softeners are made from oils that decrease the absorbency of diapers and may be harmful to your baby's health. Pour a quarter-cup of vinegar into your laundry machine during the rinse cycle to keep baby clothes soft and to help remove soap from the clothing fibers. Never use chlorine bleach to whiten clothes. It is incredibly damaging to the environment and harsh against your baby's skin. Use hydrogen peroxide or natural sunshine to whiten and brighten whites.

If possible dry baby clothes on a clothesline. Indoors or outdoors, using a clothesline will help you save money on your electric bill and reduce your impact on the environment. And clothes that are dried on an outdoor clothesline can use the brightening, drying, and freshening power of the sun and outdoor air to boost cleaning power.

CHAPTER 16

The Diaper Dilemma

For years, new parents have been vexed in their efforts to choose an environmentally friendly diaper. Cloth diaper fans have long insisted that theirs is the better choice because cloth is reusable and therefore doesn't take up space in landfills. Disposable diaper devotees, on the other hand, counter that disposables are more eco-friendly because they don't need to be washed and therefore save both water and energy. Are you confused about the diaper dilemma? Check out this chapter to sort out which diaper will work best for you.

Diaper Options

For all of the joys that a new baby brings in to your life, changing diapers is not likely to be one of them. Newborn babies need to be changed every two to three hours. As babies become toddlers, that schedule will ease up a bit, but you can still expect to change from 5,000 to 8,000 diapers from the time your baby is born until she is potty trained. So it is important to take a good long look at the diapering options that are available so that you can choose the one that will work best for you and your family.

Independent studies over the years have consistently come to the conclusion that there is no significant difference in the environmental impact between disposables and cloth. So what's an eco-minded parent to do?

Disposables

Prior to the 1960s, new parents had only one option for diapering their children—cloth. But times changed once disposable diapers hit the market. New parents were suddenly relieved of the extra laundry and accidents that came along with cloth diapering, and the disposable market boomed as a result. Today, 95 percent of all babies in America wear disposables rather than cloth. But these diapers come with a number of environmental and human health costs that bear consideration.

When the first diaper statistics were gathered, in 1970, American babies were going through 350,000 tons of disposable diapers each year. Today, 27.4 billion disposable diapers are used each year in the United States (that translates into more than 3.4 million tons of waste dumped into landfills). According to the London-based Women's Environmental Network, disposable diapers alone will make up about one-half the garbage by volume for an average family with one baby.

Another problem with disposable diapers is the number of trees that are cut down to make them. Two hundred fifty thousand trees are consumed every year to make disposable diapers for American babies. Disposable diapers are generally filled with fibers called cellulose. Cellulose, made from pine trees, draws the liquid into the center of the diaper and away from the baby's bottom. This virgin paper pulp then goes straight from your baby into the landfills.

Many disposable diaper packages remind parents to flush solids in the toilet before disposing of a diaper in the trash can. But this is a rare occurrence. About five million tons of untreated body excrement, which may carry over 100 intestinal viruses, is brought to landfills via disposable diapers every year, contributing to groundwater contamination and attracting insects and pests that breed disease.

In addition, some research has examined whether disposable diapers, with their petroleum-based covers, raise the temperature of a baby's genitals during use. Researchers speculate that this increased temperature could be particularly harmful to baby boys, leading to adult infertility. One recent study, published in the *Archives of Disease in Childhood*, probed this theory by monitoring the temperatures inside the diapers of forty-eight boys over the course of two days. The study found that the scrotal temperature was higher in the boys wearing disposable diapers compared to the boys who wore cloth diapers.

FACT

A typical baby goes through 6,000 disposable diapers before they're potty trained. Ninety-five percent of Americans use disposable diapers. In the United States alone, that adds up to almost 18 billion new diapers each year, just sitting in our landfills for the next 500 years!

The production of disposable diapers also uses a slew of toxic chemicals, and is responsible for even more toxic chemical byproducts. Keep reading to learn more about disposable diapers and their chemical side effects.

Green Disposables

If you are set on using disposable diapers, you may want to consider a disposable eco-diaper that is used just like a disposable but is made without the use of dyes, fragrances, chlorine-bleached papers, and other toxic chemicals. Some are even made from wood pulp harvested from sustainably managed forests. Seventh Generation (*www.seventhgeneration.com*), diapers are chlorine, fragrance, and latex free. However, they do use a chemically based absorbent gel that contains sodium polyacrylate. Even better, try

Tushies (*www.tushies.com*) cotton-blend diapers made with chlorine-free, sustainably harvested wood pulp that contain no extra chemicals or gels.

Cloth Diapers

From the moment the first disposable diapers were introduced, new parents tossed aside their cumbersome, leaky, and labor-intensive cloth diapers in favor of these newer, easy-to-use diapers. Today, cloth diapers make up just a little over 4 percent of the American diaper market.

Fortunately, cloth diapers *have* changed dramatically since the days of plastic pants and safety pins. Over the last few years they have become more convenient to use and precious to look at then ever before. Cloth diapers now come in a huge array of colors, shapes, and styles with designs from brands like Fuzzi Bunz (*www.fuzzibunz.com*), bumGenius (*www.bumgenius.com*), Kissaluvs (*www.kissaluvs.com*), and Happy Heinys (*www.happyheinys.com*). Traditional plastic pants that were used to give cloth diapers their waterproof covering, have been replaced with water-resistant covers made of merino wool, nylon, or polyurethane laminate. Instead of safety pins, new cloth diapers use velcro, buttons, or snaps. Here's a look at some of the different styles of cloth diapers available today.

Flat. Flat diapers are the original, old-fashioned choice when it comes to cloth diapering. They are found in many big-box and department stores as one-layer diapers, generally made out of 100 percent cotton gauze that are fastened with safety pins and covered with some type of waterproof pants.

Prefolds. Prefolds are similar to flats, but have multiple layers in the middle of the diaper to aide in absorption. They come in a wide variety of sizes and thicknesses to fit children from preemies to toddlers. Like flats, prefolds must be fastened with safety pins and covered with a waterproof pant.

All-in-Ones (AIOs). As their name implies, all-in-one diapers (or AIOs), combine the absorbent cloth diaper with the waterproof cover to form an easier-to-use product. The advantage of AIOs is that they are less time-consuming and cumbersome to use. However, these types of diapers do tend to be rather bulky and therefore take a longer time to dry than other types of cloth diapers.

Pocket diapers. Pocket diapers are cloth diapers that have an opening (or pocket) in the back that can be stuffed with any absorbent layer. Pocket diapers are easy to use and change. They are also flexible in that you can control the thickness of the absorbent layer inserted in the pocket—using thicker layers at night and lightweight layers during the day. But you have to remember to remove the inner layer before washing and reinsert it when the diapers are dry.

Hybrid Diapers

The latest option in diapering is referred to as the hybrid diaper, which combines a washable cloth pant with biodegradable and flushable insert liner. The primary hybrid brand, gDiapers (*www.gdiapers.com*) consist of three parts: outer pants with a Velcro closure in the back, snap-in nylon liners, and flushable pads. The used pads are removed from the liner, stripped apart by hand, dropped into the toilet, stirred with a swishstick to break up the contents, and flushed. The outer pants and nylon liners are washed and reused.

FACT

It does take a little practice to get the hang of using and flushing gDiapers. If you decide to try these hybrid diapers, check out their website (*www.gdiapers.com*) for detailed instructions and a video demonstration. Or call their toll-free number (866) 55-FLUSH to talk to a live mom/diaper therapist who will walk you through the procedure.

Unlike disposable diapers, hybrid diapers don't use any elemental plastics or landfill space. They also use less of the water and energy used to wash standard cloth diapers. And hybrid diapers biodegrade in 150 days (compared to 500 years for disposable). If you have a compost pile that you don't use for food plants, you can toss wet liners directly on the pile.

The Chemicals Used to Make Disposables

The biggest benefit of disposable diapers is that they are able to wick moisture away from a baby's skin and lock it away. But did you ever stop and think about just how disposables can accomplish this goal? Chemicals—and lots of them. And many of these chemicals have been linked to some serious health effects.

When disposable diapers first hit the market in the 1960s, they were comprised of a plastic diaper with a lot of paper fluff inside. Today's disposables, on the other hand are constructed of a waterproof plastic outer layer, an absorbent pad with super absorbent chemicals, and an inner liner. The super absorbent chemical, sodium polyacrylate, absorbs and holds fluids in the diaper. Sodium polyacrylate crystals can absorb up to 800 times their weight in water—turning into gel when wet. This chemical was tested by the Cosmetics Review Panel (an industry-run review panel), and was found to be safe for use based on the assumption that it will not be absorbed through the skin. No studies have ever evaluated the long-term health effects of a baby's exposure to sodium polyacrylate (on her reproductive organs) for twenty-four hours a day for the first two to three years of her life.

ALERT

The sodium polyacrylate used to make disposable diapers so absorbent is the same chemical that used to be found in tampons. But several decades ago, researchers linked sodium polyacrylate to toxic shock syndrome. It has been banned for use in feminine hygiene products since 1985.

Disposable diapers can also contain a volatile mixture of dyes and fragrances, which can lead to allergic reactions, asthma, and other forms of respiratory irritation in babies. In one 1999 study, mice were exposed to disposable diapers from several different brands and monitored for changes in breathing patterns. After exposure the mice showed reduced lung function similar to the symptoms of asthma. The mice that breathed emissions from cloth diapers, on the other hand, did not have these respiratory problems. The researchers also analyzed the emissions from the disposables and found several chemicals that are known to cause respiratory distress such as ethylbenzene, styrene, and toluene.

Dioxin, a toxic carcinogen, is also released during the production of disposable diapers. It is released as a byproduct of the bleaching of paper required in the manufacture of disposables. Dioxin is a persistent organic pollutant that accumulates in the environment and is not readily broken down. It can cause cancer as well as other health problems, and is found in meat, fish, dairy, and in human breast milk.

A Cost Comparison of Cloth versus Disposable

Take one look at a cloth diaper catalog or website and you may feel a bit of sticker shock. No doubt, investing a hundred or so dollars up front in cloth diapers is more expensive than buying a pack of disposables for twenty dollars. But just think how quickly those twenty dollar packages will add up.

The average baby is likely to need a new pack of disposables every two weeks. Do the math—you will spend $240 in disposables diapers in just six months. The fact is that using cloth diapers can save you thousands of dollars over the course of your child's diapering years.

Here is a rough estimate of the cost comparison between cloth and disposable diapers:

CLOTH DIAPERS
- Diapers Needed: 24
- Cost per Diaper: $17.95
- Total Cost: $430.80

DISPOSABLE DIAPERS
- Diapers Needed: 6,000–8,000
- Cost Per Diaper: $ .32
- Total Cost: $1,920–$2,560

For even more detailed information about the breakdown of costs of various kinds of cloth diapers such as prefolds or all-in-ones, check out Diaper Decisions (*www.diaperdecisions.com/cost_of_cloth_diapers.htm*).

Cleaning Cloth Diapers

The method you choose to wash your cloth diapers will have a major influence over the environmental impact of your diapering choice. A lot will depend on the services and facilities in your local area.

Washing Diapers at Home

Washing cloth diapers at home is as simple as tossing the contents of your laundry pail in the washing machine. Use your regular nontoxic laundry detergent to get diapers clean. You might also want to add a few drops of tea tree oil to the rinse cycle to remove odors.

ESSENTIAL

Do not use fabric softener or dryer sheets on cloth diapers. These products coat diapers with an oily film to make garments soft. However, they could weaken the absorbency of your diapers. To keep diapers soft, add a quarter-cup of vinegar to the rinse cycle during washing.

Cloth diapers can take the environmental edge over disposables with some energy- and water-saving washing techniques. Wash full loads of diapers in warm water whenever possible, skipping the pre-soak option. Line dry cloth diapers to minimize the energy needed to dry.

Diaper Services

Many new parents turn to a diaper service to handle the cleaning and care of their baby's cloth diapers. Diaper services are professional laundries that deliver clean cloth diapers and pick up soiled diapers on a weekly basis. These services rent diapers to families of infants, hospital nurseries, and day-care centers. The cost of a diaper service will vary depending upon your location and the number of diapers you sign up for each week.

The major plus of diaper services is that you will never have to launder your baby's diapers directly. Just toss the dirties in the pail and hand them over in exchange for a pile of freshly laundered and ready to use cloth diapers. Diaper services allow you to choose the number and size of diapers you require for your baby each week, so you can be flexible according to your baby's needs. The down side is that you may not be able to choose specialized styles of cloth diapers as many services tend to be limited in the variety that the offer.

QUESTION

Can I continue to use a cloth diaper service when traveling?
Yes. Contact your diaper service ahead of time to order any extra diapers you might need for your trip and to let them know that you will not need a diaper pick up while you are gone. Seal used diapers in a waterproof bag (like a large zip-top bag) and pack them in your luggage. Schedule a pick up and delivery immediately upon your return.

From an environmental standpoint, it is a toss up as to whether using a diaper service is greener than washing cloth diapers at home. It really depends on the diaper service facility. Some businesses go all-out to be green, using nontoxic cleaners, washing the fullest loads possible, and even delivering diapers via eco-friendly cars. On the other hand, some diaper services use bleach and extremely hot water to launder diapers.

Contact the National Association of Diaper Services (*www.diapernet .org*) to find a business in your area. Before you sign up with a diaper service, ask them these questions to make sure that they will help you minimize the impact created by your baby's diapers.

- What type of diapers do you offer?
- How many diapers do you recommend that I order per week?
- How much is the cost and when will the bill come?
- How do you launder your diapers?
- Do you take any steps to green your business? (Electric vehicles, carbon offsets, green cleaners?)

If you do decide to use a diaper service, it is a good idea to schedule a pre-birth delivery of diapers to arrive a couple of weeks before your due date. That way you will have diapers at home ready to use.

Diaper Bags, Wipes, and Pails

Essentially, you can use any type of bag to haul around the items you will need to care for your baby on the go. But many parents like the convenience of carrying a specially designed diaper bag that has a built in changing pad, enclosed pouch for dirty diapers, and plenty of pockets for toys, pacifiers, bottles, and spare clothes.

Gently used diaper bags are easy to find at yard sales and thrift stores and on online auction websites such as eBay (*www.ebay.com*). If you decide to purchase a new bag, be wary of the materials used in its production.

A recent study from the Center for Environmental Health found excessive levels of lead in many major name-brand diaper bags. For their research, the group bought sixty diaper bags from leading retailers, tested their vinyl changing pads for lead, and found that six of the products exceeded the federal safety standard of 600 parts per million.

Steer clear of vinyl and other petroleum-based products by choosing diaper bags made from recycled materials. The Re-Run bag from Fleurville (*www.fleurville.com*) is made from recycled plastic water bottles. Even better, Wee Generation (*www.weegeneration.com*) bags are made from 100 percent post-consumer recycled plastic bottles and have received the exclusive cradle to cradle certification of environmental friendliness.

Green Diaper Wipes

Traditional baby wipes are disposable cloths used to cleanse a baby's bottom during diaper changes. Many parents also keep them on hand to wiping sticky fingers and hands or even clean up spills on the go. Disposable diaper wipes are infused with a number of chemicals in order to improve their cleaning power. Unfortunately, these chemicals include toxic detergents, fragrances, preservatives, and even alcohol. Disposable wipes are also usually sold in disposable plastic tubs that add to their waste.

Eco-Wipes

Look for nontoxic diaper wipes like those from Seventh Generation (*www.seventhgeneration.com*). According to their website, Seventh Generation diaper wipes contain the following ingredients: water, Polysorbate 20 (a cleansing agent derived from sugar), glycerin (soothes and cleanses skin, vegetable-oil derived), citric acid (provides stability and pH balance), potassium sorbate (a natural preservative), aloe barbadensis gel (helps heal skin), and tocopherol acetate (Vitamin E acetate, which helps heal skin.)

Homemade Wipes

Save money and the planet by making your own all-natural baby wipes at home. Here's how:

INGREDIENTS
Water (boiled and cooled)
Cleanser (eco-baby wash) or grape seed oil extract
Lotion (aloe vera, organic olive oil)
Small scraps of reusable cloths

Mix first three ingredients together and store in an air-tight container or spray bottle.

When changing diapers, simply wet cloths with the solution and use to clean you baby's bottom. Place the wipes, along with diapers in the laundry.

ESSENTIAL

Need to freshen that stinky diaper pail? Don't reach for wasteful plastic bags or commercial air fresheners that contain VOCs and artificial fragrances. Instead, look for natural air fresheners such as a squeeze of lemon, a sprinkle of baking soda, or a teaspoon of vinegar to remove odors.

Diaper Pails

The greenest diaper pail is one that you already have in your house. For cloth diapers, any garbage pail with a good lid will work great. To make washing easier, line your trash can with a durable cloth liner that can be washed right along with the diapers. You might even want to have two so that you can wash one and line the can for new diapers right away.

When using cloth diapers, toss solids in the toilet before placing diapers in the pail. Sprinkle with a bit of baking soda to reduce odor before washing. You might also want to fill your diaper pail with water and baking soda to allow diapers to soak before washing. However, unless you plan on washing diapers frequently, pass on this method to avoid keeping a pail of stagnant water in your home.

Elimination Communication

Some parents have eschewed diapers all together and turned to a method called "elimination communication" where parents learn to "read" their baby's cues and rush them to the potty when they appear ready to go. Inevitable messes aside, this method is unquestionably better for the environment because it doesn't require the water, energy, or landfill space of diapers. However, it is not for the faint of heart. If you cannot devote your full attention to watching your baby for "cues," save yourself and your baby some frustration and use another method.

For more information about Elimination Communication, check out Diaper Free Baby (*www.diaperfreebaby.org*) or Natural Birth and Baby Care (*www.naturalbirthandbabycare.com*).

CHAPTER 17

The Nursery

One of the most fun things to do during pregnancy is to set up a nursery for your new baby. Whether you love animals or funky patterns, there are nursery themes and color schemes to match any style of *décor*. But whether you decide to give your baby her own room, or section off a corner of yours, the most important thing about setting up a nursery will be ensuring that it is a safe and comfortable place for your baby to rest.

Sleep Options

Although it may not seem like it at first, newborn babies actually sleep for about twenty hours each day. By the end of his first year, that may dwindle to about sixteen hours. During the day, you may choose to wear your baby in a sling or baby carrier for naps. Or you may decide to let him nap in a car seat, stroller, or crib. At night, you will have four options for putting your baby to sleep: a crib, a bassinet, a co-sleeper, or directly in your own bed.

Essentially, where and how you put your baby to sleep will be determined by your family's needs and the amount of space available to you. It is a personal choice and one you and your partner can discuss before your baby is born. But be flexible, your baby may have his own thoughts about where (and how often) he likes to sleep and it's often easier to follow his lead than to subject him to your will.

Remodeling or Adding On

Need a new addition to accommodate your family's new addition? Think green while remodeling or adding on to improve the air quality, energy efficiency, and comfort of your home while saving you a fortune on future energy, water, sewer, and maintenance bills.

Green Design

Don't wait until the construction has begun to start thinking green. Ask your designer or architect to incorporate green building into the design of the project to make the best use of energy efficiency, waste reduction, water conservation, and use of recycled materials.

ESSENTIAL

You may be able to earn rebates or credits by incorporating green designs or products into your home. Check with your local energy supplier and water utility to see if they offer discounts for installing energy-saving devices and gadgets. Or check the Database of State Incentives for Renewables and Efficiency (*www.dsireusa.org*) for energy efficiency incentives in your state.

Check out *Green from the Ground Up: Sustainable, Healthy, and Energy-Efficient Home Construction* by David Johnston and Scott Gibson for detailed instructions on building green. On the web, look for green building and design information at Green Building Solutions (*www.greenbuilding solutions.org*).

Salvage What You Have

If you are remodeling a room to use as a nursery, seek out ways to salvage the materials that you already have. Old floor tiles could be used as a decorative wall mural while old curtains could be turned into blankets, pillows, or cleaning rags. Salvaging what you already have, saves you money on materials and keeps these resources out of landfills.

Banish Toxins

Conventional building materials emit VOCs and other toxins that are harmful to the environment and your family. Green building techniques minimize the emission of VOCs and other pollutants so that you, your kids, and your contractor can all breathe a little easier.

ALERT

Be careful about starting a construction project in your home while you are pregnant. Some of the chemicals used and debris created during the process may be harmful to you and your baby. Talk with your health care provider about the work you intend to do and precautions you should take to stay safe.

Keep toxins out of the air by avoiding formaldehyde-based adhesives, as well as toxin-emitting paints, carpeting, and finishes. Breathe easier by replacing these solvent-free adhesives, water-based wood finishes, and low-VOC paints and carpets.

Reuse and Recycle Construction Waste

After your new room is finished, keep extra materials out of the landfill by making sure they are reused or recycled. In many cases, your contractor will be happy to take the materials off your hands for use on a future project. If not, post an ad on Freecycle (*www.freecycle.org*) or contact your local recycling facility or builder's exchange to ensure that extra materials are put to good use.

Paints and Finishes

When thinking about painting you new baby's room, you are probably thinking about one thing: color. Will you go with a traditional blue or pink or something more bold like a pattern or mural design? These decisions are all part of the fun of planning for your new baby. Just be sure that the finishes you use to add color to your room are healthy for your whole family.

The Lowdown on Lead

Prior to 1978, most homes were painted with lead-based paint. According to the EPA, lead-based paint that is in good condition is not a hazard to your family's health. However, lead paint that is deteriorating in any way (peeling, chipping, cracking, or chalking) is an immediate health hazard to you, your baby, and the environment.

Dust and paint chips from lead-based paint accumulate on floors, and near door jams and window sills. They can be inhaled or ingested through the mouth, and are particularly hazardous for little babies who tend to crawl on the floors and then put their hands in their mouths.

ALERT

If your home has lead-based paint, do not peel, scrap, sand, or agitate it in any way. Disturbing lead-based paint increases the likelihood that you or your baby will inhale lead-based dust, which is extremely harmful to unborn and newborn babies.

If you think your home might have lead-based paint, get it tested. Check out the EPA's website (*www.epa.gov/lead*) to find a list of EPA-certified labs where you can send in your paint chips to be tested. If the paint in your home does contain lead, call the National Lead Information Center (1-800

-424-LEAD) to find out what you need to know about removing lead-based paint and avoiding exposure. On the EPA website you can also find a list of local businesses that specialize in removing or sealing lead-based paints.

Why Is Paint so Toxic?

Even after lead was removed from paints in 1978, a slew of chemicals remained that can be harmful to the health of you and your baby. The airborne chemicals released during painting, after the paint is dry, and as paint is removed, fall into a category of pollutants known as VOCs. VOCs are responsible for the harsh odor associated with fresh paint. They are potentially carcinogenic chemicals that evaporate easily and pollute the air. VOCs are released in the highest concentrations when the paint is still wet, but most paint will continue to emit harmful fumes for years afterwards.

The health hazards associated with VOCs are well documented. Because of this, the EPA has required all paint manufacturers to reduce the levels of VOCs in their commercial products. Still, some are better than others, so be sure you check your paint label carefully to make sure you find a product that will be healthy for your home.

Low and Zero-VOC Paints

Because of the environmental regulations set forth by the EPA and increasing consumer demand, many paint companies have developed new house paints that emit little or no VOCs. These paints use water instead of petroleum as a base and therefore reduce the level of harmful emissions. These paints also contain no or low amounts of VOC-emitting heavy metals and formaldehyde. Low-VOC paints must meet the EPA standard of a maximum 200 grams of VOCs per liter of paint or 300 grams of VOCs per liter of varnish. This is less than half the typical VOC content of standard paints.

AFM (*www.afmsafecoat.com*) and Sherwin-Williams (*www.sherwinwilliams.com*) both offer a wide range of low-VOC paints.

ESSENTIAL

If you have a problem with chemical sensitivities and allergies, you may want to opt for milk or natural paints that emit fewer odors.

Even better than low-VOC paints are zero-VOC paints that contain five grams of VOCs or less per liter of paint. Try Safe Paint (*www.safepaint.net*) or American Pride (*www.ecosafetyproducts.com*).

Natural Interior Paint

Natural paints and wood finishes are often composed of natural plant dyes, oils, and waxes. Common ingredients include citrus, balsam, clay, chalk, and talcum. They do not contain any heavy metals or VOCs, so most natural paints do not emit any odors or biocide gasses. They are available as paint, primer, finish, sealer, stain, wax, although these products do tend to cost more than comparable products.

Clay Paint

One of the most common natural paints available today is clay paint. Clay paints are made primarily from earth-based minerals and use mostly water as a solvent. Colors range from natural earth tones to an assortment of blue, white, and orange tints. Clay paints adhere readily to most surfaces found inside a house and like most standard paints they require only two coats for full coverage.

The biggest drawbacks to clay paints are that they do not come in as many colors as standard paints, nor can they be cleaned as easily. Clay paints are also significantly more expensive than petroleum-based paint, so keep that in mind as you are planning the budget for your remodeling.

Lime Wash

Another eco-alternative to the standard petroleum-based paint is to use a lime wash. Limestone, a calcium-based mineral, is combined with water to form a simple, natural paint that is the basis of all whitewashes. Lime wash can be used indoors or outdoors and forms a unique, glowing finish that comes in a variety of colors. Unlike traditional paint products, lime wash actually sinks into the surface it's covering. Because of this, lime wash can only be used with porous materials such as brick, wood, plaster, and concrete; but not on drywall or previously painted surfaces.

To apply lime wash correctly, you will need to use several thin coats. And even though it is a 100 percent natural product, limestone is corrosive to both eyes and skin, so wear gloves and goggles during application.

Milk Paint

Another time-tested natural paint is milk-based paint. Milk paints are made with milk protein, or casein, which is separated from the milk and mixed with water, clay, and earth pigments to form a natural, eco-friendly paint. Milk paints are packaged in powdered form, making it lighter and easier to ship. The powder must be mixed with water and then used immediately (usually within hours to days) to prevent clumping. Milk, like clay, can only be used as an interior paint. But unlike clay, milk-based paints now come in a wide variety of colors.

Recycled Paint

Another eco-option when it comes to paints is recycled paint. A number of manufacturers have developed recycled content latex paint and primers. By incorporating unused stock and recovered paint into the mix, these paints are often less expensive than virgin paints while reducing the use of new materials and keeping the old paints out of the waste stream.

Paint Removers

It may be necessary to remove old paint (that is not lead-based) before adding new colors (especially if you are refinishing a piece of furniture). Standard paint strippers are petroleum-based and contain a particularly harmful chemical called *methylene chloride* or *dichloromethane*.

Look for a methylene-free remover at your local hardware store. When performing your paint removal project, make sure the workspace is well ventilated and use gloves to keep unwanted compounds from absorbing through the skin. Do not attempt to use these chemicals if you are pregnant and keep young children out of the room where they are used for several days to reduce exposure.

Floor Coverings

Your floor is one of the largest surface areas in your home. And while you may not spend a whole lot of time on the floor, your baby will. Babies crawl on the floor, touching it with their hands, their knees, their bellies, and often, their faces! And as much as you try to control where your baby will crawl, you will soon find her getting into places you never expected. Even after the crawling stage, toddlers and young children spend the majority of their time sitting, resting, and playing on the floor.

Most floor covering, whether its carpet, tile, or finished wood, is manufactured with synthetic materials, adhesives, binders, coatings, and backings that contain VOCs that cause indoor air pollution and are hazardous to your family's health.

Traditional flooring is also damaging to the environment as the extraction of raw materials, processing of materials, and manufacture and transportation of it all add up to high consumption of energy and resources and a huge production of waste. Disposal of old flooring is an ecological nightmare as synthetic flooring does not degrade in a landfill. When you are searching for flooring, your priorities might be durability, comfort, aesthetics, hygiene, stain resistance, etc. Why not add nontoxic to that list as well?

Wood

Adding hardwood floors or cabinets to a room? Use reclaimed or Forest Stewardship Council (FSC)–certified wood to minimize your impact on old-growth forests. FSC-certified wood comes from forests that have been managed sustainably to protect the forest, the availability of wood resources, and the local economy. Reclaimed wood is high-quality wood that has been salvaged from other demolished or renovated buildings. You or your contractor can find reclaimed wood at building material exchange stores or via online sources such as Craigslist (*www.craigslist.org*) or Freecycle (*www.freecycle.org*). Reclaimed wood reduces the use of virgin materials, eases the burden on landfills, and often costs less than new materials.

Rapidly Renewable Flooring

The swell of eco-design has brought with it a number of renewable flooring options such as bamboo, cork, and natural linoleum. These options are considered rapidly renewable because they come from plants that can be grown, harvested, and replanted quickly with minimal disturbance to the environment. Bamboo is a fast-growing grass that is as beautiful and durable as hardwood. Cork is harvested from the outer bark of the cork oak tree. Cork can also be used as an underlayment or as a wall covering to reduce noise between rooms. Natural linoleum is produced from such materials as cork, wood flour, and linseed oil.

Low-Toxin Carpets

Conventional carpeting is often produced using a slew of chemicals that off-gas into your home for months after installation. Your best bet is to steer clear of carpets altogether or minimize their use by choosing area rugs in place of wall to wall carpeting. When you do purchase carpets and rugs, look for products that are labeled as emitting low or very-low levels of toxins such as acetaldehyde, benzene, formaldehyde, naphthalene, toluene, and vinyl acetate.

Window Coverings

The products you use to cover your windows will not only affect the aesthetics of the room, they will also affect the room's air quality as well as the heating and cooling costs of your room.

Curtains

Drapery fabrics can be made of either natural fibers like cotton, linen, silk, and wool, or petroleum-based synthetics like polyester, nylon, and rayon. As you might expect, synthetics are more damaging for the environment and more likely to be loaded with harmful chemical residues.

In addition to choosing a better fabric, it is wise to avoid curtains coated with stain treatments and flame retardants, as these chemical treatments off-gas VOCs into your home. Also, look for curtains that have been colored with less toxic, low-impact dyes, or opt for naturally pigmented fabrics such as color-grown cotton.

Curtains with a light-colored lining will help to reduced energy costs by deflecting the sun's rays in the summer and minimizing air leaks in winter. If your favorite curtains don't have linings, they can always be added later by a skilled seamstress.

Window Blinds and Shades

Faux wood and plastic blinds typically contain polyvinyl chloride (PVC), which has a pretty destructive environmental lifecycle. PVC releases carcinogenic dioxin into the air during manufacture (and after disposal, if it is incinerated), and it contains plasticizers called phthalates, which can trigger respiratory problems and interfere with the body's hormonal systems. In 1996, vinyl mini blinds were also found to contain lead, a neurotoxin used as a UV stabilizer that leaches out of vinyl blinds as they age. The Consumer Product Safety Commission asked the window-covering industry to switch to a safer stabilizer, and now an undisclosed tin compound is commonly used, according to the trade group Window Covering Safety Council.

If heat gain in the summer is your problem, wood shutters, preferably external, will do the most to cut your energy bills. But in either situation, you can increase the efficiency of your window by installing low-emittance (low-E) glazing, which you can find at most local hardware stores.

Furniture

When a new baby is on the way, it is easy to succumb to all of the adorable products and furnishings that are marketed as baby care essentials. But what do you really need? And how do you choose products that are safe for your baby and for the environment? Conventionally produced furniture causes a shocking amount of chemical pollution, old-growth forest depletion, and waste. The glues, stains, and finishes used to make most items of furniture are chock full of the volatile organic compounds (VOCs) that off-gas into your home. Children in particular (because of their developing immune systems) are especially susceptible to VOCs. The wood that is used to create furniture often comes from poorly managed forests. Not to mention the fact that all of these large pieces of furniture need somewhere to go when they die.

Fortunately, eco-furniture is becoming as common as your average recliner, as most of the major furniture manufacturers are changing the way they design and produce their collections. Powder-based finishing coats, which not only are VOC-free, but require less energy and create less waste, can now be used in place of paint. Furniture giants, such as Hermann Miller and Knoll, are using FSC-certified sustainable wood and recycled-content in some of their pieces. And furniture makers are looking past the showroom floor and designing furniture that can be easily disassembled for repair or recycling. That means that we as consumers won't have to give up function or style to go green. Here's what you need to know to green your baby's nursery.

Don't Go Overboard

Contrary to the marketing hype, you do not need all of the baby furniture that comes in most sets. Talk to your friends and family about which items they found most useful, and skip the rest.

Buy Vintage

The next time you are looking for new furniture, consider buying a vintage or pre-loved piece. Pre-loved furniture does not require the use of additional resources, and it lightens the load on landfills. In addition, furniture that has been around awhile has probably finished off-gassing, keeping those nasty VOCs out of your home.

Buy It to Last

If you purchase an item that is flimsy to begin with, it probably won't last long in a house filled with kids. Invest in durable furniture that will save you money over the long run in replacement costs.

Along those same lines, look for items that will grow with your child, such as cribs that convert to toddler beds or changing tables that become dressers. These items will save you a fortune in the long run and keep your old stuff from ending up in a landfill.

No VOCs

Did you ever notice how a new piece of furniture stinks when you first bring it home? That stink is the gases seeping out of the furniture's glues, paints, and finishes, and it is loaded with chemicals that you really don't want to breathe, like VOCs and formaldehyde. Babies, with their fragile and developing immune systems, are especially susceptible to the potential health risks associated with VOCs. Keep these toxins out of the air and out of your home by selecting furniture that uses water-based adhesives and natural treatments.

Buy a Green Crib

If you can get a secondhand crib from a reliable source that meets all of today's safety requirements, you have hit the jackpot! You will save money and the environment. But if you do need to purchase a new crib, be very selective. Cheap furniture, while tempting for the budget, typically contains formaldehyde and high-VOC particle board. Steer clear of products that carry the warning "known to the state of California to cause cancer or reproductive toxicity," as they likely contain these toxins. If your budget allows, look for a crib that uses FSC-certified wood.

Check out Lifekind (*www.lifekind.com*), Ikea (*www.ikea.com*), and Sage Baby (*www.sagebabynyc.com*) for nontoxic cribs and baby furniture.

Pass It On

Don't send your furniture off to the landfill graveyard. Even if it is broken, you will likely be able to find someone who will be glad to take it off of your hands (and even pay you for it) at a yard sale or at sites such as Craigslist (*www.craiglist.org*) or eBay (*www.ebay.com*). If those options don't work, try giving it away for free at your local thrift store or on Freecycle (*www.free cycle.org*). Last resort: Stick it in your front yard with a FREE sign on it.

Bedding

Pesticides, synthetic fertilizers, and harmful dyes are all used to create standard crib mattresses and sheets. These chemicals are harmful to the planet in their production and harmful to your baby each time she sleeps. In a recent report published in the *American Journal of Public Health*, researchers found that the use of bedding that contains no synthetic materials appears to reduce the risk of developing wheezing in infants.

Crib Mattresses

The materials used to make a modern conventional crib mattress pose a serious health risk to the sleeper. Take a close look at the small white tag attached to a crib mattress and you will find that it is labeled "Do Not Remove." Mattress manufacturers are required by law to list the contents of the mattress, broken down by percentage, on this little tag. This label may tell you what your mattress is made *of*, but it does not tell you what those materials are made *from*. For example, polyurethane foam is one of the most common materials used to make crib mattresses. This material may be listed on the content label, but you will not receive any information about the potential hazards that can be caused by the chemicals that are used to make polyurethane foam. Nor is there any information about the byproducts of these chemicals, or what will happen as they break down over time.

ALERT

All flexible polyurethane foam is created in either a mold or slab process by reacting chemicals known as *isocyanates* and *polyols* with other chemicals that act as stabilizers, catalysts, surfactants, fire retardants, colorants, stain repellants, and blowing agents. Each of these chemicals is associated with a host of environmental and human health hazards.

You baby will spend the better part of his first few months sleeping in his crib, so it's important to be very selective when shopping for a crib mattress. The ideal choice is an organic wool mattress that is naturally resistant to dust mites and mold and made without the use of synthetic pesticides. Check out Lifekind (*www.lifekind.com*), Eco Bedroom (*www.ecobedroom.com*), or Eco Baby (*www.ecobaby.com*) to find an organic crib mattress to suit your baby's needs.

Sheets

Similar to baby clothing, the sheets you use in your baby's bed should be free of chemical pesticides. Lay your baby down on environmentally sound, organic bedding options that will ease your worried mind while he rests. Try Lifekind (*www.lifekind.com*) and Sage Baby (*www.sagebabynyc.com*) for organic cotton baby bedding in a variety of styles and colors.

CHAPTER 18

The Green Baby Shower

You are almost ready to welcome your new baby to the world. All you need now is a green baby shower to help you stock up on eco-savvy supplies and celebrate your baby as simply and naturally as possible. The main purpose of any baby shower is to welcome a new baby into the world. And what better way to do that then to make sure your shower is also respectful to the planet that new baby will be inheriting.

Greening a Baby Shower

Historically, baby showers were a way to "shower" a mommy-to-be with the practical items she would need during her pregnancy and after her baby was born. A green baby shower is one that honors this tradition of celebrating a new mom and baby while minimizing the gathering's impact on the planet. In most cases, a friend or family member will throw a baby shower for you to help celebrate your pregnancy and your new baby. If that's the case, bookmark this chapter and hand it over to your host so they will have all of the tools they need to plan a green event.

FACT

The Oregon Environmental Council (*www.oeconline.org*) has put together an online green baby shower kit with tons of resources to help you plan an eco-savvy party. And while many of the vendors listed are specific to the Portland, Oregon, area, you can utilize many of the tips for party planning and preparations no matter where you live.

You don't have to break the bank on so-called eco-friendly food, decorations, and presents. The essence of a green baby shower is to keep things simple and gentle on the planet. Look for ways to minimize waste and conserve resources throughout the party planning process.

Invitations

Whether you send them by mail or over the web, you will need to send out invitations to any guests who you want to attend your shower. The invitation should include all of the pertinent details of the party (who, what, where, when) as well as details about the "theme" of the event.

There are a number of great eco-savvy choices when it comes to inviting guests to a green baby shower. The greenest method is to send evites (*www.evite.com*), or e-mail invitations. Evites can be customized with the colors, styles, and pictures of your choosing, and sending them in lieu of paper invites conserves resources and reduces waste. Another green option is to send invites made from green materials such as recycled content paper, bamboo, sugar cane, or plantable paper, which is paper that contains embedded flower seeds, after the invitation is used, the recipient can plant it in a garden.

The initial invitation is a great place to let shower guests know about the mother-to-be's desire to go green. Either by politely asking for second-hand or nontoxic gifts or by listing the eco-retailers where she is registered, you can help your guests prepare for the shower accordingly.

Preparations

If the baby shower will be held in your home or in the home of a friend or family member, you will have more control over the shower's environment. Prepare for the party by cleaning with nontoxic household cleaning products. Use vinegar and hot water to clean counters, bathrooms, and tables. Wet-mop floors to remove toxins that have been brought in on shoes. If weather permits, open windows for a few hours before the party begins, to reduce the amount of toxins in indoor air. During the party, set up recycling bins for glass, plastic, and aluminum beverage containers near trash cans so that you guests will be more likely to use them.

ESSENTIAL

Avoid waste by thinking conservatively when planning the quantity of food to serve guests. You will save a bundle of time and money in food preparation and cleanup. Be sure to donate any extra non-perishable items to your local food shelter. And wrap up leftovers for your guests in wax paper or non-PVC cling wrap.

Food Dishes

If possible, use reusable dishes, utensils, and cloth napkins while entertaining guests. If you do need to use paper products, look for ones that are compostable or made from recycled paper. Rent or borrow items that you won't need more than once, like large punch bowls, chaffing dishes, or insulated beverage containers.

Keep the foods simple and green by serving dishes made from local ingredients. If your shower will be catered, ask the chef to do the same. Serve organic fruit juices and filtered water from a pitcher.

Decorations

Skip the paper and plastic and decorate with natural items from your backyard such as plants, flowers, and pine cones. If you use a florist, ask the staff to use flowers that have been grown locally and without pesticides. Use soy candles in recycled glass jars or used baby food containers.

Activities

There are lots of fun activities you can do at a baby shower that are easy on the planet and reinforce the green theme. Here are a few ideas:

1. **Make a mobile:** Ask your guests to bring a "favorite thing" that has been in their home or has special meaning, to be hung on a mobile for the new baby. You can incorporate a theme, such as *love* or *ocean*, to help guide your guests' choices. Use recycled materials such as ribbons or pieces of foil molded into shapes to provide color and reflect light.
2. **Create a tee:** Purchase new or gently used organic baby T-shirts and have guests decorate with soy-based paints. Use an organic T-shirt or baby blanket as a guest book for shower attendees to inscribe special messages or thoughts to the new mom.
3. **Add-a-bead:** Ask each guest to bring a bead to string onto a bracelet that the new mom can wear during labor and after her baby's birth to remind her of her circle of support.

Choose activities that match the interests of the mom-to-be and the interests and desired activity-level of the party guests.

Party Favors

To minimize waste and make sure your guests stay happy, go for eco-friendly party favors such as consumables (cookies, cupcakes, or other baked goods are always a hit as are plants or flowers) or reusables (picture frames or art supplies). Check out Creative Baby Shower Ideas (*www.creative-baby-shower-ideas.com*) for ideas on making simple, eco-savvy baby shower party favors.

Green Baby Shower Themes

The basic premise behind any green baby shower is to minimize the party's impact on the planet while celebrating the expecting mom and her new baby. Here are a few theme ideas for green baby showers:

The No-Gifts-Please Party

It is possible (and sometimes preferable) to have a party with friends, family, and games without involving gifts. If this is not the new mom's first baby, she may not need all of the stuff that a first-time mom might need. But that doesn't mean that she shouldn't have a baby shower to welcome this baby. Nor does it mean that guests need to go out a purchase items that may just wind up in the trash can.

ESSENTIAL

In lieu of gifts, you might want to ask guests to bring wish-list items for a favorite charity such as blankets, toys, or books for children in a nearby children's hospital. After the party, the guest of honor can deliver the donations and take a picture to include in her thank-you notes.

Some expecting moms may wish to circumvent the baby shower ritual altogether and involve friends and family in a picnic, hike, or other decidedly non-showery celebration.

Or they may choose to have a traditional baby shower gathering without all of the traditional gifts. Skip gifts altogether by suggesting "*no gifts, please,*" on the party invitation. Without the hassle of gifts, party goers can come together to celebrate the new mom and her baby without worrying about who gave the best present. The downside is that not everyone will abide by your request.

Blessingways

A blessingway is an old Native American tradition that honors a mother-to-be. During this type of shower, attendants gather together to tell stories, sing songs, share birth stories, and offer parenting wisdom. Participants can also write out wishes or blessings for the new addition that the host can make into a keepsake book. To learn more about blessingways, check out *www.blessingwaybook.com*.

Share-the-Love Party

A share-the-love party is a great way to green a baby shower and still ensure that a new mom receives all of the items she will need and want while raising her baby. For this kind of shower, simply request that attendants bring along secondhand gifts, passing along treasures from their own babies. Guests that haven't had babies in the last few years could be encouraged to bring gently used toys, clothes, or books from a local thrift store.

It would be helpful if the host of the shower coordinates gifts to avoid duplicates. If there is one main thrift store in your area, you may even be able to ask them to keep a running register of gifts to help guests make better choices about what to purchase.

Baby-Book Party

At a green baby-book shower guests can bring along one or two of their favorite children's books. A baby will treasure books long after she grows out of those cutesy clothes or noise-making bouncy seat.

Food-Freezing Fete

Another great idea for a green baby shower is one in which the attendants bring along prepared foods such as casseroles, desserts, or snacks that can be frozen until the baby is born. That way, the new parents won't have to worry about cooking for those first few sleep-deprived weeks of caring for a newborn.

How to Ask for Green Gifts

You know that you want to raise your baby in a green and healthy environment, but many of the guests at your baby shower may not entirely grasp your eco-ethic. The question that you are faced with is whether or not it's polite to ask for green gifts for the baby shower.

Fortunately, the very nature of a baby shower is to help expecting parents gather the items they will need to care for their baby. So don't be afraid to suggest that guests bring gently used gifts, organic cotton bedding, or nontoxic toys. Another option is to register for green gifts through an eco-friendly retailer.

FACT

A recent survey on the website The Green Parent (*www.thegreen parent.com*) asked thousands of parents to weigh in on whether or not it is polite to ask for green gifts. 65 percent thought it was acceptable to ask for green gifts, 24 percent thought it was tacky to ask for any gift, and 11 percent thought it would be appropriate only in certain situations (like baby showers).

Green Gift Registries

Wish lists or gift registries can help ensure that a mother to be gets the gifts she needs and wants for her new baby. Depending on the situation, the host can ask guests for specific gifts or donations toward one meaningful gift. There are a number of green gift registries that you can use to help guide your guests in making their gift selections.

Register at Baby Earth (*www.babyearth.com*) and your registry can be forwarded to family and friends at the click of a button. Fresh & Green (*www .freshandgreen.com*), EcoExpress (*www.ecoexpress.com*), and Nature's Crib (*www.naturescrib.com*) also offer green baby gift registries.

Green Baby Shower Gift Ideas

The greenest baby shower gifts are those that are gentle on the planet and will be useful and cherished by the recipient. Here are a few ideas for eco-savvy gifts that you may want to suggest:

- **Consumables:** Consumable gifts such as cookies, organic teas, or fresh flowers make a thoughtful gift for almost any occasion and produce very little waste. And besides, who doesn't love a batch of gooey, fresh-baked cookies or a crispy loaf of fresh-baked bread?

- **Offer up your services:** Ask friends and family members to skip the material gift and offer their services instead. They can babysit, make dinner, clean the house, weed the garden, or run an errand (the possibilities are endless).
- **Offer up someone else's services:** Gift certificates for a service such as a massage or a green housecleaner make the perfect eco-friendly gift.
- **Support a cause:** For the expecting mom who already has everything she needs, ask guests to consider donating to a charity that is near and dear to the recipient's heart such as the local children's hospital or Heifer International (*www.heifer.org*), a worldwide organization that helps to feed the world's hungry.
- **Green goodies:** Ask guests to keep the environment in mind when they purchase gifts by looking for fair-trade, organic, or locally grown options whenever possible. Friends and family members can fill a reusable shopping tote to the brim with nontoxic cleaning products or eco-savvy baby care supplies to really help a new mom out.
- **Make it yourself:** Guests that are skilled in sewing or crafting could make a handmade gift that is much more likely to be cherished (and retained) by the mom-to-be through the years. A knitted baby blanket, a pregnancy scrapbook, a photo frame, or a handmade organic onesie make easy, low-impact gifts.
- **Buy local:** Ask guests to look for gifts that are produced close to home. Whether it is a basket of fresh vegetables from a local farm or a wooden toy made by an area crafter, locally produced gifts reduce the emission and packaging involved in shipping.
- **Buy pre-loved:** Encourage guests to hit their local thrift shop, flea market, or vintage boutique to find a wide range of unique and time-tested gifts. If necessary, the item can be refurbished later with a new coat of eco-friendly, nontoxic paint or a well-placed ribbon to turn it into a treasure.
- **No-waste gifts:** Gift cards to a favorite restaurant or store are easy to give and popular to receive. Other no-waste gift ideas include tickets

(movies, theater, or sporting events), club memberships, or charitable donations.

- **Give green toys:** Ask guests to look for FSC-certified wood and organic fabrics when choosing green toys for kids. Steer clear of soft plastic toys that are likely to contain polyvinyl chloride (PVC). The European Union recently banned the sale of toys containing PVC after studies found that these toys leached phthalates that may disrupt the natural development of hormones.

ESSENTIAL

Try to avoid giving gifts that will continue to produce waste or require electricity. If you have to give a power-hungry gift, throw in a solar charger or a package of rechargeable batteries and a battery charger to eliminate the gift's future waste.

It's a Wrap

Regular wrapping paper costs a bundle and lasts but a few minutes before it hits the trash bin. Consider a green alternative such as a reusable bag or basket, a scarf, or recycled materials such as newspaper or brown paper bags. You can make your package beautiful with natural adornments such as flowers or pinecones. If you need to mail the package, replace plastic bubble wrap and Styrofoam peanuts with eco alternatives such as crumpled newspaper, pine needles, or straw. Ask guests to bring gifts, new or gently used, wrapped in baby blankets instead of wrapping paper.

Thank-You Notes

After the party is said and done, the mom to be will need to send her thanks to party goers for their love, support, and gifts. To make life easier for her, purchase eco-friendly thank-you cards ahead of time and address them as guests arrive. You can ask each guest for her e-mail address so that your guest of honor can send her thanks online.

part four

Baby's First Year

CHAPTER 19

Healthy Mom/Healthy Baby

Congratulations! Your new baby is here. Now the real work (and fun!) will begin. In these first few days together, your efforts will be focused on caring for and bonding with your baby and helping your own body recover from childbirth.

At the Hospital or Birthing Center

Your world will change profoundly from the moment your new baby is placed in to your arms. And all your efforts in diet, exercise, and preparation will pay off once you see this sweet little bundle that is now yours to care for. Many couples plan the labor and delivery of their new baby for months. But once that baby is born, the real work will begin, and it is important for a new mom and baby to rest and recuperate as much as possible in the first few days after birth.

If you have decided to have your baby at home, you will benefit from the fact that all of your familiar comforts are already around you. And you won't be disrupted by hospital staff and other patients as you care for your baby. However, you may also be tempted to care for other chores like dishwashing and laundry when your focus should be on rest and your newborn.

If you have your baby in a hospital or birthing center, your subsequent stay will allow you time to relax and to regroup before you go home with your baby. Take advantage of any and all of the resources available to you there. Talk to your health care provider and the center or hospital staff about what you should expect of your body and how best you can both rest and bond with your baby during your stay.

Healing from Childbirth

Immediately after childbirth, you may feel contractions similar to menstrual cramps, as your uterus returns to its original size. These contractions may become more intense as you nurse your baby. These after-birth pains are perfectly normal and help you heal more quickly. Talk to your midwife or OB/GYN if the pain becomes intense or increases in severity.

Whether you had a vaginal or Cesarean delivery, you will be checked closely by your health care provider for the first few hours following the birth of your baby. As you recover, your urine output may be checked to ensure your kidneys and bladder are working properly. The staff will check any incisions that you had (from an episiotomy or a Cesarean) to make sure they are healing properly. Your blood pressure and the amount of bleeding will also be monitored as you recover.

Eighty percent of new moms experience a condition called the *baby blues* after their baby is born. Symptoms include exhaustion, sadness, and a feeling of helplessness. The baby blues usually dissipate after a few days. If you continue to experience these symptoms, in combination with mood swings, anxiety, and feeling of guilt or hopelessness, you may be experiencing a more serious condition called postpartum depression (PPD).

ALERT

Postpartum depression usually begins two to three weeks after giving birth, but can start any time during the first few days, weeks, or months post-delivery. The condition affects 10 to 20 percent of new moms. It is a serious condition and you should talk to your health care provider about the best ways to alleviate it.

If you are hungry, go ahead and eat a well-balanced, nutritious meal to keep you healthy and boost your energy level. Drink lots of fluids. If possible, don't sit in one spot for very long. Get up, stretch your legs, and walk around a little bit (but don't push it) to improve your circulation and relieve soreness more quickly.

If your labor and delivery were normal, it is likely that you will be discharged within a day or two after your baby's birth. Use the time you have at the hospital to rest, heal, and bond with your baby.

Caring for Your Baby

If your baby was delivered via a routine vaginal birth, he will likely be placed directly on your abdomen afterward. He'll be dried off, covered with a warm towel or blanket and given a cap to keep him from losing heat through his head. Skin to skin contact between you and your baby will help you bond with your little one while you keep him warm.

After you deliver the placenta, your health care provider will clamp the umbilical cord in two places and then you or your partner can cut the cord between the two clamps. Your caregiver will collect a tube of blood from the cord to check your baby's blood type.

At one and five minutes after birth, your baby will be given an Apgar assessment to evaluate his heart rate, breathing, muscle tone, reflex response, and color. Your caregivers can do this assessment while your baby is resting on your belly.

If you had a nonmedicated delivery, it is likely that your baby will be very alert immediately after birth. So if you are both ready, now is a good time to try breastfeeding. If this is your first baby, don't be afraid to ask questions of the nurses or other hospital staff about the best ways to feed, diaper, and swaddle your baby. But don't forget to trust your own instincts either. This is your baby and you may be amazed at how quickly you begin to understand his needs.

FACT

The Apgar assessment is a simple test developed by anesthesiologist Virginia Apgar in 1952. It is used by modern hospitals worldwide to rate a baby's appearance, pulse, responsiveness, muscle activity, and breathing with a number between zero and two (with two being the strongest rating). The totaled numbers will determine if your baby needs further assessment.

Feeding your baby for the first time, whether you are breastfeeding or bottle feeding, may feel a little scary. Take your time, breathe deeply, and trust in the knowledge that in no time at all, you and your baby will handle feedings like a couple of pros.

Getting the Rest You Both Need

When a new baby is born, family and friends all rush to be first in line to meet her and congratulate the new parents. And while it is wonderful to visit with loved ones and share your new baby with the world, you might want to limit the number or length of visits for at least the first few days.

The best way to care for yourself and your new little baby is to ensure that you both get all of the rest you need during your first few days together. That may mean limiting phone calls and visitors initially. It may also mean putting off other tasks (like housework and laundry) until you are able to rest. For the first few days, all you should worry about is eating, sleeping, and caring for your new baby.

In order to achieve the rest you need when the baby is born, it is a good idea to have everything as organized as possible before you go into labor.

Set up a schedule with your friends and family so that they can come and help with the household duties and cooking. Make a list of chores that need attention, such as feeding pets, dishes, and grocery shopping and do not be afraid to ask people to help (or take them up on their offers to help) whenever you can.

ESSENTIAL

You will probably hear the same advice time and time again: Sleep when your baby sleeps. Take this advice to heart and take it one step further by also resting while your baby is nursing. If possible, lay down to nurse your baby for the first few days so that you can bond and snuggle while catching a few zzzs.

Finding a Green Pediatrician

Just as you found a health care provider for yourself, you will want to find the very best pediatrician to care for your baby. It is more than likely that your baby's pediatrician will be the one you turn to for advice on feeding, diapering, and child development, as well as medical care. So it is important to find a health care provider who you feel comfortable with and with whom you can ask questions and discuss your child's care.

FACT

After you have narrowed down your list of potential pediatricians, check with the Federation of State Medical Boards (FSMB) to see if there have been any serious disciplinary actions, or professional peer reviews against your candidates. Online, you can browse the FSMB website at (*www.fsmb.org*) or call 1-817-868-4000 to find out how to contact your state board.

Questions to Ask Your Pediatrician

After your baby is born, she will need to be checked out and cared for by a health care provider. If you have other children, you may have already established a relationship with a pediatrician. If not, you will need to seek out a reliable provider who will work with you to care for your child's health.

Ask friends, family, and coworkers for recommendations. And before your baby is born, make an appointment with the top candidates to discuss your baby's care. In addition to questions about fees, scheduling, and emergency contacts, here are some questions you might want to ask to determine how well a pediatrician's eco-savvy views align with your own.

1. What is your opinion on the importance of vaccinations?

Find out what the pediatrician thinks about vaccines and the schedule through which they are typically administered.

2. How do you recommend treating ear infections?

Ear infections are a common ailment among babies. In the past, pediatricians treated every ear infection with a prescription for antibiotics. But today, health care providers think differently. According to the American Academy of Pediatricians, most ear infections will actually heal better on their own. So instead of a prescription for antibiotics, your child might simply need an over-the-counter pain medication to help prevent discomfort until the infection heals.

3. What kinds of cleaners do you use in your office?

The types of cleaners that a health care provider uses to clean his office are a good indication of whether or not he is concerned about the health and safety of toxins in the environment.

4. What steps do you take to make your office green?

Does the staff at the office make an effort to conserve paper, recycle, drink filtered (instead of bottled) water, or reduce energy use? Ask your health care provider about the efforts made to minimize the impact of the office on the environment.

Use these questions as a guide to discussing a few of the key issues that may come up during your child's care.

The Vaccination Decision

No parent wants to see her child get sick. Fortunately, your child will grow up in a time when modern medicine and vaccines can help prevent a number of previously fatal diseases such as polio and measles. But there are also many red flags that have been raised about the safety of the vaccines themselves. So what's a concerned parent to do?

The most important thing you can do to ensure your child's safety is to find out as much current information as you can about the safety and efficacy of vaccines. And talk to your child's pediatrician about the best ways to protect him from disease.

FACT

In 1962, the year before the measles vaccine was introduced, almost 500,000 cases of measles were reported in the United States. Ten years later, there were about 32,000 cases, and by 1982 there were fewer than 2,000. In 1998 and 1999, only about 100 measles cases were reported each year.

Alternative Shot Schedules

The Centers for Disease Control and Prevention (CDC) has developed a set schedule by which they believe children should receive their immunizations. According to this schedule (*www.cdc.gov/vaccines/recs/schedules/downloads/child/2008/08_0-6yrs_schedule_bw_pr.pdf*), babies should receive as many as twenty-five immunizations by the time they are eighteen-months old.

Dr. Robert Sears, a world-renowned pediatrician and author of *The Vaccine Book: Making the Right Decision for Your Child,* has developed an alternative vaccine schedule dubbed *the Sears Schedule* that encourages parents and health care providers to give babies all of the shots they need, but spread out over the first few years of life, instead of bunching them all up in the first eighteen months. According to the Sears Schedule, babies will receive fewer vaccines at a time, concentrating on the most important vaccines first, and slightly delaying the less important vaccines.

Check Titers

According to the CDC schedule, children should receive boosters to certain vaccines, such as the chicken pox vaccine, to boost the baby's immunity received from a previous shot. Some children, however, may have received adequate immune system protection from the first shot and therefore would not need these additional boosters.

If you are concerned about the number of boosters your child is slated to receive, talk with your health care provider about performing a blood test to check a child's titers. By *checking titers* the pediatrician can measure the amount of antibodies in your child's blood, giving an indication of whether or not your baby is immune to the disease. If enough antibodies are present, you child will not need additional boosters for that vaccine. If you do decide to go this route, be sure to find out in advance if the titers test will be covered by your health insurance plan.

Split up Combination Shots

Many parents and health care providers question the necessity of giving babies a number of shots at a time. According to the CDC schedule, your baby should receive five shots at her two-month checkup and then another five at four months.

Many of these vaccinations are combined into one shot. For example, measles, mumps and rubella are put together into one injection called MMR, and diphtheria, tetanus, and pertussis are put together into one shot called DTaP.

Some health experts argue that it is better for babies to spread these immunizations out over several visits. Yes, this may mean more injections for your baby. But it could also minimize her reactions to the vaccines. The MMR vaccine is available as three separate injections that could be given to your baby over the course of several weeks or months. Talk to your health care provider about the possibility of separating and spreading out these vaccines.

Finding Green Childcare

Finding a high quality childcare center can be a daunting and overwhelming task for many new parents. There are so many questions to ask and factors to consider, such as location, price, number and age of enrollees, and the number of hours you will need care. One major factor that you should keep in mind is the environmental practices of the facility.

A green childcare center is one that takes measures to ensure that its practices are gentle on the environment and safe and healthy for children. Even if your town does not have a facility that labels itself as *green* there may be some steps they are already taking (or would consider taking) to make their childcare centers as eco-friendly as possible.

ESSENTIAL

To get a feel for a childcare center visit the facilities and talk with other parents who send their children there. Check out the ratio of staff to children, the cleanliness of the facility, and whether or not babies are cared for in the same rooms as older children. Ask staff how they deal with unexpected illnesses or children who misbehave.

The Oregon Environmental Council (*www.oeconline.org*) has developed an Eco-Healthy Child Care Checklist with twenty-five environmental health criteria for daycare centers. The two most important are the use of nontoxic techniques to control pests and prohibition of smoking anywhere on the center's premises. Here are the other factors to consider when choosing a green daycare facility:

- **Pesticide use:** Any product used to deter or kill pests, insects, and weeds should be nontoxic to children whether they are used inside or outside of the day care facility. If a more toxic product is required, be sure the facility has a policy in place to notify parents in advance and minimize children's exposure after application.
- **Mold and mildew:** Make sure the child care center has proper ventilation and humidity controls so as to avoid the buildup of mold and mildew.
- **Green cleaning:** The chemicals found in common household products used for cleaning and disinfection can be harmful to children and the environment. A green daycare center should use only nontoxic

and biodegradable cleaning products in its facility. In addition, scented candles and chemical air fresheners should be prohibited.

- **Lead:** If the childcare center you are considering was built before 1978, there is a good chance that its walls are covered with lead-based paint. Find out what steps have been taken to test for the presence of lead and abate it if necessary. Also find out about the risks for exposure to lead through drinking water.

- **Play areas:** Look for a childcare center that will help your children get outdoors as often as possible. They may have a garden, a nature trail, or special play equipment to encourage outdoor play. Just make sure any outdoor playground equipment is not made from treated wood. Indoors, the facility should have a number of nontoxic toys that encourage creative play. Plastic toys should be at a minimum and those that are available should be labeled PVC- and BPA-free.

- **Mercury:** A green childcare center should use digital thermometers instead of mercury-based thermometers.

- **Furniture and carpets:** Look for a childcare center that does not have wall-to-wall carpet and make sure that nontoxic cleaners are used to clean all carpets. Rugs and carpet should be vacuumed daily. Furniture should be solid wood instead of off-gassing particleboard. In addition, children and guests should be encouraged to remove shoes and wear slippers indoors to minimize the number of toxins that are tracked inside.

- **Art supplies:** The Art and Creative Materials Institute (ACMI) provides an approved list of nontoxic art supplies. A green daycare facility should stock paints, crayons, craft dough, and other art supplies that carry the ACMI seal.

- **Recycling and garbage storage:** The childcare center should have facilities in place to recycle items like glass, paper, plastic, and aluminum. Stored garbage should be kept covered to reduce the incidence of pests.

CHAPTER 20

Healthy Home Remedies

Your baby's first year is likely to be marked by a number of ailments, such as diaper rash, eczema, and teething. These conditions may be upsetting at the time, causing pain, irritation, sleeplessness, or difficulty eating. But more often than not, the common conditions that will affect your baby in her first year will go away on their own with only minor treatments or assistance. This chapter will discuss some of the common ailments you may see in your baby's first year and some natural remedies you can try to alleviate them.

The Green Medicine Cabinet

Take a look at the children's section of any drug store and you will see a ridiculous number of products that claim to heal everything from gas to sleeplessness. The problem is that the manufacturing, use, and disposal of many of these products is significantly contributing to environmental pollution. Everyday use of nanoparticles, pharmaceuticals, antibiotics, and hormones can have serious side effects on both your baby's health and that of the planet.

Many prescription medications are lifesavers and absolutely necessary. But there are also many occasions when prescriptions are overused and avoidable. For these minor ailments, it is much better to try a natural, at-home remedy first before reaching for a prescription medication.

Cradle Cap

Many babies develop a common condition called cradle cap, which is characterized by redness and scaly patches on the scalp. Cradle cap is similar to dandruff in that it is caused by overactive oil glands on the scalp and face. And though it may look unsightly, it usually is not bothersome to your baby. Cradle cap is not contagious and in most cases it is not considered a serious condition. If your baby develops cradle cap, try one of these natural home remedies to reduce or eliminate the buildup of scales and restore your baby's head to its natural beauty. For severe cases of cradle cap or unusual amounts of spreading, talk to your baby's pediatrician to make sure that the skin does not become infected.

Gentle Washing

If your baby develops cradle cap, it does not mean that his hair is dirty, but the condition may be alleviated by frequent gentle washing and massaging of the scalp. Use warm water and a very gentle shampoo to cleanse the area and a soft brush to brush the scales away. Repeat this procedure for several days until you see a lessening in the buildup of scales.

Oils

Try massaging a small amount of a natural oil such as olive oil or tea tree oil into your baby's scalp. Rub the oil on your baby's head, use a soft brush to brush the flakes out, and then cleanse the area with a gentle shampoo.

Colds

Colds are very common in young children, especially those who are prone to put their fingers and toys in their mouths. And although they can be annoying, most colds are minor and will clear up on their own with rest and good nutrition.

For many years, parents used decongestants and antihistamines to treat their baby's colds. But the common thinking now is that these medications do nothing to ease the congestion, runny nose, and sneezing that accompany the colds, and they can in fact cause dangerous side effects instead. According to the Centers for Disease Control and Prevention, over-the-counter cold and cough medications are no more effective than a placebo in reducing cold symptoms in children younger than two.

A safer remedy for colds is to try saline nose drops that will loosen the mucous in your baby's nose so that it can be easily removed with a bulb syringe or a tissue. It is also a good idea to help your baby rest in a slightly elevated position so that the mucous will flow out of her nostrils naturally. And a vaporizer or humidifier may be helpful in thinning mucous and soothing a dry, sore throat.

QUESTION

Is it a cold or allergies?
It can be tricky to tell a cold from allergies. In general, colds are marked by a runny nose with clear mucus that may thicken and turn gray or yellow or green over several days. A cold may also be accompanied by a cough or low-grade fever. Allergies, on the other hand, are characterized by itchy, watery eyes, sneezing, and a runny nose that only runs clear.

It can be difficult for a baby with a congested nose to eat, as both breast-feeding and bottles block her only source of air. So try feeding her immediately after using the saline nose drops and take frequent breaks if necessary for her to catch her breath.

Gas

Most babies suck in and swallow air as they eat (whether they eat from a breast or a bottle) which can cause gas bubbles to form in the baby's stomach. If these gas bubbles are allowed to pass through the stomach and into the gastrointestinal tract, they may cause painful bloating and discomfort. The best way to relieve the pain caused by gas is to help it find a way out, either through burping or by passing gas.

QUESTION

Does my baby have colic?
All babies cry, but sometimes a baby will cry for hours at a time, for what seems like no reason at all. This extreme type of crying in a baby between three weeks and three months of age may be due to colic. Doctors usually diagnose colic when a healthy baby experiences intense crying for more than three hours a day, at least three days a week, for at least three weeks in a row.

Preventing Gas

If your baby develops gas frequently, here are a few techniques you can try to keep him from swallowing so much air while he eats:

- **Change position:** Hold your baby at about a 45-degree angle while you feed him so that gas will stay above the liquid and be more easily burped out.
- **Change bottles:** If you feed your baby through a bottle, try one that is a different design or shape. Try switching bottles, nipples or both.
- **Burp frequently:** Burp your baby halfway through feeding to prevent the buildup of gas bubbles.

- **Don't overfeed:** Let your baby determine how much he needs to eat at any given time. Forcing him to eat more can lead to discomfort and gas.

Try these simple techniques first to alleviate gas. If after a few days, your baby is still bothered, talk to your health care provider about other ways to naturally relieve your baby's discomfort.

Ear Infections

Next to the common cold, ear infections are the most commonly diagnosed childhood illness in the United States. More than three out of four children will have at least one ear infection by the time they reach three years of age.

An ear infection is characterized by a buildup of fluid in the eardrum that leads to redness, swelling, and pain. Ear infections can be quite painful for little ones who react with crying, sleep disturbances, and ear pulling. So it is no wonder that many parents head straight to their health care provider to ask for a prescription medication that will alleviate their baby's distress.

But according to *Raising Baby Green: The Earth-Friendly Guide to Pregnancy, Childbirth, and Babycare,* of the 10 million antibiotic prescriptions handed out to treat ear infections each year, roughly 9 million did not actually help the children they were given to. In fact, antibiotics should only be used in to treat the most severe ear infections. In most cases, ear infections will dissipate on their own just as quickly without antibiotics.

ALERT

Ear infections are more common in boys than in girls, in kids whose families have a history of ear infections, and during the winter season when colds are most prevalent. Babies who are exposed to cigarette smoke, who are bottle-fed, or who attend daycare are also more likely to develop ear infections than those who don't.

If your baby is under six months, she should be seen by her pediatrician, particularly if her ear infection is combined with a fever. For older babies though, ear infections are often better treated with pain relief and rest, unless her condition is accompanied by a high fever and/or severe symptoms.

Diarrhea and Constipation

For the first few months of a baby's life, when she is eating only formula or breast milk, it is unlikely that she will have many problems with diarrhea or constipation. However at around six months, when solid foods are introduced, you may notice changes in your baby's stools as she adjusts to certain new foods.

The key to avoiding gastrointestinal problems is to introduce new foods to your baby's diet slowly, allowing her to try small amounts of one new food first before moving on to the next one. If your baby does become constipated or has problems with diarrhea, try a different food for a few days until her system has had a chance to adjust.

If constipation becomes a problem, try feeding her a small amount of diluted, pureed prunes. Make sure she is drinking plenty of breast milk or formula and getting plenty of rest as well. If your baby is old enough to crawl, give her plenty of opportunity to move her body and allow waste to move through her system naturally. Talk to your health care provider if your baby is younger than six months, if her symptoms are severe, or if they persist for several days.

Diaper Rash

Almost every baby will develop diaper rash at some point during his diaper-wearing years. A diaper rash is a very common condition that occurs when a baby's bottom becomes irritated in his diaper area. It can be extremely uncomfortable for your baby, but in most cases, it will clear up in hours or days with a few simple tricks. Here are some natural remedies you can use to alleviate and avoid diaper rash.

Fresh Air

The best remedy for diaper rash is to take off your baby's diaper and let his bottom get some fresh air. Let your baby go diaper-free for as often as possible each day, and make sure to change her diaper frequently.

Diaper Creams and Ointments

A generation ago, the traditional remedy for diaper rash was a healthy dose of talcum powder applied directly to a baby's bottom during diaper changes. However, health experts now know that talc-based powders contain tiny particles that can irritate a baby's skin and delicate lung tissue.

ESSENTIAL

Some health experts argue that disposable diapers are better for babies prone to diaper rash because they keep a baby's bottom drier. Others argue that cloth diapers are better because parents tend to change cloth diapers more frequently. The truth is that neither cloth nor disposable diapers are better at preventing irritation. The key to preventing diaper rash is frequent changes, regardless of whether you use cloth or disposable diapers.

Today, there are tons of creams and ointments on store shelves that claim to alleviate diaper rash, but many of these should be viewed with caution. Conventional diaper rash treatments contain preservatives and parabens that may be harmful to your baby's health. Instead, look for zinc-based creams and ointments made without harsh ingredients such as the products made by California Baby (*www.californiababy.com*), Badger (*www.badgerbalm.com*), and Terressentials (*www.terressentials.com*). Apply diaper cream liberally during each diaper change until symptoms are eliminated.

Teething

Somewhere around your baby's six-month birthday, she may begin cutting teeth. The primary teeth, which form before the baby is born, usually begin to push through the gums around six months of age. But, like many milestones there is a wide range of normal when it comes to teething. So don't be surprised if your baby's first tooth shows up when she is two months old, or if she is still toothless at twelve months old.

Teething is an exciting milestone that you will certainly want to mark down on your baby's calendar. Unfortunately, your baby may be less than happy about this new development. The process of teething, whereby the teeth push through and erupt through the gums is marked by drooling, as well as swelling and pain in the gums. Your baby may be abnormally cranky and have trouble sleeping and eating for a few days. Some babies may also spit up or develop mild diarrhea due to the increased amount of saliva they are swallowing. Other babies develop a rash on their cheeks, chin, neck, and chest from the excessive drooling. Teething may also cause a mild fever, congestion, and ear pulling—symptoms that look similar to an ear infection.

FACT

In general, teeth begin to appear on the following schedule: the central incisors (the teeth right in the middle of the jaw on the top and bottom), come in at six to twelve months; lateral incisors at nine to thirteen months; canine (cuspeds) at sixteen to twenty-two months; the first molars at thirteen to nineteen months; and the second molars at twenty-five to thirty-three months. Most children have all of their primary teeth by age three.

If your baby develops severe symptoms, or you are concerned about his condition for any reason, talk to your health care provider to ensure that his symptoms are normal. Teething is a normal process that all babies must endure, and the best thing that you can do to help him get through it is to find ways to minimize the pain and irritation.

Some parents swear by over-the-counter oral analgesics to ease the pain of teething. However the relief from these products only lasts for a few minutes and many carry a small risk of allergic reaction and decreased gag reflex.

Instead, try the following natural teething remedies to ease the pain and swelling associated with teething.

Gum Massage

Irritated, swollen gums are often soothed by gentle massage. Using one clean finger, slowly massage your baby's gums with gentle but firm pressure until the pain subsides.

Nontoxic Teethers

Many companies make teething products for babies to chew on when their teeth are coming in. These can be great for helping to alleviate the pain of teething, but you have to watch out for teethers made from toxic plastics. Instead, opt for teethers made from natural fibers, such as organic cotton, that can be washed and used over and over again. Cool the teether in the refrigerator for extra numbing relief.

A cold banana or bagel may also make a good teether in pinch, but keep a close eye on your baby to make sure that she doesn't bite off a piece that is too large for her to swallow. Cold spoons and organic cotton washcloths are also great teethers.

Eczema

It is not uncommon for a baby to develop eczema or other minor skin irritations. The most common treatment for eczema is a steroid cream, such as hydrocortisone. However, these creams can be damaging to the skin, especially if they are used for prolonged periods of time. Fortunately, there are natural remedies that work just as well as steroids at alleviating eczema, if not better.

Prevention

Prevention is the best remedy when it comes to eczema and other skin irritations. So if your baby is prone to these conditions, try making a few changes to minimize her exposure to irritations.

- **Diet:** Rashes and eczema are often caused by a reaction to one of these foods: cow's milk, soy, peanuts, eggs, fish, or wheat. Remove these foods from your baby's diet (or your diet if you are nursing) for a week to see if the irritation clears up. If it does, then slowly reintroduce each food one by one watching carefully for further outbreaks.
- **Chemical exposure:** If your baby has sensitive skin, try to minimize her exposure to fragrances, preservatives, and other chemicals that may

be present in personal care products, laundry detergents, or household cleaning agents.

- **Dryness:** Eczema and other skin irritations are often caused by dry skin. Help keep your baby's skin soft and supple by cleansing in warm water only and applying a gentle moisturizer while her skin is still damp to lock in moisture. If your home is particularly dry, consider using a humidifier or vaporizer to add moisture.

Hopefully, these tips will prevent the onset or aggravation of skin irritations. If your baby does develop a rash or outbreak of eczema, try applying a nontoxic moisturizing lotion to the affected area several times each day. Talk to your health care provider if the condition worsens or persists.

Baby Massage

Massaging your baby is a great way to help you both relax and bond. It can be especially helpful to a baby who is suffering from a bothersome ailment such as a cold or diaper rash.

Choose a moment during which you and your baby are relaxed, well-fed, calm, and unlikely to be interrupted. Wait about a half hour after the baby has eaten to avoid causing an upset stomach. If the room is warm, undress your baby completely. If it is chilly or damp, be sure to cover the parts of her body that are not being massaged with a warm blanket. Place your baby on a soft surface like a bed or thick blanket.

Rub some nontoxic baby lotion or cream between your hands to make them soft and warm.

Starting at the head, use soft gentle touches to massage your baby. Rub her head, face, shoulders, arms, hands, fingers, chest, stomach, legs, feet, and toes. Talk to your baby in a soft, soothing voice. If your baby wants to change position let her move around. Don't worry if you miss one area, you can always go back to it later on or try it again another time.

If at any time your baby seems uncomfortable or distraught, stop massaging her for a little while and hold or feed her instead. A baby massage should be a comfortable, relaxing experience for both of you, not something that is forced or distressing.

CHAPTER 21

Baby Foods

The foods you feed your baby throughout her first year will go a long way toward helping her grow and develop. In her first few weeks of life, you can bond with her every time she eats as you provide her with the comfort of security of healthy, nourishing food. The foods you give your baby in her first year will also provide a firm foundation for sound eating habits as she grows.

Breast Milk or Formula?

Choosing whether to breastfeed or formula feed your baby is one of the first decisions a new mom must make. And it is a decision that many moms become extremely passionate about.

Health experts and organizations, such as the Academy of Pediatrics, the American Medical Association, the American Dietetic Association, and the World Health Organization, recommend that babies be breastfed exclusively for the first six months and that breastfeeding should continue until at least twelve months if both the mother and baby are able.

The health and emotional benefits of breastfeeding are well documented. Still, for some mothers and babies it is simply not an option. The important thing to remember is that every mom has to do what works best for her and for her baby.

Breastfeeding Advantages

Breastfeeding your baby is an extremely rewarding and loving experience that benefits both a mother and her baby. It provides the ideal nourishment for a growing baby and creates a unique bonding experience that many nursing mothers cherish. Here's a look at some of the many advantages of breastfeeding.

ESSENTIAL

To ensure success with breastfeeding, you should learn as much about it as possible before delivery. The first attempts at nursing should being immediately after delivery. Nursing should continue, on demand, about every two hours, until you and your baby fall into a breastfeeding routine. Steer clear of supplements and artificial nipples until your baby has learned how to breastfeed.

Ideal Nutrition

Human breast milk is the perfect food for human babies. It contains the precise ratio of protein, calories, and fats as well as vitamins, minerals, and nutrients that a baby needs to grow and thrive. Breast milk is more easily digested than formula so that breastfed babies have fewer incidences of diarrhea or constipation. As a group, formula-fed infants have more difficulty with digestion than do breastfed infants. A mother's breast milk also changes to meet the needs of her growing baby.

The FDA requires formula manufacturers to ensure that they provide all the known necessary nutrients in their formulas. And while commercial formulas are a fine alternative to breast milk, they do not offer an identical match to the ingredients and composition of the real thing. This is because scientists have not yet been able to identify or duplicate some of breast milk's more complex substances.

Infection Fighting

Antibodies passed from a nursing mother to her baby can help lower the occurrence of many conditions, including ear infections, diarrhea, respiratory infections, and meningitis. Research shows that formula-fed infants have more infections and more hospitalizations than do breastfed babies. Breastfeeding boosts a baby's immune system by increasing the barriers to infection and decreasing the growth of organisms like bacteria and viruses.

ALERT

If you are nursing, pay close attention to what you put in your body. Drugs, nicotine, alcohol, and even some foods can be secreted in breast milk. You may need to increase your calorie intake; nursing requires about 600 extra calories a day. And drink plenty of fluids to increase your milk supply.

Studies also show that breastfeeding is particularly beneficial for babies who are born prematurely and it may help to protect children against allergies, asthma, diabetes, obesity, and sudden infant death syndrome (SIDS).

Sucking at the breast promotes good jaw development as well. Its harder work to get milk out of a breast than a bottle, and the exercise strengthens the jaws and encourages the growth of straight, healthy teeth. The baby at the breast also can control the flow of milk by sucking and stopping. With a bottle, the baby must constantly suck or react to the pressure of the nipple placed in the mouth. Recent studies also suggests that children who were exclusively breastfed for six months have IQs in the range of five to ten points higher than children who were formula fed.

Cost

One of the best benefits to breastfeeding is that unlike costly commercial formulas, breast milk doesn't cost a cent. Nor does it require any additional apparatus in the form on bottles, bottle warmers, and nipple sterilizers.

In addition, breastfed babies are sick less often than infants who receive formula. That translates to fewer trips to the doctor's office and less money doled out for medications. In a study published in the April 1999 issue of the journal *Pediatrics*, researchers determined that infants who were never breastfed would incur additional medical costs of $331 to $475 per year.

Convenience

Breast milk does not have to be prepared in any way before it is served at mealtime. There is no mixing, no heating, and no bottles to sterilize. Nursing moms are often particularly grateful during middle of the night feedings because there is no formula to prepare or heat up. And breastfeeding mothers generally have an easier time getting out and about with their babies because they don't have to worry about running out of food or finding a place to heat it up on the go.

Postpartum Weight Loss

Recent studies indicate that breastfeeding might help prevent childhood and adult obesity. According to the National Women's Health Information Center, babies who are breastfed tend to gain less unnecessary weight, which may prevent obesity into adulthood. Breastfeeding also burns calories and helps shrink the uterus, so nursing moms may be able to return to their pre-pregnancy shape and weight quicker.

Better Bonding

Breastfeeding allows new moms to bond closely with their babies through skin-to-skin contact. For many, it helps to enhance the emotional connection between a mother and her infant. In addition, studies show that breastfeeding helps lower the risk of premenopausal breast cancer and also may help decrease the risk of uterine and ovarian cancer.

Breastfeeding Challenges

Breastfeeding does have many fantastic benefits for a mom and her baby, but it is not without its challenges as well. For some new moms and babies, nursing comes very easily. But for others, it may require a bit more patience and persistence. Here are some of the common challenges that you may experience when breastfeeding.

Discomfort

Breastfeeding a baby is a new experience and it may initially feel uncomfortable until you get the hang of it. While it shouldn't hurt, latch pain is normal for the first week or two until you and your baby grow accustomed to the process. If pain or discomfort is a problem, seek out the help of a lactation consultant, or your baby's pediatrician to help diagnose and alleviate the problem.

ALERT

Watch out for infection! While it is natural for breastfeeding to be slightly uncomfortable at first, you should seek medical attention if you experience fever or painful lumps and redness in your breasts. These symptoms indicate the presence of an infection that may require medication and/or an altered nursing schedule.

Time Investment

Breastfeeding is very convenient in that a new mother always has a supply of food ready for her baby. But the time investment required can also be a bit of a challenge. If you decide to formula-feed your baby, your partner and other family members will be able to share in the feeding responsibilities, giving you a much-needed break.

Even if a new mom decides to pump her breast milk, lactation experts recommend that a breastfeeding baby should not be introduced to a bottle for the first several weeks until he is more comfortable with breastfeeding. That means that for the first few weeks, the new mother will need to be available for nursing every few hours around the clock. There's no question that this can be exhausting, especially when you are also trying to recover from labor and delivery.

Some women are also concerned that nursing will make it hard for them to work, run errands, or travel because of a breastfeeding schedule or a need to pump breast milk during the day. Another factor to consider is that breastfed babies need to eat more often than babies who are fed formula, because breast milk digests faster than formula.

Diet

The foods you eat will travel from your bloodstream directly in to your breast milk. So there are a number of foods and beverages that you should avoid if you plan to breastfeed your baby. Nursing mothers must be careful to avoid the following items:

- Alcohol
- Caffeine
- Cow's milk
- Gas-inducing vegetables (broccoli, cabbage, or beans)

Talk to your health care provider or your baby's pediatrician if you have any concerns about the foods you can eat while nursing.

Formula Advantages

Breastfeeding is wonderful, but, for a variety of reasons, it may not be a good fit for every mother and baby. In these situations, commercially prepared infant formulas are an excellent alternative. Commercial formula is manufactured under sterile conditions, and regulated by the FDA to ensure that it comes as close as possible to the complex combination of proteins, sugars, fats, and vitamins found in breast milk. If you decide not to breastfeed your baby, it is important that you use only a commercially prepared formula and that you do not try to create your own. Here are some of the primary advantages to using formula.

Convenience

The main benefit of feeding a baby formula is that it can offer you a break from the rigors of caring for your new baby. Either parent, or other friends and family members, can feed the baby a bottle at any time, allowing you to share the responsibilities of feeding your baby. If you need to care for other children, work, or travel frequently, formula feeding may make it easier for you to leave your baby with your partner or caregiver for extended periods. And formula-feeding moms don't need to worry about finding a private place to nurse in public.

QUESTION

Can I breastfeed my baby if I am on medication?
Even mothers who must take daily medication for conditions such as epilepsy, diabetes, or high blood pressure can usually breastfeed. But you should talk with your baby's pediatrician about medications you are taking while nursing. When you do need to take medication, minimize your baby's exposure by taking the drug just after nursing or before your baby sleeps.

Frequency of Feedings
Because formula digests slower than breast milk, formula-fed babies usually need to eat less often than do breastfed babies. However, this varies depending upon the needs of each individual baby.

Diet
New moms who feed their babies formula don't have to worry about the things they eat or drink affecting their babies.

Formula Disadvantages

Commercially prepared formula offers a number of benefits for moms and new babies. But as with breastfeeding, there are some challenges to consider when deciding whether to formula feed.

Preparation
Unlike breast milk, which is ready at all times, formula must be prepared and heated in sterilized containers for each feeding. Bottles, nipples, and utensils used to prepare formula must be washed before and after each

feeding. Ready-to-feed formulas that can be poured directly into a bottle without any mixing or water tend to be very expensive and wasteful.

Less Complete

Although formula manufacturers do their best to duplicate the complex ratio of proteins, fats, and nutrients found in breast milk, they have yet to duplicate the complexity of breast milk, which changes as the baby's needs change. In addition, formulas do not contain any of the important disease-preventing antibodies that are commonly found in breast milk. According to the FDA, human milk contains at least 100 ingredients not found in formula.

Cost

While breast milk is free and available in a virtually unlimited supply, formula can be a costly expense. Powdered formula is the least expensive, followed by concentrated, while ready-to-feed formula products are the most expensive. If your baby requires a specialty formula, such as a soy-based or hypoallergenic formula, the cost will be even greater. During the first year of life, the cost of basic formula can run about $1,500.

Gas and Constipation

Formula-fed babies may have more gas and firmer bowel movements than breastfed babies.

Nursing Gear

Technically, your breasts and a good supply of milk are all you really need to breastfeed your baby. But to make the process easier on yourself you may want to invest in some basic nursing gear, such as nursing bras, a breast pump, and nipple cream.

Nursing Clothing

If you plan to breastfeed your baby, pick up a couple nursing bras with detachable straps that will help you get easier access to your goods as needed. Look for bras made from 100 percent organic cotton with no underwire.

You don't need a special wardrobe for nursing. Button down shirts, large T-shirts, and tank tops all work well for breastfeeding your baby. Choose shirts made from natural organic fabrics that wick moisture easily and are safe for your baby to rest against.

FACT

La Leche League International (*www.lllli.org*) is an international non-profit organization dedicated to supporting the needs and rights of breastfeeding mothers. Check out their website for tips of nursing, for information about breastfeeding laws, and to find out when and where to find breastfeeding support in your local area.

If you wear your baby in a sling, it will serve double duty as a blanket to cover your breasts during nursing. While it's not necessary that you cover up to nurse, you may feel more comfortable with some extra cover when you breastfeed your baby in public. Keep a spare receiving blanket in your diaper bag to give you and your baby some privacy. Or try the fun nursing cover like the Hooter Hider from Bebe au Lait (*www.bebeaulait.com*).

Breast Pumps

A breast pump allows you to pump your breast milk either to relieve engorgement or to store your breast milk for later feedings. A breast pump can be a costly expense, but if you plan on offering your baby breast milk it a bottle frequently, it may be a wise investment. Alternatively, you can borrow or rent a breast pump from your hospital or birthing center. Most offer both electric and hand pump models.

Nursing Pads and Nipple Creams

Nursing pads come in disposable or reusable varieties. The reusable ones are often made of cotton and are very absorbent. They can be washed and reused just like cloth diapers. Disposable pads, on the other hand, are made from bleached paper products and are generally not as soft as the fabric pads. In your baby's first few weeks, you will probably use nursing pads regularly to absorb leakage as your breasts adjust to your baby's changing needs. But as you and your baby establish a regular nursing routine, you may only need nursing pads at night, if at all.

You may also notice that your nipples become dry, cracked, and sore when you first start breastfeeding. Use a quality nipple cream such as Lasinoh Lanolin by Ameda, which is a safe, nontoxic cream that you can use to soothe aching nipples.

Organic Formulas

If you do decide that formula feeding is the best choice for you and your baby, you might want to consider going with an organic baby formula that is made from ingredients that are free of pesticides and genetically modified ingredients. Earth's Best (*www.earthsbest.com*), Similac Organic (*http://similac .com/baby-formula/similac-organic*), and Baby's Only (*www.naturesone .com*) all make organic formulas that might work well for your baby.

BPA-Free Baby Bottles and Sippy Cups

Over the past few years, environmental groups and health experts have grown increasingly alarmed about a chemical that is commonly found in infant baby bottles and toddler sippy cups. Bisphenol A, or BPA, is a hormone-mimicking chemical that is used in polycarbonate plastics to make them rigid and shatterproof.

Studies suggest that BPA has estrogenic properties that, in animal tests, led to health problems such as prostate and breast cancer, reproductive disorders, obesity, Type 2 diabetes, and neurobehavioral problems such as Attention Deficit Hyperactivity Disorder (ADHD). Many leading experts and the FDA argue that the use of BPA is safe to the human public. However, many moms are not willing to take the risk.

Consumer pressure forced many of the major manufacturers to come out with a BPA-free line of baby bottles and sippy cups. Check out the BPA-Free Bottle and Sippy Cup Cheat Sheet from Safe Mama (*http://safemama .com/2007/11/22/bpa-free-bottle-and-sippy-cup-cheat-sheet*) for the latest information on this issue.

Introducing Solid Foods

About the time that your baby reaches her six-month birthday, it will be time to introduce her to solid foods. When the time comes, she should be giving you clear signs that she is ready to move beyond her liquid-only diet. Your baby is ready for solid foods when she:

- Can keep her head in a steady, upright position.
- Stops using her tongue to push food out of her mouth.
- Sits well when supported.
- Has doubled her birth weight and is at least four to six months old.
- Seems curious about what you are eating.

To introduce solid foods for the time, start by nursing or bottle feeding your baby. If she is too hungry, she will only be cranky and agitated. Next, sit her up in a comfortable position and give her one or two teaspoons of food mixed with enough formula or breast milk to make it liquidy. Start with just a small amount of food on the tip of the spoon.

Begin with a one feeding of solid food per day, adding more food, and more settings as your baby's appetitive increases. Gradually thicken the consistency of her food as she adjusts to the idea of eating from a spoon.

When introducing new foods, it is best to do so one at a time, then wait a few days to make sure your baby shows no signs of allergic reaction.

Homemade Baby Food

Homemade baby food is the healthiest and most economical way to feed your baby solid foods. Use fresh, locally grown and produced foods whenever possible. Keep it simple. Opt for easy cooking techniques like steaming and baking that preserve the foods' natural nutrients. And remember that your baby's taste buds are very sensitive, so it is unnecessary to add butter, salt, sugar, or other spices to flavor his foods. Some excellent first foods to try are rice cereal, cooked sweet potatoes, avocado, or ripe mashed bananas.

After your baby's food is cooked, you can puree it with a blender, food processor, or hand-cranked food mill. Add a little breast milk or formula to get the food to the desired consistency. For baby's first foods, make the meal as runny as possible. You can increase the texture as your baby gets older.

ALERT

While you want to expose your baby to a wide range of foods during her first year, there are a number of foods that you should avoid until your baby's first birthday. These include honey, cow's milk, egg whites, citrus fruit and juices, nuts (especially peanuts), fish, shellfish, sesame seeds, and any unpasteurized foods.

Storing Homemade Baby Food

After you get the hang of cooking and serving your baby's first few meals, you will probably want to start cooking his food in batches, so that you will have a small, homemade meal ready for him whenever he gets hungry.

ESSENTIAL

Commercially prepared baby food does come in handy at times, especially when you are on the go. Remember to look for brands that are free of added flavors, salt, sugars, and preservatives. Earth's Best (*www.earthsbest.com*) and Gerber (*www.gerber.com*) both make an organic line of baby foods that can be found at retail stores nationwide.

The simplest method for storing a batch of homemade baby food is to pour it into an ice cube tray after it has cooled and freeze it. Once the food is frozen, remove the individual food portions from the tray, wrap in waxed paper, and transfer them to a freezer-safe sealed container labeled with the type of food and the date it was prepared. Each cube of food will weigh in at about once ounce. To serve, just warm the cube in a double boiler.

CHAPTER 22

Caring for Baby's Skin

It is incredibly soft and kissable, and it is also your baby's main source of protection from the outside world. Your baby's skin is thinner and less oily than an adult's, making it more prone to damage and less resistant to harm. It also produces less melanin, the substance that helps ward off sunburn. Every product you use to care for your baby's skin will be absorbed directly into her delicate body, so make sure that it is mild, healthy, and pure.

Green Your Baby's Bath

The first bath with a new baby can be a nerve-wracking experience. New-born babies are so small and wiggly as it is—get them wet and it seems almost impossible to hold on to their slippery little bodies. But after a few tries, you will probably master the art of gently cleansing your baby in the bathtub.

When babies are first born they are usually covered in a creamy white coating called the *vernix caseosa*, a collection of dead cells and mucus that cover him throughout your pregnancy. If you deliver your baby in a hospital or birthing center, he will probably be given his first bath immediately after birth. A gentle bath with warm water will help remove blood and other fluids while leaving the vernix intact. Once he is dried off, massage the vernix coating into your baby's skin to keep it soft and protected. If you have had a cesarean delivery, or if you and your partner are not able to bathe your baby yourselves, request that the hospital staff sponge your baby off with warm water only, leaving the vernix intact.

ALERT

Never leave your baby unsupervised, even for a minute. A baby can drown in under once inch of water, and in less than sixty seconds. If the doorbell or phone rings and you feel you must answer it, scoop him up in a towel and take him with you.

For your baby's first few weeks, you will probably only need warm water to get her clean. If she is particularly dirty, you might try using a small amount of a mild, nontoxic baby wash. Look for dye-free, fragrance-free baby skin care products that contain the least amount of harmful chemicals. Here's how to choose the safest skin care products for your baby:

- **Read the label:** You don't have to have a degree in chemistry to know that skin care products with a long list of chemical ingredients are probably bad for your baby's delicate skin. Look for products with just a few simple ingredients. If the ingredient list is long, or if you cannot pronounce most of the ingredients on the list, you should pass. Steer clear of products that contain parabens, phthalates, petroleum byproducts (like petrolatum or petroleum distillates), sodium laurel sulfate, and triclosan, as these chemicals can irritate a baby's skin and immune system.

- **Go fragrance free:** Fragrances and dyes are harsh chemicals that could irritate a baby's delicate skin and immune system. Choose products that are free of these toxins.
- **Go organic:** Organic skin care products are free of pesticides, genetically modified ingredients, and other toxic residues that can be harmful to a young infant. While personal care products themselves cannot be certified as organic, a product can bear the organic label if it contains primarily organic ingredients (like avocado or olive oil).
- **No animal testing:** Look for baby skin care products that carry the Leaping Bunny logo indicating that they have never been tested on animals.

Baby Skincare Products

The next time you are browsing in the baby aisle of your favorite store, take a look at how many different types of soaps, cream, lotions, and potions are made to care for a baby's skin. Just how many of these products will your baby really need? Keep your vanity stocked with the following products and you will have all you need to care for your baby's skin:

- Baby-safe sunscreen
- Diaper cream
- Mild liquid soap
- Natural baby lotion

These four items are all you need to keep your baby's skin clean, soft, and sweet-smelling.

Washing Baby's Delicate Skin

For the first week to ten days after your baby is born, until his umbilical cord stump falls off and the area heals, it is best to stick to sponge baths using an organic washcloth that has been moistened in warm water. For these baths, concentrate on wiping down your baby's face and hands frequently and thoroughly cleaning his genital area.

ESSENTIAL

Talcum powder can irritate a baby's lungs when inhaled, so don't use it anywhere near your baby. If diaper rash is a problem, try using a cornstarch-based powder. But keep a close eye on baby's bottom. Yeast, which sometimes causes diaper rash, can feed on cornstarch.

After his belly button heals, you can start giving your newborn tub baths. With tiny newborn babies, it may be easier to use the kitchen sink or a small plastic baby tub instead of a full-sized standard tub. Until your baby is crawling around and getting into messes, you probably don't really need to bathe him more than once a week. But if your baby enjoys taking a bath, and if he is not prone to sensitive skin, you may decide to bathe him every day for the sheer pleasure of it.

Baby Wash

For your baby's first few weeks of life, you really just need to use warm water to rinse and clean his delicate skin. After that, you may want to use a mild cleanser when he gets particularly dirty. Read baby-wash labels carefully, many contain the foaming agent sodium laurel sulfate, which can be damaging to your baby's immune system. Instead, look for products that use coconut, or other plant-based cleansers, as these natural ingredients will be safer for baby's skin.

Homemade Baby Lotion

Massaging your baby gently with baby lotion is a great way to help her relax and to bond with her. Just be sure that baby lotion does not contain petroleum or petroleum byproducts. Food-based baby lotions, such as those made from apricot-seed, aloe vera, avocado, coconut, olive oil, sunflower, safflower, or vitamin E, are a great choice for babies.

You can also make your own baby lotion using the following recipe:

INGREDIENTS
½ cup honey
½ cup cream

Combine honey and cream in a saucepan and cook slowly over medium heat. Stir continually until the two are well blended. Let the mixture cool for five minutes. Store in an airtight container (preferably glass) in the refrigerator for up to one week. Allow mixture to cool completely before using. Remember, babies younger than twelve months old should not ingest honey for any reason.

Homemade Bubble Bath

Once your baby is a few months old, she will be able to sit up and enjoy her bath on a whole new level. Babies at this age delight in the sensations and sights of a bubble bath. Unfortunately, most commercially prepared bubble bath formulas use sodium laurel sulfates and petroleum byproducts. Who wants their baby soaking in that? A better bet is to make your own home-made bubble bath. It is so easy to make and use that you will wonder why you ever bought a commercial product.

INGREDIENTS
1 cup baby shampoo or eco-friendly liquid soap
¾ cup water
½–1 teaspoon glycerin

Combine baby shampoo or eco-friendly liquid soap, water, and glycerin in a reusable plastic bottle. Add a few drops to running water at bath time for a fun, bubbly, nourishing bath.

Bath Toys and Books

Bath time is playtime for babies. You will find that as your baby gets older, she'll enjoying splashing around in the water even more, and may even like the addition of some bath toys and books.

Can babies have acne?
Yes. Baby acne is completely normal. But it is not caused by dirt or blocked pores. Baby acne is primarily caused by hormones passed through the placenta prior to birth. It will go away on its own as these hormones are metabolized and leave the body.

Many bath toys are made with #3 plastic, or polyvinylchloride (PVC), which is not only damaging to the environment in its production but may expose kids to lead and other neuro-toxic heavy metals and phthalates. Plastic bath toys also generally contain phthalates in order to make them more flexible. Look for bath toys that are made from healthy materials such as organic cotton or PVC-, BPA-, and phthalate-free plastics. Try the Original Natural Rubber Duck by Rich Frog (*www.thesoftlanding.com*), Organic Cotton Bath Toys from EcoExpress (*www.ecoexpress.com*), or Sassy Count and Spell Bath Appliqués (*www.thesoftlanding.com*). These toys are all BPA-, PVC-, and phthalate-free. But your baby won't care about that. He'll just love that they make bath time such a blast!

Cleaning Bath Toys

The damp environment of the bath can be a breeding ground for dirt and mold buildup, especially in bath toys that are difficult to keep dry. To keep your bath toys clean and mold-free, soak them in a mixture of water and white distilled vinegar for at least ten minutes, rubbing gently to remove dirt and grime. Rinse with water and let dry completely. If mold is present, soak toys in vinegar overnight, scrub, rinse with water, and let dry completely.

Squirty toys, which will probably be very popular in your baby's bath, have a tendency to grow mold inside where they are difficult to clean. To keep the mold out, clean them regularly by squeezing out all of the water and filling them up with straight vinegar. Squeeze out the vinegar and let the toy dry completely. If mold is present, soak the toy with vinegar overnight. In the morning, squeeze out the vinegar, refill, and repeat until you no longer see gunk coming out.

Sun Protection

Until you baby is at least six months of age, you will need to take great care to ensure that she is not exposed to any more than a few minutes of sun each day. Her thin, delicate skin is extremely sensitive to the sun's ultraviolet rays, yet too fragile to handle the ingredients in sunscreen, even a nontoxic variety.

ALERT

Friction between baby's clothing and skin, or where areas of skin rub together, may cause chafing. Chafed skin may be tender and look red and irritated. Remove clothing that is tight or rubs against your baby's skin. And be sure to keep spots that are prone to chafing, like under the chin and around the genitals, clean and dry.

After six months, you can cautiously use sunscreen to protect her from the sun. Still, you may be surprised to learn that your favorite brand of sunscreen may not be as effective as you thought. In fact, an extensive sunscreen survey, conducted by the nonprofit Environmental Working Group, found that of the 1,026 sunscreen brands tested, 86 percent offer inadequate protection from the sun, or contain ingredients with significant safety concerns. Here's how to choose an effective, safe, sunscreen to protect your baby.

Chemical versus Mineral

Chemical-based sunscreens are designed to absorb the sun's rays with compounds such as benzophenone, homosaläte, padimate-0, parsol 1789 (avobenzone), and octyl methoxycinnamate (octinoxate). Unfortunately, these chemicals are as bad as they sound. For starters, they have been linked to health effects such as hormonal changes and DNA damage. In addition, most chemical sunscreens only protect against the sun's UVB rays (the cause of sunburns) not its UVA rays (those responsible for skin cancer and accelerated aging).

ALERT

While sunscreen is a good way to protect your baby's skin, an even better bet is to avoid sun exposure whenever possible. Keep your baby out of direct sunlight when the sun's rays are strongest (between 10 A.M. and 4 P.M.). When she is out in the sun, make sure she wears a hat at all times and protective clothing.

Mineral sunblocks that use titanium dioxide or zinc oxide are a better choice for sun protection because they block both UVB and UVA rays. They are healthier than chemical formulas because they are designed to lay on top of the skin rather than being absorbed into it. But because of this, they leave a layer of white on the skin. (Ever see a lifeguard with a white nose? That's mineral sunblock.)

The Nano Effect

In an effort to minimize this white-nose effect, some mineral sunscreen manufacturers are using formulas containing nanometer-sized particles of their chemical components. This allows the product to be absorbed into the skin more readily (so that it becomes transparent); however, titanium and zinc oxide are two chemicals that you really don't want to absorb into your skin. For instance, unlike larger particles of titanium oxide, nanoparticles can enter the bloodstream and damage brain cells.

Choose Healthier Ingredients

There are lots of sunscreens out there that claim to be natural or to contain organic ingredients. But many still contain parabens, preservatives, and petroleum byproducts. Look for sunscreen products that are preservative-free or those with milder preservatives such as potassium sorbate. And choose products that use natural emollients such as olive oil, sunflower, jojoba, shea butter, or cocoa butter instead of petroleum.

The Bottom Line

Sun protection is not something you want to do without. Just keep it healthy by choosing a mineral-based sunblock that aims for transparency without nano-particles. Here are a few brands to try:

- Alba Botanica (*www.albabotanica.com*)
- Avalon Organics (*www.avalonorganics.com*)
- Burt's Bees (*www.burtsbees.com*)
- California Baby (*www.californiababy.com*)
- Dr. Hauschka (*www.drhauschka.com*)
- Jason Natural (*www.jason-natural.com*)

The important thing to remember is that these products won't do you any good at all if you leave them at home while you and your baby are out in the sun. Keep a spare bottle of sun block in your diaper bag so that you will actually have it ready when and where you need it!

Natural Bug Repellents

Nothing ruins a fun day at the park faster than a swarm of pesky bugs. But while many conventional bug sprays are effective at keeping the bugs away, they also use an extremely toxic chemical as their active ingredient, DEET. Also known as *N, N-diethyl-meta-toluamide,* DEET is a powerful insecticide that can peel paint, damage rayon and spandex, and melt plastic. Up to 56 percent of DEET applied to the skin enters the bloodstream, and reactions to it include skin rashes, lethargy, muscle spasms, nausea, seizures, and irritability. So this is not something you want anywhere near your little baby.

FACT

Ticks, the carriers of Lyme disease, are among the most worrisome pests. If you live in, or are traveling to an area known for Lyme disease (according to the Centers for Disease Control, this includes the Atlantic states and Northern California), contact the American Lyme Disease Foundation at 1-800-876-5963 for preventive advice.

To keep bugs from ruining your next day at the park, use a natural bug repellent that bothers bugs—not your baby.

There are a number of natural alternatives to DEET, made primarily from plant essential oils, that you can use to protect your baby from bugs. Most natural insect repellents are made with citronella, a tall, aromatic grass indigenous to Southern Asia. Its pungent, lemony fragrance is pleasant to most people but objectionable to mosquitoes. Other aromatic essential oils commonly found in natural insect repellents include cedarwood, lemongrass, eucalyptus, peppermint, pennyroyal, lavender, and bergamot.

ALERT

Insects are attracted by perfumes and scented personal care products (such as shampoos and lotions), as well as by sweet foods such as ice cream, fruit juices, and watermelon. Avoid insects naturally by using unscented products on your baby and steering clear of sweet treats while in insect-prone areas.

To make your own natural insect repellent, mix one part garlic juice with five parts water in a small spray bottle. Shake well before using. Spray lightly on exposed body parts. You could also try mixing rubbing alcohol, witch hazel, vodka, or olive oil with one of the essential oils listed below.

- Catnip
- Cedarwood
- Citronella
- Geranium
- Lemongrass
- Pennyroyal
- Tea Tree Oil

Mix these ingredients in a ratio of one part essential oil to ten parts base in a clean spray bottle and shake well before using. Also remember that essential oils are only to be used externally. And to ensure that your baby is not allergic, you should test the spray on a small area of her skin first. If she does not show any signs of a reaction, lightly spray exposed body parts with the repellent.

If biting flies are a problem, you can make your own flypaper with this simple recipe: Mix one-quarter cup syrup, one tablespoon granulated sugar and one tablespoon brown sugar in a small bowl. Cut strips of brown kraft paper and soak in this mixture. Let dry overnight. To hang, poke a small hole at the top of each strip and hang with string or thread.

Treating Bites

Despite your best efforts, it is likely that your baby will get a bug bit or two in her lifetime. Most bites will be minor causing a little redness, swelling, and itching. You can minimize these symptoms by applying a small amount of undiluted tea tree oil, cold compresses, lavender essential oil, or calamine lotion to the bites.

For bee and wasp stings, you will need to remove the stinger while being careful not to squeeze the venom sac. You can do this by scraping the stinger with the edge of a credit card or dull butter knife. Apply a cold compress to the area, watch your baby for signs of a reaction (such as wheezing, difficulty breathing, or diarrhea), and call your health care provider immediately if you become concerned.

CHAPTER 23

It's Play Time

It may seem like all fun and games, but there's more going on than you think when your child is playing. All of that lifting, dropping, looking, pouring, bouncing, hiding, building, and knocking down adds up to a whole lot of fun, indeed. But it is also the way your baby is learning about the world around her. Children learn major concepts like reading, math, physics, and geometry every time they play.

Green Arts and Crafts for Baby

Can an orange crayon be green? It can if it is made from natural ingredients like soy or beeswax instead of petroleum. The same goes for that red marker or rainbow watercolor paints.

In addition to their contribution to global warming, traditional art supplies also contain a slew of dubious chemicals and solvents. Nontoxic art supplies are not only better for the planet, they're also better for your family's health as they don't off-gas noxious chemicals.

The good news is that there are green options available for just about any color of your budding Picasso's palette. Here's how to find eco-friendly art supplies.

Raid the Pantry

Some of the best art supplies are recycled materials from your own kitchen. With a few swipes of glue, an egg carton can be transformed into a caterpillar, a soda bottle can be turned in to a birdfeeder or a boat, and an empty paper towel tube can become a telescope or a flute.

ESSENTIAL

Children don't need a lot of toys to have fun. More often than not, they will simply want to play with you. Playing with your baby teaches her that she is loved, important, and fun to be around. It builds the self-esteem and self-confidence that your baby will to continue building loving and supportive relationships throughout her life.

It is easy to go to a big box craft store and end up spending a fortune on new supplies to nurture your child's creativity, but it is not necessary or eco-friendly. Teach your kids reduce, reuse, recycle by buying less, using what you already have at home in new and creative ways, and putting unused items in their proper place at the end of their lifecycle.

Seal the Deal

The Art and Creative Materials Institute (ACMI) is an international organization that works to promote nontoxic art and creative materials for children and adults. The group evaluates art supplies and products, conducting extensive toxicological tests to determine toxicity. Look for the ACMI seal (*www. acminet.org*) on everything from paints to crayons to glue to ensure that your baby's art supplies are nontoxic and safe.

Recycle It

Your baby's doodles and scribbles will look just as good on recycled paper as they would on a clean sheet. Keep a special box in your office or kitchen to hold used paper, envelopes, and cardboard that can be used again as art supplies. When you need to buy new, look for 100 percent post-consumer waste paper, and teach your children to use it sparingly.

DIY It

Cannot find eco-friendly art supplies in your area? Make your own instead! Check out the Green Parent (*www.thegreenparent.com*) for video demonstrations on making your own recycled paper, organic play dough, recycled crayons, or eco-friendly finger paints.

There is literally no end to the number of craft projects you can try with your baby. More often than not, if you simply set out a few materials, your baby's natural creativity and curiosity will kick in and get her going. If you need a little inspiration, learn how to make twig baskets, clay pots, potato stamps, and dozens of other eco-friendly projects from the book *Nature's Art Box* by Laura C. Martin. Online, check out Kinderart (*www.kinderart.com*) or Kaboose (*www.kaboose.com*).

Touch and Feel

You don't need a houseful of toys to entertain your baby. More often than not, she will delight in exploring the touch and feel of common items around your home. Make up a small batch of spaghetti, allow it to cool, and let your baby play with it. She'll love the way it wiggles and slide through her fingers. Toss the spaghetti on the compost pile when finished. Or make up a batch of slippery silk, also known as *gloop*, by mixing corn flour with a little water and letting her squish it through her fingers.

Another idea is to make your baby a treasure basket containing everyday touchy-feely objects, such as a brush, a piece of bark, sea shells, crinkly paper, sponges, or fine-grade sandpaper.

Outdoor Play

In the not-so-distant past, children spent the better part of their days outside, playing, digging, building, and exploring their way through the natural world. But according to Richard Louv, author of *Last Child in the Woods: Saving Our Children from Nature-Deficit Disorder*, today's children have become increasingly alienated from the natural world, with disastrous implications, not only for their physical fitness, but also for their long-term mental and spiritual heath.

In today's technological age it is more important than ever to encourage children to play outdoors. And there's no better time to start then when children are young. Get your baby outdoors and help him develop his own personal relationship with the outdoor world.

Grow a Garden

Gardening with your baby is a great way to introduce her to nature, and help her make the connection between the food in the ground and the food on her plate! A vegetable garden is an easy start. When your baby is young, carry her in a sling or let her rest on a blanket nearby while you plant and weed your garden. Talk to her about the types of flowers, herbs, and vegetables you are planting and why. As she gets older, she can help you dig holes, plant, seeds, and even pick the harvest. Be sure to point out any vegetables that she may find on the dinner table. If your yard is not big enough for a garden, trying growing a few potted plants near a sunny window in your home.

Take a Hike

Even the little children can enjoy the nature and wonder of the outdoors by going on a hike. Carry your baby in a sling or front-facing baby carrier and let him explore the world from the safety of your arms. As your baby gets older and begins taking his own steps, hold his hand as you take short walks through the woods.

Your local park, a nearby playground, and even your backyard will open up a world of wonder, observations and questions when viewed through a baby's eyes. Be sure to point out the sights, sounds, and smells of your trip as you walk.

Go On a Treasure Hunt

Even before your baby can say the words, she will be able to recognize the sights and sounds of her world. Take her on a treasure hunt and challenge her to point out the things that she sees and hears. Ask her to spot a tree, a bird, a squirrel, or a flower. When she gets a little older, see if she can spot a yellow flower, or a gray rock, or if she can hear a bird that's way up in the trees.

Playgrounds

A safe, well-constructed playground can be a wonderful place for young children to get exercise, fresh air, and unstructured play. But be aware that many outdoor playgrounds were constructed using treated lumber that often contains arsenic, and can be dangerous to children. The arsenic penetrates the wood, and runs off into the soil around it. If your neighborhood has a playground, talk with local park officials to make sure that it was not made from treated lumber.

Baby Toys

It is so much fun to introduce a baby to a new toy. But how can you trust that a toy will be safe for your baby? In recent years, the number of toy recalls has increased dramatically due to the number of toys that are now mass produced using dubious materials. With the myriad toys on store shelves to choose from, there's no need to settle for those that are poorly made, potentially dangerous, or made from toxic materials.

There are a number of toy manufacturers that take great pride in producing high-quality children's toys that are fun, educational, and safe. The key is to find toys that suit your child's interests as well as your budget. Look for companies that use responsible manufacturing methods and nontoxic materials. Remember, until your child is about three years old, any toy he plays with will likely wind up in his mouth. So make sure that every toy in your home is made from safe and nontoxic materials.

Check out the following websites to find high-quality toys for your baby made from materials you can trust: Mamas Earth (*www.mamas earth.com*), Under the Nile, (*www.underthenile.com*), the Soft Landing (*www.thesoftlanding.com*), and Nature's Crib (*www.naturescrib.com*).

Wooden Toys

Many of the wooden toys you see on store shelves are made of plywood or particleboard held together with toxic glues and finished with petroleum-based sealers, paints, preservatives, and pesticides. Skip these toxic toys and look for high-quality, unfinished solid wooden toys. If possible, choose wooden toys that bear the FSC seal, since they are made with solid wood harvested from sustainable sources. You can tell if a toy is made from solid wood by looking at its unfinished edges. If you can see layers, it's made from pressed wood or particle board.

Make sure the paint on your baby's wooden toys is nontoxic. A wooden toy that is strong-smelling or decorated with bright paints is likely laden with chemicals. The safest bet is to choose unpainted wooden toys with beeswax or nontoxic oil finishes.

Stuffed Animals

Babies love to snuggle up with a favorite stuffed toy or animal. You may even have a few of your own still hanging around from your own childhood days. To make sure a stuffed animal is safe for your baby to cuddle, look for products made from natural, organic fabrics such as cotton, hemp, or wool. Unlike conventional stuffed toys, organic stuffed toys have not been exposed to synthetic chemical pesticides, fertilizers, dyes, or finishes.

Plastic Toys

Be very wary of toys that are made from plastic. Not only are they petroleum-based, but they also contain a number of toxins like bisphenol (BPA), polyvinyl chloride (PVC), and phthalates that are harmful to children and the planet. Most plastic products contain PVC, a chemical compound that has been linked to cancer and other serious health problems.

BPA is used to make plastic toys that are stiff and shatterproof, like toy bottles or dolls. While phthalates are added to plastics that need to be soft and pliable such as that used for teething rings and pacifiers.

The manufacturing of plastics also takes a toll on the environment. Plastics' manufacturers are the single largest users of chlorine, a chemical that reacts in the environment to create the dangerous byproduct dioxin. In addition, heavy metals like lead and cadmium are used as stabilizers in soft vinyl products and packaging. These metals are unsafe for children and harmful to the environment when they are released during manufacturing and disposal.

To be safe, opt for toys made from natural fibers or untreated wood instead of plastics. When you do purchase plastic toys, be sure they are labeled BPA-, PVC-, and phthalate-free.

QUESTION

How often should baby toys be cleaned?
Get in the habit of cleaning your baby's toys as you would the other areas of your home. In particular, make sure toys get cleaned whenever they are noticeably soiled, whenever your baby is recovering from an illness such as diarrhea or a cold, or after a playdate; especially if the other children have put your baby's toys in their mouths.

Cleaning Baby Toys

Babies are constantly touching and chewing on their favorite toys, so they can pick up germs and illnesses easily. You can reduce your baby's chance of catching illnesses by keeping his toys and play area clean. Most toys can be cleaned with a mixture of nontoxic soap and hot water. For deep cleaning, small plastic toys can be cleaned and sanitized in a dishwasher while fabric toys can take a spin through the laundry machine (just make sure you are washing full loads!).

Homemade Baby Play

Is it not amazing that no matter how many fancy toys you buy or are given for your baby, they always prefer the box or bag it was packaged in instead? Save money on fancy toys and make your own fun play things for baby. You just need a little creativity and the items you probably already have in your recycling box or pantry. Here are a few ideas.

ESSENTIAL

Check Make Baby Stuff (*www.make-baby-stuff.com*) to learn how to make all kinds of baby toys at home. The site has instructions for making homemade puzzles, doll furniture, teddy bears, and even wooden blocks. It is incredibly rewarding to watch your baby play with a toy that you personally made.

Homemade Bubbles

Babies love to watch someone blowing bubbles. It must look like magic to such young eyes to see something so unusual form out of thin air. Steer clear of the commercially prepared bubble products that are made from dubious chemicals, and make your own bubble liquid instead. That way, you and baby will always be ready for a moment of magic!

INGREDIENTS

½ cup nontoxic dish soap

1½ cups water

2 teaspoons sugar

Gently mix the dish soap, water, and sugar together in a cup or empty yogurt container. Stir well. Pour a small amount of the mixture into your baby's next bath and stand back as she giggles and squeals with delight!

Organic Play Dough

Play dough can be a feast for a young baby's senses. The colors and textures make for fabulous exploration. And the supple material helps young children practice moving their little fingers by rolling, breaking, and smooshing it.

Traditional store-bought play dough is made from petroleum byproducts that are harmful to the planet and can be just as harmful to your baby if ingested. And their containers create mountains of disposable waste. Here's how to make your own play dough that is safer for everyone:

INGREDIENTS
1 cup organic flour
½ cup sea salt
2 tablespoons cream of tartar
1 cup filtered water
1 tablespoon vegetable oil

1. Mix flour, salt, and cream of tartar in a saucepan.
2. Combine water and oil in a small bowl. Stir into the flour mixture gradually.
3. Cook over medium heat for 5 minutes or until very thick, stirring constantly. Remove and allow to cool for a few minutes. Knead until smooth. Store in an airtight container.

ALERT

Don't take your eyes off of that organic play dough! It will burn very easily when cooking, so be sure to assemble all ingredients and make sure baby is in a safe place before you begin. Stir the mixture quickly and constantly over low heat to avoid sticking.

To add color to your play dough, separate the mixture into portions and add a little food-grade dye to each.

Homemade Finger Paint

Finger painting is a popular activity for babies and young children because it gives them a chance to express themselves through color even before they develop the fine motor skills necessary to handle a brush. It is also a great way to get messy! Steer clear of petroleum-based finger paints that off-gas VOCs and look for those made from natural pigments and oils such as Livos SALIS Natural Hemp Finger Paints (*www.kidbean.com*). Better yet, make your own eco-savvy finger paints to keep those little fingers safe, happy, and busy!

INGREDIENTS
1½ tablespoons white sugar
½ cup dry cornstarch
½ teaspoon salt
1 cup of cold water
1 box of food coloring with red, green, yellow, and blue

1. Mix the sugar, cornstarch, salt, and water in a medium saucepan over low heat. Stirring constantly, gradually add a few drops at a time of food coloring until it reaches the desired color.
2. Continue to cook and stir for 10 minutes. The ingredients will gradually thicken from a runny consistency to a more paint-like consistency. Once the mixture thickens, remove the pan from heat.
3. Once cool, transfer paint to a recycled glass jar (such as a baby food jar) for storage, or to a recycled plastic container (such as a yogurt) for immediate use.

Great Green Reads for Baby

There is nothing quite like snuggling up with your baby and a good book. Reading to him, even at this young age is a great way for you both to relax and bond. And it also helps to boost your baby's brain power and expose him to language and concepts from the world around him.

Studies show that language skills and intelligence are directly related to how many words an infant hears each day. In one study, babies whose parents spoke to them an average of 2,100 words an hour scored higher on standardized tests when they reached age three than did children whose parents hadn't been as verbal. A running commentary throughout your day is a great way to keep the conversation flowing. And reading is another fun way to add variety to your verbal interactions.

ALERT

Babies need to feel an emotional connection with the words they hear throughout the day. So steer clear of books on tape, as well as radio and television. In fact, a recent study from the American Academy of Pediatrics shows that watching videos as a toddler may lead to Attention Deficit Hyperactivity Disorder (ADHD).

So read to your baby as often as possible, especially from books that will help to spark his interest in the environment. Here are a few great green reads to share with your little one:

- *The Lorax* by Dr. Seuss (Random House Books for Young Readers, 1971).
- *The Great Kapok Tree: A Tale of the Amazon Rain Forest* by Lynne Cherry (Sandpiper, 2000).
- *Over in the Jungle: A Rainforest Rhyme* by Marianne Berkes (Dawn Publications, 2007).
- *If I Ran the Rain Forest: All about Tropical Rain Forests* by Bonnie Worth (Random House Books for Young Readers, 2003).
- *Eco Babies Wear Green* by Michelle Sinclair Colman (Ten Speed Press, 2009).
- *Babies in the Bayou* by Jim Arnosky (Penguin Group, 2007).
- *Little Monkey* by Kimberly Ainsworth (Simon & Schuster Children's Publishing, 2008).

CHAPTER 24

Baby's First Birthday!

Hooray, it is your baby's first birthday! Your baby has marked off some major milestones in this first year—her first smile, her first tooth, and maybe even her first step. And now it is time for her first birthday party! You've earned this party too with 365 days (and nights) of sleep deprivation, diaper changes, and round-the-clock feedings. So go ahead and get ready to celebrate! This chapter will show you how to make your baby's first birthday party fun, memorable, and gentle on the planet.

Throwing a Great Green Party

It can be tempting to go all out for your baby's first-ever birthday party. After all, you want it to be an event that you will remember for your baby's lifetime. But remember, all of the decorations, food, and activities you use to celebrate your baby's big day will take a heavy toll on both your wallet and the planet.

According to the Clean Air Council, every day 43,000 tons of food are thrown out in the United States, and each year Americans toss out enough paper and plastic cups, forks, and spoons to circle the equator 300 times. That kind of waste can be a real party pooper!

Instead, why not make your baby's first birthday party a fun, simple, eco-savvy event that honors her and her environment? Reduce waste, save money, and eliminate hassle by hosting a great green birthday party to ring in your baby's first year!

Planning the Party

The first step in planning your baby's party is to choose a location for the event. You can have the party at your home, the home of a family member, or at a commercial location. Just be sure to choose a spot where your baby will feel comfortable. A party at your local zoo may sound like fun, but if your baby has never been there before, it may scare her more than it delights.

If the weather permits, an outdoor party can be a lot of fun for both kids and adults. It helps kids get fresh air and exercise and reduces the inevitable mess that comes with children's parties. A local park or beach that your baby enjoys is a great place to host her first birthday party.

As for the timing, the ideal party should be short—one to one and a half hours is about the most a one year old can handle without getting over stimulated and cranky. Schedule the party around your baby's nap time. A late morning party that follows her morning nap will ensure that she is well rested and ready to receive her guests.

Keep It Safe

Make sure your party space is safe for your own baby and other young guests by thoroughly baby proofing the area. Do a quick check on hands and knees for small cords, tags, choking hazards, or breakable items that might have been overlooked while decorating. Be extra thorough if you are having the party at a commercial location where they may not cater strictly to toddlers.

Make it easy for your guests to recycle to increase the chances that they'll actually do it. Line decorative baskets with clear plastic shopping bags and label clearly. Set up recycling areas near your trash cans for cans, paper, and glass.

Clean Green

Use nontoxic cleaners to ensure that your party space is a clean, green space for children to play. Wipe down toys, countertops, and tables with hot water and vinegar to kill germs and wet-mop floors to remove toxins brought in on shoes. If your party is held in a commercial location, bring along a spray bottle filled with vinegar and some clean cotton rags to wipe down the area before your guests arrive.

Invitations

Many parents spend a fortune on elaborate party invitations that their guests will look at once before they toss them in the trash can. Why not save money and save a tree, by opting for green invites instead? Here's how.

The Guest List

Chances are, your baby has made lots of new friends throughout her first year. And it can be tempting to invite every single one of them to celebrate with you at her first birthday bash. Just keep in mind that every guest you invite will increase the cost and resource use of your party and add to the potential over-stimulation of your baby.

Keep your baby's temperament in mind as you put together the guest list for her first birthday party. If your baby is particularly shy or easily frazzled, be sure to limit the number of guests to just a few close family and friends. It is not worth throwing an elaborate birthday party for tons of guests if the guest-of-honor spends the entire party in tears. If you decide to invite other families with babies or toddlers, limit the number to one to five families at most.

ALERT

Even if you are only hosting a small gathering, keep in mind that you will probably be caring for your baby (changing diapers, nursing, soothing) throughout the party. If possible, consider hiring a neighborhood teenager to help you with the preparations and cleanup for the party.

Sending Invites

Skip the usual paper invites that cost a fortune to mail and take forever to fill out. Instead, e-mail an invite to your friends for free through a website like Evite (*www.evite.com*). For friends and family members that don't have Internet access, send invitations by snail mail that are printed on recycled paper. Even better, look for paper-free cards like the Poo-poo (*www.poo poopaper.com*) cards made from elephant dung!

You can also make your own eco-savvy party invitations using recycled paper. Here are a few ideas:

- **#1:** Cut a large number 1 from piece of recycled paper. Write your child's name on the front of the number and the details of the party (time, location, etc.) on the back.
- **Photo cards:** Choose a favorite photo of your child, make a few extra copies, and write the party details on the back. Family and friends alike will cherish the photo much more than they would a paper invitation.
- **Baby art:** Cut a few pieces of your baby's artwork into postcard-sized notes and write the details for the party on the back.
- **Diaper invites:** Cut a piece of recycled paper into a square, fold it in half to make a triangle, and fold corners of the triangle toward the center to make your invitation look like a cloth diaper. Fasten a real

safety pin at the top to hold the triangles together. Write the party details inside the diaper.

Hand-deliver invitations to friends and family members that you see frequently to save money on postage and eliminate the waste and pollution caused by shipping.

Food

Although it is not necessary to provide a full meal for your guests, it is always a good idea to at least have a few snacks and treats on hand, especially for your baby and other young guests. Here's how to minimize the waste and cost of the food your serve without scrimping on the taste.

Keep It Local

Serve locally grown foods to your party guests. Shipping ingredients from another part of the world requires a tremendous amount of fuel. So check out your nearest farmers' market or CSA (community-supported agriculture) for in-season fruits and vegetables, as well as meat, eggs, and dairy products. These selections are fresher, tastier and often cheaper than their store-bought cousins.

Check for Allergies

If you are inviting other families with children, make sure you find out if any of the other guests have allergies. You may not be able to accommodate everybody's food requests, but it may help you better prepare the food list. If all of your party guests have a peanut allergy, you probably won't want to serve peanut butter and jelly sandwiches for lunch!

Ninety percent of food allergies are caused by a reaction to one of these foods: eggs, milk, peanuts, wheat, soy, tree nuts (like walnuts, Brazil nuts, and cashews), fish (such as tuna, salmon, and cod), and shellfish (like lobster, shrimp, and crab).

Plan It

Most people go overboard with the food when throwing a party. The point is to offer your guests a meal or a snack, not to ensure that they cannot eat another bite for a week! Avoid waste by thinking conservatively when planning the quantity of food to serve guests. You will save a bundle of time and money in food preparation and cleanup.

Finger-Licking Good

Finger foods are perfect for little ones. Animal crackers, cream cheese sandwiches (cut into quarters), cheese, and cut-up pieces of soft fruits and vegetables make great choices to serve young guests.

A Healthier Cake

Your baby will probably not have had much experience with cake before his first birthday. So don't forget to get lots of great shots of him diving in to his first yummy treat. But if his exposure to sweets has been limited up to this point, this may not be the time to hit him with all of the processed sugars and preservatives found in a traditional cake. Try one of these healthier cake options instead.

The Egg-Free Cake

Most health experts recommend that babies not eat egg whites until they are twelve months old. So if your baby has not yet had whole eggs by her first birthday party, this may not be a good time to give them a try. Egg substitutes won't help, as most still contain eggs. Instead, look for vegan cake mixes and frostings that are free of all animal products. Or search the web for a good homemade vegan cake recipe such as this Vegan Chocolate Cake recipe from Allrecipes.com (*http://allrecipes.com/Recipe/Vegan-Chocolate-Cake/Detail.aspx*), which uses simple ingredients you probably already have in your pantry.

Low-Sugar Cakes

If this is your baby's first taste of sweets, you might want to cut back on the sugar a bit to avoid giving his system such a shock. If you are making the cake at home, simply reduce the amount of sugar your recipe requires.

Another option is to choose a fruit-based cake, such as banana cake, apple-sauce cake, or carrot cake. Cakes that contain fruit usually have less sugar. If you are having the cake made, just ask the staff at your bakery to reduce the sugar as much as possible.

ESSENTIAL

To make homemade whip cream, beat one cup chilled heavy cream with an electric mixer until it thickens. Add one teaspoon vanilla and two tablespoons sugar, and continue beating until soft peaks form. Turn the beaters off and pull them up. The whip cream is ready when it forms stiff peaks. Keep refrigerated. Makes two cups.

Healthier Frosting

Look for healthier frosting choices like organic yogurt thickened with cream cheese or a traditional cream cheese frosting. Or try dusting the cake with powdered sugar instead of frosting. You can also use homemade whip cream instead of the traditional frosting. Homemade whipped cream is very simple to make and it uses much less sugar than the frosting you will find at the store.

Donate Leftovers

If you do have party leftovers, offer them to guests on their way out to ensure they won't go to waste. And be sure to donate any extra nonperishable items to your local food shelter.

Decorations

You don't need a lot of fussy decorations at this party. Remember, the guest of honor will more than likely tear, chew, or play with any decorations you decide to use.

Keep it simple and natural by skipping the wasteful paper and plastic decorations that will fill up your trash can once the party is over. Be resourceful and use things you already have in original ways. You will save money and time, reduce waste, and have unique and unexpected decorations that your guests (the guest-of-honor included) are sure to love.

ALERT

According to SAFE Kids USA, children under age eight can choke or suffocate on uninflated or broken balloons. Balloons that are accidentally released into the environment are also dangerous to the animals, birds, fish, and reptiles that may mistake them for food. If you must use balloons, keep them out of reach of children and discard them immediately after use.

Natural Decor

Decorate with natural items from your backyard such as plants, flowers, and pine cones. Steer clear of sharp items or choking hazards such as small rocks, pointed sticks, or thorned stems that could be harmful to your baby to touch.

Reusables

Look around your house or hit the thrift store for reusable decorations such as pillows, scarves, and other fabrics that will add festivity to the party space and serve as fun toys for the children to play with.

Pictures

Select a number of pictures and mementos from your baby's past year. Tape them onto sheets of recycled construction paper to frame them; then tape the pictures on the walls in chronological sequence.

Table Settings

Use reusable dishes, utensils, and cloth napkins, if possible, to eliminate the waste created by disposable table settings. If you do need to use disposable products, seek out those with the highest recycled paper content or look for compostable products that will break down quickly in a compost pile.

Whole Foods stores (*www.wholefoods.com*) carry durable plates and bowls that look like sturdy paper ones but are actually made from renewable and biodegradable sugar cane. Another option, try the plates and bowls from Recycline (*www.recycline.com*) that are made entirely of recycled plastic yogurt cups and are sturdy enough to be reused several times.

ESSENTIAL

Save space and money by renting or borrowing items that you will only need occasionally, such as large punch bowls, pitchers, chaffing dishes, or insulated beverage containers. Hit your local thrift store to pick up extra dishes, bowls, and serving utensils that will add to the eclectic flair of your party.

For utensils, look for Cereplast (*www.cereplast.com*) forks, spoons, and knives, which are made from a biodegradable bioplastic consisting of 80 percent corn-based starch and 20 percent green fillers. You can throw them straight in to the compost pile after the party and they'll break down in about three months.

Entertainment

There will be so much going on at your baby's first birthday party that you may find there is not time for any set activities. Even so, it is always a good idea to have a few activities prepared ahead of time in case your younger guests get antsy. If your child and her guests seem ready for some entertainment, try a few of these fun party activities:

- **Story time:** Read or tell the children one of your child's favorite stories. Capture their attention by using props like a stuffed animal or toy train to tell the story.
- **Home movies:** Show a home video of baby's first year (just be sure you've edited it to no longer than ten minutes!).
- **Art stations:** Set out crayons and coloring books on a low table for children to color as the inspiration strikes.

- **Ball rolls:** Have children sit in a circle with legs apart and roll a large ball, or several small balls, back and forth to one another.
- **Wagon rides:** Decorate a wagon and pull children for rides.
- **Box village:** Decorate several large cardboard boxes and allow children to climb in and through boxes.
- **Finger painting:** Make up a batch of eco-friendly finger paints, and set up a station with old T-shirts for smocks and an old curtain liner as a tarp for the kids to paint.
- **Piñatas:** Blow up a latex balloon and cover it with nontoxic glue and one-inch strips of recycled newspaper. Allow glue to dry, pop the balloon (be sure to discard properly), and cut a small flap in the piñata so that you can fill it with eco-friendly treats like small boxes of raisins, stickers, or organic candies.

Keep the atmosphere of the party relaxed and let your baby's temperament be your guide to the activities you decide to try. Don't try to force your baby through a lineup of activities if she is content to simply play with a toy on the floor.

Party Favors

Most parents dread the bags of gift junk that accompany their children home from birthday parties. All too often, these bags are filled with cheap and poorly made trinkets that were harmful to the planet to produce and harmful to children to play with.

ALERT

According to the American Academy of Pediatrics, the follow items should be kept out of the hands of infants and young children to reduce the incidence of choking: latex balloons, coins, marbles, toys with small parts, toys that can be compressed to fit entirely into a child's mouth, small balls, pen or marker caps, and small button-type batteries.

Replace these bags of junk with eco-friendly gifts that are gentle on the planet and healthy for small children. Consumable gifts, such as cookies or muffins, are always a hit for kids. Plants or flowers make great waste-free gifts for adults. Useful items such as a picture frame or a small board book will also make a thoughtful gift.

Another idea is to have a craft activity at your party that the kids can take home with them as a favor. Party guests can paint a T-shirt with nontoxic finger paints, decorate a picture frame, or make a birdfeeder by spreading a pine cone with peanut butter and rolling it in bird seed.

Thank-You Notes

Even if your schedule is hectic, it is always nice to stop and say thanks to those who helped you celebrate your baby's first birthday. But that doesn't mean you need to generate mountains of waste by sending out tons of expensive thank-you cards that are time-consuming to fill out. Instead, send a simple, heartfelt, and personal e-mail to each of your guests expressing your appreciation.

If you do decide to send out a paper thank-you, scan your child's latest artwork into your computer and use it to create your own unique recycled paper cards. Check out Conservatree (*www.conservatree.org*) for a listing a retailers that sell blank eco-friendly note cards.

Green Glossary

Air pollution Contaminants or substances in the air that interfere with human or environmental health.

Alternative energy Energy from sources other than fossils such as wind, solar, or geothermal. Usually eco-friendly.

Biodegradable A product that will break down in the environment. This label is sometimes misleading applied to products to make them appear eco-friendly.

Birth plan A written document that outlines the preferences and wishes that expecting parents would like to strive for during the labor and delivery of their new baby.

Carbon dioxide Also known as CO_2, this natural gas is has been found in increasing concentrations in the atmosphere as a result of human activities, such as the burning of fossil fuels. These increased concentrations contribute to global warming.

Carbon footprint A measure of your impact on the environment in terms of the amount of greenhouse gases produced, measured in units of carbon dioxide.

Carbon offsetting *See* offsets.

Chlorine A toxic and highly reactive gas that is used for water disinfection and the production of plastics. Chlorine is responsible for more household poisonings annually than any other toxin. It also causes ozone depletion.

Climate change A change in global temperature and weather patterns that can be linked to human activities like the burning of fossil fuels.

Composting A process of decomposing organic wastes, like food scraps and paper, naturally, to produce a fertilizer rich in minerals that is useful for gardening and farming.

Conservation The act of preserving and protecting the environment and resources found in nature.

Doula A person trained to offer a mother physical and emotional support during labor and delivery.

Energy efficient A service or technology that can reduce the amount of electricity or fuel used to do the same work.

Environmentally preferable A misleading label often applied to make products or services appear green.

Fossil fuel Coal, oil, and natural gas.

Global warming An increase in the average temperature of the Earth's climate.

Greywater Waste water that does not contain sewage or fecal contamination and can be reused for watering plants or irrigation after filtration.

Hemp Plant fiber used for making cloth and rope.

Landfill Area where waste is dumped and covered with dirt and topsoil.

Lead A heavy metal that is toxic to humans and harmful to the environment. Found in paints, pipes, and other products.

Low-emission vehicles Cars (or other motorized vehicles) that emit less pollution than comparable models.

Natural A product that contains no synthetic ingredients. This label is often applied to products to make them appear green, but the term is not regulated; therefore, it is meaningless.

Nontoxic Describes a product or material that is not harmful. This label is often applied to products to make them appear green, but the term is not regulated; therefore, it is meaningless.

Off-gassing The release of airborne chemicals as byproducts of toxins.

Offsets Products or services, such as the planting of trees or use of renewable energy, used to compensate for the emission of carbon.

Organic On product packaging, this term is used to describe items that have been produced without the use of synthetic chemicals or genetically modified ingredients. The use of the word *organic* is regulated and must be certified by the U.S. Department of Agriculture.

Phosphates A natural element that can be harmful to the environment if present in high concentrations. Phosphate is often used in detergents to enhance their effectiveness and has been found in large quantities in lakes and waterways.

Plastic Human-made durable and flexible synthetic-based product. Composed mainly of petroleum.

Post-consumer waste Waste that is collected after the consumer has used and disposed of it.

Recycling The process of reusing raw materials by collecting, sorting, and reprocessing them from the waste stream.

Reduce Consuming less as a means of conservation.

Renewable energy Energy sourced from sources such as wind or sun that can keep producing energy indefinitely without being used up.

Reuse Finding another way to use an object before throwing it away or recycling it.

Sustainable Able to last over a long period of time without becoming depleted or damaging the environment.

Toxic Poisonous or harmful.

VOC Volatile organic compound. Toxic when off-gassed into the environment.

Vermi-composting The process of composting using worms to slowly decompose materials.

Green Resources

Books

Carson, Rachel. *Silent Spring*. (Boston, MA: Houghton Mifflin, 1962.)

Gore, Al. *An Inconvenient Truth: The Crisis of Global Warming*. (New York, NY: Rodale, 2006.)

Gow-McDilda, Diane. *The Everything Green Living Book: Easy Ways to Conserve Energy, Protect Your Family's Health, and Help Save the Environment*. (Boston, MA: Adams Media, 2007.)

Imus, Deirdre. *The Essential Green You: Easy Ways to Detox Your Diet, Your Body, and Your Life*. (New York, NY: Simon & Schuster, 2009.)

Mason Hunter, Linda. *Green Clean: The Environmentally Sound Guide to Cleaning Your Home*. (New York, NY: Melcher Media, 2005.)

McDonough, William. *Cradle to Cradle: Remaking the Way We Make Things*. (New York, NY: North Point Press, 2002.)

McKibben, Bill. *The End of Nature*. (New York, NY: Random House, Inc., 1989.)

Rider, Kimberly. *Organic Baby: Simple Steps for Healthy Living*. (San Francisco, CA: Chronicle Books, 2007.)

Savedge, Jenn. *The Green Parent: An Eco-Friendly Guide to Earth-Friendly Living*. (Seattle, WA: Kedzie Press, 2008.)

Uliano, Sophia. *Gorgeously Green: 8 Simple Steps to an Earth-Friendly Life*. (New York, NY: Harper Collins, 2008.)

Vann, Lizzie. *Organic Baby and Toddler Cookbook: Easy Recipes for Natural Food*. (New York, NY: DK Publishing, 2000.)

Websites

In addition to all the websites listed in the text you can also visit the following sites.

Beauty

COMPACT FOR SAFE COSMETICS
Check out this link to download a list of companies that have pledged to keep personal care products cruelty-free.
www.safecosmetics.org

THE CONSUMER'S UNION GUIDE TO ENVIRONMENTAL LABELS
This site provides detailed information about the labels on your favorite personal care products.
www.greenerchoices.org/ecolabels

SKIN DEEP, ENVIRONMENTAL WORKING GROUP
This is the site for the comprehensive campaign to inform consumers about the toxins in personal care products.
www.cosmeticsdatabase.com

Building

BUILDING GREEN
Check out this site for green building news and a directory of green building products.
www.buildinggreen.com

DSIRE, DATABASE OF STATE INCENTIVES FOR RENEWABLES AND EFFICIENCY
This site gives a state by state listing of grants and incentives for renewable and energy efficient technology.
www.dsireusa.org

EFFICIENT WINDOWS COLLABORATIVE
This site offers information about energy-saving windows.
www.efficientwindows.org

GREEN HOME GUIDE
This site is a very informative and independent source for green building product reviews from industry professionals.
www.greenhomeguide.com

U.S. GREEN BUILDING COUNCIL
This site is a great resource on green building standards.
www.usgbc.org

Cars

GRASSOLEAN
Check out this site for information on veggie-based fuels.
www.grassolean.com

GREEN CAR CONGRESS
This site provides information about the technologies, issues, and policies of alternative fuels.
www.greencarcongress.com

GREENERCARS.ORG, AMERICAN COUNCIL FOR AN ENERGY-EFFICIENT ECONOMY
This site gives lots of great information about efforts to make cars greener.
www.greenercars.org

HYBRIDCARS
Check out this site for the latest information on hybrid cars.
www.hybridcars.com

NATIONAL BIODIESEL BOARD
Use this site to find a directory of biodiesel stations across the United States.
www.biodiesel.org

U.S. DEPARTMENT OF ENERGY, ALTERNATIVE FUELS DATA CENTER
This site offers information on alternative fuels.
www.eere.energy.gov/afdc

U.S. DEPARTMENT OF ENERGY, FUEL ECONOMY INFORMATION
Compare the fuel efficiency of different model cars and learn more about saving fuel at this site.
www.fueleconomy.gov

U.S. ENVIRONMENTAL PROTECTION AGENCY, GREEN VEHICLE GUIDE
Check out this site to learn about eco-savvy vehicles.
www.epa.gov/greenvehicles

Cleaning

EARTH 911
This link provides a list of dry cleaners that use the wet-cleaning method.
www.earth911.org/master.asp?s=ls&serviceid=139

FIND CO₂
Use this link to find a national directory of CO_2 dry cleaners.
http://findco2.com

GREEN EARTH DRY CLEANERS
This site provides a directory of green earth dry cleaners.
www.greenearthcleaning.com/rostersearch.asp

U.S. ENVIRONMENTAL PROTECTION AGENCY, ENVIRONMENTALLY PREFERABLE CLEANERS
Check out this site to find out government regulations on green cleaning.
www.epa.gov/epp/pubs/products/cleaning.htm

WASHINGTON TOXICS COALITION
This site provides in-depth information on environmental toxins.
www.watoxics.org

Clothing

CO-OP AMERICA
This site offers excellent information about sweatshops.
www.coopamerica.org/programs/sweatshops

THE GLASS SLIPPER PROJECT
Chicago residents can use this site to find out where to donate prom dresses and accessories.
www.glassslipperproject.org

GOODWILL INDUSTRIES INTERNATIONAL
Use this site to find a Goodwill thrift store in your area.
www.goodwill.org

LOTUS ORGANICS
An excellent resource for information about sustainable clothing and organic fibers.
www.lotusorganics.com

THE PRINCESS PROJECT
Use this website to find a drop-off location for prom dresses and accessories in the San Francisco Bay area.
www.princessproject.org

THE SALVATION ARMY
Check out this site for more information about the Salvation Army and to locate a shop near you.
www.salvationarmyusa.org

SOLES 4 SOULS
This site offers information about where to donate gently used shoes for children and adults in need.
www.soles4souls.org

Energy

AMERICAN WIND ENERGY ASSOCIATION
This site offers information about alternative wind energy.
www.awea.org

CHEERS (CALIFORNIA HOME ENERGY RATING SERVICES)
California residents can use this site to find a home energy auditor in their area.
www.cheers.org

HOME ENERGY SAVER
This site provides info and tips for saving energy around the home.
http://hes.lbl.gov/hes

RESNET (RESIDENTIAL ENERGY SERVICES NETWORK)
Use this website to find a home energy auditor near you.
www.resnet.us

SOLAR ENERGY INTERNATIONAL
This site offers information about alternative solar energy.
www.solarenergy.org

SOLAR LIVING INSTITUTE
This site is a great resource on solar energy.
www.solarliving.org

U.S. DEPARTMENT OF ENERGY
Check out this site for tips on saving energy.
www.energy.gov

U.S. DEPARTMENT OF ENERGY, ENERGY EFFICIENCY AND RENEWABLE ENERGY
Check here for information on renewable energy.
www.eere.energy.gov

U.S. ENVIRONMENTAL PROTECTION AGENCY, ENERGY STAR PROGRAM
Check this website for the latest information about Energy Star–rated products.
www.energystar.gov

Food

LOCAL HARVEST
Use this site to find out more about locally grown food in your area.
www.localharvest.org

SUSTAINABLE TABLE
Check out this site for a seasonal list of locally grown foods.
www.sustainabletable.org

UNITED STATES DEPARTMENT OF AGRICULTURE (USDA)
This site offers more information about the national standards for organic certification.
www.ams.usda.gov/nop

Gifts and Parties

CARE2
Check out this link for twenty-five great consumer-less gift ideas.
www.care2.com/greenliving/25-great-consumer-less-gift-ideas.html

THE NATURAL RESOURCE DEFENSE COUNCIL
Check out this green gift-giving guide for eco-savvy gift ideas.
www.nrdc.org/cities/living/ggift.asp

SIERRA CLUB
Use this link for some great green gift ideas.
www.sierraclub.org/e-files/gift_ideas.asp

Green

THE GREEN GUIDE
This site offers information for National Geographic of green living.
www.thegreenguide.com

THE GREEN PARENT
The site is the author's blog and an excellent resource for kid-friendly information about eco-friendly living.
www.thegreenparent.com

GRIST, ENVIRONMENTAL NEWS AND COMMENTARY
This site offers the latest in eco-news and information.
www.grist.org

THE LEAGUE OF CONSERVATION VOTERS
Use this site to see how your elected officials rate on the National Environmental Scorecard.
www.lcv.org

MOTHER NATURE NETWORK, FAMILY BLOG
This blog offers up-to-date information on raising a green family.
www.mnn.com/family

TREEHUGGER
This site is a great resource for environmentally friendly information.
www.treehugger.com

Lawn Care

BEYOND PESTICIDES
This site gives detailed information about the dangers of chemical pesticides.
www.beyondpesticides.org

COMPOST GUIDE
Check out this site to learn all about composting.
www.compostguide.com

HOW TO COMPOST
This site provides great information on composting.
www.howtocompost.org

KIDS RECYCLE! VERMI-COMPOSTING RESOURCES
Check out this site to learn more about vermi-composting.
www.kidsrecycle.org/worms.php

NORTHEAST ORGANIC FARMING ASSOCIATION
This site provides information about organic farming.
www.nofa.org

ORGANIC GARDENING
Use this site as your guide for starting an organic garden.
www.organicgardening.com

PESTICIDE-ACTION NETWORK
This site is a great resource of information about pesticides.
www.panna.org

THE NATIONAL PESTICIDE INFORMATION CENTER
This site offers detailed information about pesticides.
www.npic.orst.edu

U.S. ENVIRONMENTAL PROTECTION AGENCY
Check out this link for some basic information on composting.
www.epa.gov/compost/basic.htm

Pets

THE HUMANE SOCIETY OF THE UNITED STATES
This site is offers excellent information about wild and domestic animals.
www.hsus.org

PETFINDER
Use this website to find an adoptable pet in your area.
www.petfinder.com

PETS 911
Check out this website to find information about your local animal shelter.
www.pets911.com

Shopping

THE COALITION FOR CONSUMER INFORMATION ON COSMETICS
This site provides information about the Leaping Bunny Label.
www.leapingbunny.org

THE CONSUMER'S UNION GUIDE TO ENVIRONMENTAL LABELS
This site provides a comprehensive guide to environmental labeling on food, personal care products, household cleaners, and paper products.
www.greenerchoices.org/ecolabels

EARTH ISLAND INSTITUTE
Check out this site for more information about the campaign for dolphin-safe tuna.
www.earthisland.org

FOREST STEWARDSHIP COUNCIL
This site offers information about sustainable forestry.
www.fscus.org

GREEN SEAL
Check out this site for information about environmentally responsible products.
www.greenseal.org

MBDC, CRADLE-TO-CRADLE CERTIFICATION
Check out this site to learn more about cradle-to-cradle certification.
www.mbdc.com

NATIONAL MARINE FISHERIES SERVICE
This site offers a wealth of information about the Dolphin Protection Consumer Information Act.
www.nmfs.noaa.gov

THE RAINFOREST ALLIANCE
Use this link to learn more about the SmartWood Program.
www.rainforest-alliance.org

RESPONSIBLE SHOPPER
Use this link to research a company's environmental and social impacts before you make your next purchase.
www.coopamerica.org/ programs/responsibleshopper

TRANSFAIR USA (TFUSA)
This site offers information about Fair-Trade Certification.
www.transfairusa.org

UNITED STATES DEPARTMENT OF AGRICULTURE (USDA)
Check out this site for detailed information about the National Organic Program.
www.ams.usda.gov/nop

U.S. ENVIRONMENTAL PROTECTION AGENCY
Use this link to learn more about the EPA's Energy Star Program.
www.energystar.gov

Vacations

THE INTERNATIONAL ECOTOURISM SOCIETY
This site offers information about ecotourism worldwide.
www.ecotourism.org

PLANETA
Check out this site for practical ecotourism information.
www.planeta.com

RAINFOREST ALLIANCE
This site is a great resource on sustainable tourism.
www.rainforest-alliance.org

Waste

EARTH 911
This site is great resource for learning about recycling and finding out where and how to recycle items in your local area.
www.earth911.org

NATIONAL RECYCLING COALITION, INC.
Check out this site for recycling facts and statistics.
www.nrc-recycle.org

U.S. ENVIRONMENTAL PROTECTION AGENCY
Check out the EPA's website for great tips on reducing waste.
www.epa.gov

Water

H2OUSE
This site is a great resource on water conservation.
www.h2ouse.org

U.S. ENVIRONMENTAL PROTECTION AGENCY, ENERGY STAR PROGRAM
Check this website for the latest information about Energy Star–rated products.
www.energystar.gov

WATER CONSERVE
This website is full of great water-saving tips.
www.waterconserve.org

WATER–USE IT WISELY
Another great water conservation website.
www.wateruseitwisely.com

Index

A

Air
    pollution, minimizing, 35–36
    quality, 34–35
Allergies and asthma, 36–37

B

Baby clothes, 173–80
    fabric finishes, 173–74
    green, 175–77
    green on a budget, 178–79
    homemade, 179–80
    layette, 173
    sleepwear, 178
    washing, 180
Baby essentials, 164–71
    checklist, 164–65
Baby food
    homemade, 247–48
    introducing solids, 247
Baby massage, 236
Baby shower, 207–14
    green gift ideas, 212–14
    green gift registries, 212
    green gifts, asking for, 211–12
    green themes, 210–11
    greening, 207–9
    thank-you notes, 214
Baby wipes, homemade, 191
Bathing baby, 250–51
    baby lotion, homemade,
      252–53
    baby wash, 252
    bubble bath, homemade, 253
    toys and books, 254–55
    washing skin, 251–52

Beauty products
    aerosols, 48
    and animal testing, 47
    antiperspirant and deodorant,
      59
    basics, 46–48
    chemicals, 48
    disposables, 48
    do-it-yourself, 60
    ingredients, 49–53
    nails, 60
    oil-free, 47–48
    perfume, 59
    reducing number, 47
    shaving, 58
    skin care and cosmetics, 54–57
    teeth, 57–58
Birth plan, 12–14
Birthday, baby's first, 272–81
    decorations, 277–78
    entertainment, 279–80
    food, 275–77
    invitations, 273–75
    party favors, 280–82
    party planning, 272–73
    table settings, 278–79
    thank-you notes, 281
Birthing location, 7–9
    birthing center, 8
    home, 9
    hospital, 7–8
Books for baby, 269–70
Bottles and sippy cups, 246
Breastfeeding, 238–42
    challenges, 241–42
Bubbles, homemade, 267
Bug
    bites, treatment, 259
    repellant, natural, 257–59

C

Car seats, 165–66
Carbon offsets, 150
Cars, 143–47
Changing tables, 168
Childbirth recovery, 218–19
Childcare, finding green, 224–26
Cleaning
    air fresheners, natural, 91–92
    chemicals, 89–91
    dishwashing, 92–93
    eco-friendly supplies, 98
    laundry, 93–95
    make your own, 95–98
    reasons for green, 88–89

D

Diapers, 182–92
    bags, 190
    cloth, 184–85
    cloth, diaper services, 188–89
    cloth, washing at home, 188
    cost comparison, 187
    disposables, 182–83
    disposables, chemicals in,
      186–87
    disposables, green, 183–84
    elimination communication,
      192
    hybrid, 185
    pails, 191–92
    wipes, 190–91

E

Energy
    home energy audits, 100–1
    household consumption, 100
    renewable, 108
    suppliers, 108
Energy conservation, 101–8
    appliances, 104–6
    gadgets, 107–8
    heating and cooling, 102–3
    lighting, 106
    water heaters, 103

F

Finger paint, homemade, 269
Food, 21–32
    additives and preservatives,
      21–23
    bacteria, 30
    beef, 29
    contamination levels, 31–32
    genetically modified ingredi-
      ents, 23–24
    miles, 30–31
    organic and free-range, 26–27
    organic, where to buy, 31
    pesticides, 24–25
    seafood and mercury, 27–29
    seafood, wild vs. farmed, 27–29
    synthetic hormones, 25–26
Formula, 242–44

H

Hair care, 53–54
Health care provider, 4–7
    doula, 5–6
    midwife, 4–5
    obstetrician, 4
    questions to ask, 6–7

High chairs and boosters, 168–69
Home remedies, 228–36. *See
also* Pregnancy ailments, home
remedies
    colds, 229–30
    cradle cap, 228–29
    diaper rash, 232–33
    diarrhea and constipation, 232
    ear infections, 231–32
    eczema, 235–36
    gas, 230–31
    teething, 233–35

L

Labor and delivery options, 9–12
    c-section, 12
    medicated vaginal delivery, 11
    non-medicated vaginal deliv-
      ery, 10–11

M

Maternity clothes, 76–84
    dry cleaning, 83–84
    fabric choice, 76–79
    organic, 81–83
    passing them on, 83
    pre-loved, 81
    using what you have, 79–81

N

Newborn, caring for, 219–20
Nursery, 193–205
    bedding, 204–5
    floor covering, 199–201
    furniture, 202–4
    paints and finishes, 196–99

    remodeling or adding on,
      194–96
    window coverings, 201–2
Nursing gear, 244–46

P

Packing for birth, 14–16
Pediatrician, green, 221–22
Pets, 152–59
    adopting, 152
    alternatives to, 158–59
    bathing, 155–56
    feeding, 153–54
    fleas, 156–57
    gear, 154–55
    spay or neuter, 152
    waste, 157
Plastics, 117–18
Play, 261–70
    arts and crafts, green, 261–63
    dough, homemade organic,
      268
    homemade play things, 267–69
    outdoor, 263–64
    toys, 264–67
Pregnancy ailments, home rem-
edies, 16–19
    constipation and hemorrhoids,
      18
    headaches, 18
    heartburn, 17–18
    morning sickness, 16–17
    stretch marks and dry skin,
      18–19

R

Resting with new baby, 220–21

S

Shopping
    bag and bottle, bring your own, 67–68
    bulk, 64–65
    buying local, 68
    disposables, 66–67
    fair treatment of workers, 63–64
    greenwashing, 72–74
    labels, 68–72
    packaging, 65–66
    pollution reduction, 62–63
    reduce waste, 62, 65–67
    savings, 64–65
Skincare, baby, 250–59
Slings and babywearers, 169–71
Strollers, 167
Sun protection for baby, 255–57
Sunscreen, 55–56

T

Toxins, 39–44
    asbestos, 42
    chlorine, 41
    dioxins, 40
    in workplace, 44
    lead, 40–41
    mercury, 43
    nitrates, 43–44
    tobacco smoke, 42–44
    volatile organic compounds, 39–40
Toys, 264–67
Transportation, 142–50
    car maintenance, 146–47
    carbon offsets, 150
    driving green, 143–45
    green car guide, 145–46
    public, 143
    walking, 142–43
Trash, 110–21
    compost pile, 114–15
    recycling, 116–21
    reducing, 112–14
    reusing, 115–16
    weighing, 121
    where it goes, 110–12
Tubs, 171

V

Vacations, 148–49
Vaccination, 223–24
VBAC, 12

W

Water, 37–39
    bottled vs. tap, 37–38
    filters, 39
    pollution, 37
    tests, 38–39
Water conservation, 123–31
    air conditioners, 128
    at home, 123–29
    at store, 129
    bathroom, 124–26
    gadgets, 129–31
    kitchen, 126–27
    laundry, 127–28
    multi-tasking, 124
    outdoors, 128–29
    rain water collection, 131

Y

Yard, 133–40
    garden, starting, 140
    mowing, 135–37
    natural fertilizers, 139–40
    planting, 133–34
    watering, 137–38
    weeding, 138–39